STUDY GUIDE
Volume I

A History of Western Society

Test Fri- 23rd
5 (c) & 7

Book Report Due Before Thanksgiving
Factual "Person or place"
Having to do with this course!

STUDY GUIDE
Volume I

James Schmiechen
Central Michigan University

A History of Western Society

Fourth Edition

John P. McKay
University of Illinois at Urbana-Champaign

Bennett D. Hill
Georgetown University

John Buckler
University of Illinois at Urbana-Champaign

HOUGHTON MIFFLIN COMPANY   BOSTON
DALLAS   GENEVA, ILLINOIS   PALO ALTO   PRINCETON, NEW JERSEY

Printed in the U.S.A.

ISBN: 0-395-55873-5

ABCDEFGHIJ-WC-96543210

Contents

To the Student

How to Study History and Prepare for Exams

The study of history can be rewarding but also perplexing. Most history courses require you to read and understand large bodies of detailed information. The history student is expected to perform many tasks—memorize information, study the reasons for change, analyze the accomplishments and failures of various societies, understand new ideas, identify historical periods, pick out broad themes and generalizations in history, and so forth. These jobs often present difficulties. This guide will make your study easier and increase your efficiency. It has been developed to help you read, study, and review *A History of Western Society*, and regular and systematic use of it will improve your grade in this course. You may use the guide in a variety of ways, but for best results you might choose the following approach:

1. *Preview the entire chapter* by reading the "Chapter Questions" and "Chapter Summary"; then quickly read through the study outline, noting the reading with understanding exercises. All of this will take only a few minutes but is an important first step in reading. It is called *previewing*. By pointing out what the chapter is about and what to look for, previewing will make your reading easier and improve your reading comprehension.

2. *Now read your assignment in the textbook.* Pay attention to features that reveal the scope and major emphasis of a chapter or section, such as the chapter title, chapter and section introductions, questions, headings, conclusions, and illustrative material (e.g., maps and photographs). Note study hint 3 on page ix about underlining.

3. After reading, *review what you have read* and check your comprehension by going over the chapter outline once again—but this time make sure that you understand all the points and subpoints. If you do not fully understand a particular point or subpoint, then you need to return to the text and reread. It is not at all uncommon to need to read the text at least twice.

4. Continue your review. *Answer the review questions* that follow the study outline. It is best to write out or outline your answer on a sheet of paper or a note card. Be sure to include the supporting facts. Reread your answers periodically. This process will help you build a storehouse of information and understanding to use at the time of the exam.

5. Now work on the definitions, identifications, and explanations in the study-review exercises provided in each chapter of the *Study Guide*. This will help you to understand and recall both concepts and specific facts. Know not just who or what, but also why the term is significant. Does it illustrate or represent some fundamental change or process? Note that if a particular term appears in the text *and* in your lecture notes, it is of special importance. Do the geography exercises found in all appropriate chapters. This is important because they will enable you to visualize the subject matter and thus remember it better. It will take a few minutes, but the payoff is considerable. (Duplicate copies of all outline maps in the *Study Guide* can be found at the end of the book.)

6. Next, *complete the multiple-choice and fill-in exercises* for each *Study Guide* chapter. Some of these questions look for basic facts, while others test your understanding and ability to synthesize material. *The answers are at the end of the Guide*. If you miss more than two or three, you need to restudy the text or spend more time working on the *Guide*.

7. The section "Major Political Ideas" will help you understand some of the political concepts that are raised in the text. Keep a special section in your notebook where you write out the answers to these questions. By the time you take your exam you will have a good understanding of what these political concepts are and how and why they developed.

8. "Issues For Essay and Discussion" sets out one or two broad questions of the type you may be asked to answer in an essay exam or discuss in a classroom discussion. Answer these by writing a one to two page essay in which you address each part of the question with a well-organized answer based on material from the text. Remember, your instructor is looking for your ability to back up your argument with historical evidence.

9. Last, "Interpretation of Visual Primary Sources" is a way for you to expand your understanding of the chapter and to help you learn how to use prints, photographs, architectural artifacts and the like in assessing historical change. Keep a section in your notebook where you answer these questions—but also use your new skills in this area when you study the other visuals in the chapter. Don't be reluctant to make reference to these visual sources when you write your examination essays.

Additional Study Hints*

1. *Organize your study time effectively*. Many students fail to do well in courses because they do not organize their time effectively. In college, students are expected to read the material before class, review, and do the homework on their own. Many history teachers give only two or three tests during the semester; therefore, assuming personal responsibility for learning the material is vital. Mark up a semester calendar to show scheduled test dates, when term projects are due, and blocks of time to be set aside for exam study and paper writing. Then, at the beginning of each week, check the calendar and your course outlines

---

*For a complete text and workbook written to meet the needs of students who want to do their best in college, see James F. Shepherd, *RSVP, The Houghton Mifflin Reading, Study, and Vocabulary Program*, Third Edition (1988).

and notes to see what specific preparation is necessary for the coming week, and plan your time accordingly. Look at all the reading with understanding exercises in this *Study Guide* and try to estimate how much time you will need to master study skills. Set aside a block of time each day or once every several days for reading your text or studying your lecture notes and working in the *Study Guide*. Despite what one observes on college campuses, studying is not done most effectively late at night or with background music. Find a quiet place to study alone, one where you can tune out the world and tune into the past.

2. *Take good lecture notes.* Good notes are readable, clear, and above all reviewable. Write down as much of the lecture as you can without letting your pen get too far behind the lecturer. Use abbreviations and jot down key words. Leave spaces where appropriate and then go back and add to your notes as soon after the lecture as possible. You may find it helpful to leave a wide margin on the left side for writing in subject headings, important points, and questions, as well as for adding information and cross-references to the text and other readings. One way to use your notes effectively is by *reciting*. Reciting is the act of asking a question and then repeating the answer silently or aloud until you can recall it easily. Above all, do not wait until the night before an exam to use lecture notes you have not looked at for weeks or months. Review your lecture notes often and see how they complement and help you interpret your reading.

3. *Underline.* Too often students mark almost everything they read and end up with little else than an entire book highlighted in yellow. Underlining can be extremely helpful or simply a waste of time in preparing for exams; the key is to be selective in what you underline. Here are some suggestions:

    a. Underline major concepts, ideas, and conclusions. You will be expected to interpret and analyze the material you have read. In many cases the textbook authors themselves have done this, so you need to pinpoint their comments as you read. Is the author making a point of interpretation or coming to a conclusion? If so, underline the key part. Remember, learning to generalize is very important, for it is the process of making history make sense. The author does it and you must learn to identify his or her interpretation as well as conflicting interpretations; then to make your own. Here is where your study of history can pay big rewards. The historian, like a good detective, not only gathers facts but also analyzes, synthesizes, and generalizes from that basic information. This is the process of historical interpretation, which you must seek to master.

    b. Underline basic facts. You will be expected to know basic facts (names, events, dates, places) so that you can reconstruct the larger picture and back up your analysis and interpretations. Each chapter of this guide includes several lists of important items. Look over these lists before you begin to read, and then underline these words as you read.

    c. Look at the review questions in the *Study Guide*—they will point to the major themes and questions to be answered. Then, as you read, underline the material that answers these questions. Making marginal notations can often complement your underlining.

4. *Work on your vocabulary.* The course lectures and each chapter in the text will probably include words that you do not know. Some of these will be historical terms or special

concepts, such as *polis*, *feudalism*, or *bourgeoisie*—words that are not often used in ordinary American speech. Others are simply new to you but important for understanding readings and discussion. If you cannot determine the meaning of the word from the context in which it appears or from its word structure, then you will need to use a dictionary. *Keep a list of words* in your lecture notebook or use the pages in the back of this guide. Improving your historical and general vocabulary is an important part of reading history as well as furthering your college career. Most graduate-school entrance exams and many job applications, for instance, have sections to test vocabulary and reading comprehension.

5. *Benefit from taking essay exams.* Here is your chance to practice your skills in historical interpretation and synthesis. Essay exams demand that you express yourself through ideas, concepts, and generalizations as well as by reciting the bare facts. The key to taking an essay exam is preparation. Follow these suggestions:

   a. *Try to anticipate the questions on the exam.* As you read the text, your notes, and this guide, jot down what seem to be logical essay questions. This will become easier as the course continues, partly because you will be familiar with the type of question your instructor asks. Some questions are fairly broad, such as the chapter questions at the beginning of each chapter in this guide; others have a more specific focus, such as the review questions. Take a good look at your lecture notes. Most professors organize their daily lectures around a particular theme or stage in history. You should be able to invent a question or two from each lecture. Then answer the question. Do the same with the textbook, using the *Study Guide* for direction. Remember, professors are often impressed when students include in their essay textbook material not covered in class.

   b. *Aim for good content and organization.* Be prepared to answer questions that require historical interpretation and analysis of a particular event, series of events, movement, process, person's life, and so forth. You must also be prepared to provide specific information to back up and support your analysis. In some cases you will be expected to give either a chronological narrative of events or a topical narrative (for example, explaining a historical movement in terms of its social, political, and economic features). Historians often approach problems in terms of cause and effect, so spend some time thinking about events in these terms. Remember, not all causes are of equal importance, so you must be ready to make distinctions—and to back up these distinctions with evidence. This is all part of showing your skill at historical interpretation.

   When organizing your essay, you will usually want to sketch out your general thesis (argument) or point of interpretation first, in an introductory sentence or two. Next move to the substance. Here you will illustrate and develop your argument by weighing the evidence and marshaling reasons and factual data. After you have completed this stage (writing the body of your essay), go on to your conclusion, which most likely will be a restatement of your original thesis. It is often helpful to outline your major points before you begin to write. Be sure you answer all parts of the question. Write clearly and directly. All of this is hard to do, but you will get better at it as the course moves along.

6. *Enhance your understanding* of important historical questions by undertaking additional reading and/or a research project as suggested in the "Understanding History Through the Arts" and "Problems for Further Investigation" sections in the *Study Guide*. Note also that

each textbook chapter has an excellent bibliography. Many of the books suggested are available in paperback editions, and all of the music suggested is available in most record-lending libraries and record stores. If your instructor requires a term paper, these sections are a good starting point.

7. *Know why you are studying history.* Nothing is worse than having to study a subject that appears to have no practical value. And indeed, it is unlikely that by itself this history course will land you a job. What, then, is its value, and how can it enrich your life? Although many students like history simply because it is interesting, there are a number of solid, old-fashioned reasons for studying it. It is often said that we need to understand our past in order to live in the present and build the future. This is true on a number of levels. On the psychological level, identification with the past gives us a badly needed sense of continuity and order in the face of ever more rapid change. We see how change has occurred in the past and are therefore better prepared to deal with it in our own lives. On another level, it is important for us to know how differing political, economic, and social systems work and what benefits and disadvantages accrue from them. As the good craftsperson uses a lifetime of experience to make a masterpiece, so an understanding of the accumulated experiences of the past enables us to construct a better society. Further, we need to understand how the historical experiences of peoples and nations have differed, and how these differences have shaped their respective visions. Only then can we come to understand how others view the world differently from the ways in which we do. Thus, history breaks down the barriers erected by provincialism and ignorance.

The strongest argument for the study of history, though, is that it re-creates the big picture at a time when it is fashionable and seemingly prudent to be highly specialized and narrowly focused. We live in the Age of Specialization. Even our universities often appear as giant trade schools, where we are asked to learn a lot about a little. As a result, it is easy to miss what is happening to the forest because we have become obsessed with a few of the trees. While specialization has undeniable benefits, both societies and individuals also need the generalist perspective and the ability to see how the entire system works. History is the queen of the generalist disciplines. Looking at change over time, history shows us how to take all the parts of the puzzle—politics, war, science, economics, architecture, sex, demography, music, philosophy, and much more—and put them together so that we can understand the whole. It is through a study of the interrelationships of the parts over a long expanse of time that we can develop a vision of society. By promoting the generalist perspective, history plays an important part on today's college campus.

Finally, the study of history has a personal and practical application. It is becoming increasingly apparent to many employers and educators that neglect of the liberal arts and humanities by well-meaning students has left them unable to think and reason analytically and to write and speak effectively. Overspecialized, narrowly focused education has left these students seriously deficient in basic skills, and an understanding of the meaning of Western culture, placing them at a serious disadvantage in the job market. Here is where this course can help. The study of the past enables us to solve today's problems. It is universally recognized that studying history is an excellent way to develop the ability to reason and write. And the moving pageant of centuries of human experience you are about to witness will surely spark your interest and develop your aptitude if you give it the chance.

Chapter 1
Near Eastern Origins

Chapter Questions

After reading and studying this chapter you should be able to answer the following questions:

What is history and what is civilization? Why is so much of the study of history involved with the process of interpretation? How did wild hunters become urban dwellers? What caused Mesopotamian culture to take root and become predominant in the ancient Near East? What contributions to Western culture did the Egyptians make? What impact did the Hittites have on Near Eastern culture?

Chapter Summary

This first chapter of the book defines the terms *history* and *civilization* and then explores how civilization in the Western world began in the Near East in the area that became modern-day Israel, Iraq, Iran, and Egypt. It was here that agriculture and the first cities emerged, where writing was invented, where law, science, and mathematics developed, and where the central religious beliefs of the modern West evolved. These developments mark the beginning of a distinctively "Western" civilization.

The two prehistoric periods, the Paleolithic, or Old Stone Age, and the Neolithic, or New Stone Age, set the stage for early civilization. Although the invention of tools, the control of fire, and the discovery of the uses of language, art, and agriculture by the Paleolithic peoples were remarkable achievements, it was the Neolithic peoples' use of systematic agriculture and settled life that was one of the most important events in world history.

As these early peoples gave up nomadic life for the settled life of towns and systematic agriculture, civilization—which meant law, government, economic growth, and religion—became possible. By around 3000 B.C., the first urban-agricultural societies had emerged in Mesopotamia, the fertile land between the Tigris and Euphrates rivers. The most important of these early communities of farmers and city builders were the southern Mesopotamians, called the Sumerians. Sumerian society was a mixture of religious ritual, war, slavery, and individual freedom. The Sumerians' greatest achievement was their system of writing, a system called cuneiform. The conquerors of Sumer, people called Semites from the northern part of Mesopotamia, spread Sumerian-Mesopotamian culture throughout the Near

East. They were followed by the Babylonians, whose city, Babylon, dominated the trade of the Tigris and Euphrates. The Babylonians united Mesopotamia and gave the world one of its most important law codes, the Code of Hammurabi. This code tells us how Mesopotamian people lived: how husbands treated their wives, how society dealt with crime, how consumer protection evolved, and so forth.

Egyptian society grew alongside the Nile River, which sheltered and isolated its people more effectively than the rivers of Mesopotamia. Egypt was first united into a single kingdom in about 3100 B.C. The focal point of all life in ancient Egypt was the pharaoh. His tomb, the pyramid, provided him with everything that he would need in the afterlife. Egyptian society was a curious mixture of freedom and constraint. Slavery existed, but ordinary people could rise to high positions if they possessed talent.

Between 2000 and 1200 B.C., Egypt and the entire Near East were greatly influenced by two migrations of Indo-Europeans that disturbed and remolded existing states. While Mesopotamia became unified under the Hittites, Egypt was first influenced by the Hyksos and then by the introduction of monotheism by the pharaoh Akhenaten. During one of the resulting periods of political disintegration a number of petty kingdoms developed, although the old culture of the Near East—especially that of Mesopotamia—lived on in the kingdoms of the newcomers.

Study Outline

Use this outline to preview the chapter before you read a particular section in your textbook and then as a self-check to test your reading comprehension after you have read the chapter section.

I. What is history and why do we study it?
  A. History is the effort to reconstruct the past.
    1. The past must be understood so we can understand the factors that shape us today.
    2. Historians reconstruct the past by posing questions about it and then attempting to answer them by studying primary and secondary sources.
      a. Herodotus, the "father of history," joined the two concepts of inquiry and research.
      b. Historians must assess the validity and perspective of each source they study.
  B. The task of the historian is to understand the evidence, then interpret it.
    1. Historians seldom have all of the facts.
    2. Interpretation is often affected by the values and attitudes of the times.
  C. Social history, the study of the basic details of daily life, is a relatively new interpretive process.
  D. *Civilization* means a people's shared way of thinking and believing.
II. Origins
  A. Darwin and ideas of human evolution
    1. Darwin's important theories ushered in a new era in history and science.
    2. Darwin believed that human beings and apes are descended from a common ancestor.
  B. Paleoanthropologists' search for the "missing link"—the point from which humans and apes went their own evolutionary ways—has led some to believe there are many links that need to be studied in order to understand evolution.

III. The Paleolithic and Neolithic ages
    A. The Paleolithic or Old Stone Age (ca 400,000 B.C.–7000 B.C.)
        1. Human survival depended on the hunt; people did not farm.
        2. Paleolithic peoples learned to control fire and make tools from stone and clothes from animal skins.
            a. Social organization allowed them to overpower animals.
            b. They had some knowledge of plants and agriculture.
            c. Kinship and tribal ties were crucial; kinship bonds were strong throughout the extended family.
            d. The tribe was a group of families led by a patriarch.
        3. The greatest accomplishments of Paleolithic peoples were intellectual: thought and language allowed experience to be passed on.
        4. Art, such as cave paintings and small clay statues, date from this time and may express a desire to control the environment.
    B. The Neolithic or New Stone Age (ca 7000 B.C.–3000 B.C.)
        1. The planting of crops and the domestication of animals—the "Agricultural Revolution"—was the age's greatest achievement.
            a. Systematic agriculture ended peoples' dependence on hunting and allowed them to settle in towns and eventually cities.
            b. Agriculture began in four areas (the Near East, western Africa, northeastern China, and Central and South America) at roughly the same time.
            c. Systematic agriculture led to population increase, trade, and the division of labor.
        2. The settled lifestyle allowed time to develop new tools and agricultural techniques.
        3. In arid regions, irrigation was undertaken, resulting in the need for a central government.
IV. Mesopotamian civilization
    A. The first cities were built in Mesopotamia (ca 3500–1700 B.C.).
        1. Mesopotamia is the level plain between the Euphrates and Tigris rivers.
        2. The peoples of the area, the Sumerians and the Semites, turned to an agricultural-urban way of life.
        3. The Sumerians made Mesopotamia the "cradle of civilization."
    B. Environment and Mesopotamian culture
        1. Geography greatly affected the political life and mental outlook of people in Mesopotamia.
            a. The land is desert; only irrigation made farming possible.
            b. Rivers provided fish and building material but also isolated Sumerian cities from one another, making them fiercely independent.
            c. Floods and droughts made life difficult and people pessimistic.
        2. The political history of Sumer is characterized by almost constant warfare.
V. Sumerian society
    A. Religion
        1. The Sumerians tried to please the gods, especially the patron deity of each city, as a means of preventing the destructive floods.
        2. A traditional priesthood performed the religious rituals.
        3. Monumental temples—the ziggurats—were built to honor the gods.

B. Government
    1. The city-states were not theocracies—a governor (*ensi*) or king (*lugal*) ruled each, and most property was held privately.
    2. Sumerian society was made up of nobles, free clients, commoners, and slaves.
    3. The king was supreme, and kingship was hereditary.
    4. The nobility—the king and his family, the chief priests, and the high palace officials—controlled most of the wealth and held most of the power.
    5. The commoners were free and had a political voice.

VI. The spread of Mesopotamian culture
    A. The short-lived empire of Sargon
        1. In 2331 B.C., Sargon, a Semitic chieftain, conquered Sumer and spread Mesopotamian culture throughout and beyond the Fertile Crescent.
        2. The Ebla tablets reveal much about Sargon's work and the extent of Mesopotamian influence.
    B. The triumph of Babylon
        1. Babylon's position as a center of commerce helped Hammurabi unify Mesopotamia.
            a. He conquered Assyria, Sumer, and Akkad.
            b. He made Marduk the god of all Mesopotamians, thus making Babylon the religious center of Mesopotamia.
        2. Hammurabi's genius enabled Babylon to become the cultural center of Mesopotamia.
    C. The invention of writing and the first schools
        1. Pictograph writing was the forerunner of cuneiform writing.
        2. Sumerian cuneiform evolved from a pictographic system to an ideogram system and then to a phonetic system.
        3. Scribal schools were centers of learning and culture.
    D. Mesopotamian thought and religion
        1. Mathematics
            a. Mesopotamians developed the concept of place value.
            b. They emphasized practical uses for math, such as construction, rather than theorizing.
        2. In medicine, evil spirits were believed to cause sickness, and treatment was by magic, prescription, and surgery.
        3. Theology, religion, and mythology
            a. The Mesopotamians believed in a hierarchy of anthropomorphic, all-powerful gods.
            b. The aim of worship was to appease the gods.
            c. The Mesopotamians created myths and an epic poem—the *Epic of Gilgamesh*—to explain the creation of earth and the origin of human beings.
            d. Their myths influenced Jewish, Christian, and Muslim thought.
    E. Daily life in Mesopotamia
        1. Hammurabi's code was based on several principles.
            a. Equality before the law did not exist: there were milder penalties for members of the nobility than for commoners and slaves.
            b. When criminal and victim were social equals, the punishment fit the crime.

      c. Individuals represented themselves, fair trials were guaranteed, and officials who failed to protect the innocent were penalized.

    2. Hammurabi's law code reflects daily life in Mesopotamia.

      a. The law provided for consumer protection and spelled out severe penalties for burglary, looting, and cheating.

      b. The code contains many laws about farming, irrigation, crops, and animals.

      c. Marriage was a business arrangement between the groom-to-be and his future father-in-law.

      d. Women had little power within the family, while husbands had absolute power.

VII. Egypt: land of the pharaohs (3100–1200 B.C.)

  A. Geography

    1. Egypt was known as the "gift of the Nile": annual flooding made crop raising easy and Egypt prosperous.

    2. The Nile unified Egypt.

    3. Egypt was nearly self-sufficient in raw materials.

    4. Geography shielded Egypt from invasion and immigration.

  B. The god-king of Egypt

    1. Egypt was politically unified under a pharaoh, or king, who was considered to be a god in human form.

    2. The greatness of the pharaohs is reflected in their tombs, the pyramids.

      a. The pyramid was believed to help preserve the pharaoh's body so that his *ka* would live on.

      b. Tomb paintings, originally designed for the *ka*, give a vivid picture of everyday life.

  C. The pharaoh's people

    1. Social mobility existed, but most people were tied to the land and subject to forced labor.

    2. Peasants could be forced to work on pyramids and canals and to serve in the pharaoh's army.

    3. The pharaoh's role was to prevent internal chaos, which could lead to war and invasion.

VIII. The Hyksos in Egypt (1640–1570 B.C.)

  A. About 1800 B.C., Semites (Hyksos) began to push into Egypt, Mesopotamia, and Syria from the Arabian peninsula.

  B. Their "invasion" of Egypt was probably gradual and peaceful.

  C. The Hyksos brought new ideas and techniques to Egyptian life.

IX. The New Kingdom in Egypt (1570–1200 B.C.)

  A. The pharaohs of the Eighteenth Dynasty created the first Egyptian empire.

  B. Akhenaten and monotheism

    1. The pharaoh Akhenaten was interested in religion, not conquests.

      a. He and his wife, Nefertiti, believed that the sun-god Aton was the only god.

      b. They attempted to impose monotheism on Egypt, in direct opposition to traditional Egyptian beliefs and the established priesthood.

    2. Akhenaten's monotheism was unpopular and failed to take hold.

X. The Hittite Empire
    A. Migration of new groups
        1. Hittites were a part of the massive Indo-European migrations that began around 2000 B.C.
            a. The term *Indo-European* refers to a large family of languages spoken throughout most of Europe and much of the Near East.
            b. The original home of the Indo-Europeans may have been central Europe.
        2. Hittite diffusion into Anatolia was peaceful, characterized by intermarriage and alliance.
    B. The rise of the Hittites and Hittite society
        1. Hattusilis I led the Hittites to conquer Anatolia and then moved eastward as far as Babylon.
        2. Hittite society was headed by a royal family and an often rebellious aristocracy.
        3. The Hittites assimilated the Mesopotamian culture.
    C. The era of Hittite greatness (ca 1475–1200 B.C.)
        1. Through wise diplomacy and war, the Hittites came to control much of the Near East.
            a. The Hittites defeated the Egyptians at the battle of Kadesh (ca 1300 B.C.), and then formed an alliance with them to prevent future wars.
            b. The Hittites often ruled through vassal-kingdoms and protectorates.
        2. The Hittites provided the Near East with an interlude of peace.
XI. The fall of empires (1200 B.C.)
    A. The period of Rameses II
        1. Following the battle of Kadesh, Rameses II used the peace to promote wealth and build great new monuments.
        2. Rameses II was the last great pharaoh of Egypt.
    B. Thirteenth-century B.C. invasions
        1. In the 13th century B.C. the invaders destroyed both the Hittite and the Egyptian empires.
            a. The "Sea Peoples," part of a larger movement of people, dealt both empires a serious blow.

Review Questions

Check your understanding of this chapter by answering the following questions.

1. What were the major accomplishments of the Paleolithic peoples? Why were their lives so precarious?
2. Why are the artistic creations of Paleolithic and Neolithic peoples so important to historians?
3. Explain the impact that systematic agriculture had on the lives of these early peoples. Why did farming and the domestication of animals constitute a revolution in human life?
4. What effect did the geography of Mesopotamia have on the lives of the people who lived between the Tigris and Euphrates rivers?
5. What importance did the Nile River have in the economic and political development of Egypt?

2. The most influential ancient Near Eastern culture was the
   a. Egyptian.
   b. Mesopotamian.
   c. Assyrian.
   d. Hittite.

3. Amon-Re was the Egyptian god (king) of
   a. the dead.
   b. fertility.
   c. the gods.
   d. agriculture.

4. The ziggurat, the world's first monumental architecture, was a monument to the
   a. pharaoh.
   b. Sumerian gods.
   c. Battle of Nineveh.
   d. Great Flood.

5. According to the Code of Hammurabi, tavernkeepers who watered down drinks were
   a. sent to jail.
   b. sold into slavery.
   c. drowned.
   d. dragged through a field.

6. The Ebla tablets, discovered in 1976, prove
   a. the close connection between Mesopotamia and Syria, plus the presence of a written language.
   b. that there was no Mesopotamian influence on the Bible.
   c. that Mesopotamian culture remained only in Mesopotamia.
   d. that no link existed between Mesopotamian literature and religion and Old Testament theology.

7. Which of the following was the goal of King Hammurabi of Babylon?
   a. To completely erase the concept of tribal kingship
   b. To unify Mesopotamia with Babylon at its head
   c. To replace the worship of the god Marduk with himself
   d. To live at peace with his neighbors, regardless of the cost

8. The Semitic chieftain who conquered Sumer in 2331 B.C. was
   a. Hammurabi.
   b. Marduk.
   c. Osiris.
   d. Sargon.

9. The law code of King Hammurabi
   a. included much legislation on agriculture and irrigation canals.
   b. handed down mild punishments for almost all crimes.
   c. treated all social classes equally.
   d. did not protect the consumer.

10. Irrigation is a special feature of
    a. Egypt.
    b. Anatolia.
    c. Syria.
    d. Assyria.

11. Geography influenced Sumerian society by
    a. making communication within the region easy.
    b. making communication within the region difficult.
    c. providing the inhabitants with everything they needed.
    d. providing an abundance of precious metals.

12. Rivers in Mesopotamia were important because they
    a. were a unifying factor.
    b. drained off excess water.
    c. kept out invaders.
    d. made irrigation possible.

13. The Sumerians responded to their environment by
    a. achieving rapid political unification.
    b. developing a pessimistic view of life.
    c. appreciating the value of floods.
    d. developing an appreciation of nature.

14. The ziggurat was
    a. an agricultural community.
    b. a temple to the gods.
    c. the king's palace.
    d. a military camp.

15. The *lugal* in Mesopotamia was the
    a. secular war leader and administrator.
    b. chief priest of the temple.
    c. council of elders.
    d. legal owner of a slave.

16. Marduk was the chief god of the
    a. Sumerians.
    b. Egyptians.
    c. Amorites.
    d. Hittites.

17. The common people of Egypt were
    a. completely without legal rights.
    b. at the bottom of the social scale.
    c. divided on the basis of color.
    d. related to the Mesopotamians.

18. The hero of the first epic poem, produced by the Sumerians, was
    a. Enlil.
    b. Osiris.
    c. Gilgamesh.
    d. Khunanup.

19. The Hittites were
    a. Persian.
    b. Semites.
    c. Akkadians.
    d. Indo-Europeans.

20. The Egyptian god Osiris was closely associated with
    a. Isis.
    b. Aton.
    c. Amon-Re.
    d. Serapis.

21. Akhenaten was interested in fostering
    a. military expansion.
    b. worship of Aton.
    c. agricultural improvements.
    d. a return to traditional values.

22. The real transformation of human life occurred when
    a. iron was discovered.
    b. religion replaced mythology.
    c. nomadic life was replaced by systematic agriculture.
    d. free citizenship evolved in Sumer.

23. The earliest known attempts to answer the question "how did it all begin" were undertaken by
    a. the lawgiver Hammurabi in his codes.
    b. the early myths.
    c. Egyptian religion.
    d. Akhenaten's monotheism.

24. Although the common folk in Egypt were often exploited, they did have
    a. release from taxation.
    b. freedom from forced labor.
    c. release from military service.
    d. the right to appeal the actions of their landlord.

25. Because of its natural resources and geography, ancient Egypt
    a. was nearly self-sufficient in raw materials.
    b. could use the Nile to gain raw materials from the south.
    c. turned to conquest to make up for its lack of resources.
    d. established trading networks along its Mediterranean coast for necessary food and raw materials.

Major Political Ideas

1. For thousands of years Paleolithic peoples roamed the earth in search of food. Why did people begin to live in permanent locations and what impact did this have on their political life? What is the difference between a tribal chieftain and an urban king?

2. The focal point of religious and political life in ancient Egypt was the god-king pharaoh, who ruled over a unified state. How did geographic and climatic factors contribute to this political structure, and what were the chief features of the pharaoh's power and of Egyptian religion? How did Akhenaten's religious beliefs threaten this system?

Issues for Essays and Discussion

1. Why did Babylon become a cultural center of Mesopotamia? Discuss this by making reference to the origins of Babylon and the contributions of Hammurabi, the Mesopotamians, and the Sumerians in law, language, and religion.

2. Much of the early history of the Near East is that of one culture established and then overthrown by another. Nevertheless, a common civilization emerged. Why? What were the political, social, religious, and economic elements of this civilization?

Interpretation of Visual Sources

Study the photograph of the city of Ur on page 14 of your textbook, particularly the ziggurat of Urnammu in the lower right-hand corner. Does the form of the structure indicate its function? What do you know about Mesopotamian environment and culture that would begin to explain the shape of the building and its materials?

Geography

On Outline Map 1.1 provided, and using Map 1.1 and Map 1.2 in the textbook as a reference, mark the following:

1. The boundaries of Mesopotamia and the location of Babylon, Ur, Uruk, the cities of Sumer, and the Fertile Crescent.

2. The location of the early Neolithic farming sites of Jericho, Çatal Hüyük, Tepe Yahya, Jarmo, and Hacilar.

3. The Nile River valley, the Nile Delta, the Nubian Desert, and the cataracts of the Nile.

Outline Map 1.1

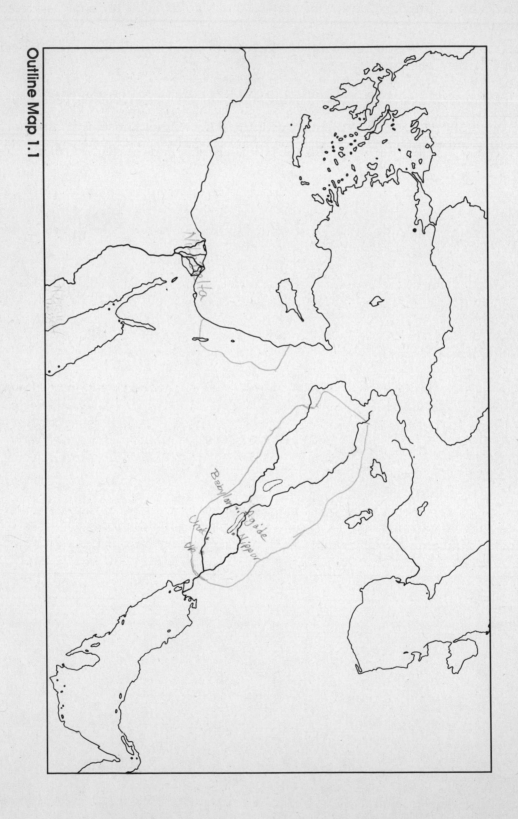

Understanding History Through the Arts

How does ancient Near Eastern art and architecture mirror the economic, social, and political life of that society? Can these aspects of civilization be used as historical documentation? Answer these questions by studying the physical nature of the city of the ancient Near East, beginning with H. W. F. Saggs, *The Greatness That Was Babylon* (1989), and S. Dalley, *Mari and Karana: Two Old Babylonian Cities* (1984). C. Desroches-Noblecourt has written an account of Egyptian art entitled *Egyptian Wall Paintings from Tombs and Temples* (1962) that is richly illustrated and informative, while C. Aldred's *Egyptian Art in the Days of the Pharaohs** (1985) examines nearly 3,000 years of Egyptian art in terms of the religious, historical, and environmental forces of Egypt. The early cave paintings, pottery, and gold ornaments of the Neolithic and Bronze Age artists and the metalwork of the Iron Age artists and others are examined in T. Powell, *Prehistoric Art** (1985).

Problems for Further Investigation

1. Precisely who were the Sumerians, and what were their contributions to the origins of civilization in Mesopotamia? The history of the discovery and study of the Sumerians is described in T. B. Jones, ed., *The Sumerian Problem** (1969). The importance of the Sumerians is the subject of S. H. Kramer's excellent survey, *The Sumerians: Their History, Culture and Character** (1984).

2. How did urban life evolve? The origins and early development of agriculture, urban life, trade, and writing in the Near East have raised questions still hotly debated among historians and archeologists. Excellent introductions to these issues can be found in a volume of readings from *Scientific American* titled *Hunters, Farmers, and Civilizations: Old World Archaeology** (1979). The history of the development of writing is the subject of C. B. F. Walker, *Cuneiform* (1987).

3. What made the pharaohs great? The life and times of the pharaohs make interesting reading. Two excellent books are L. Cottrell, *Life Under the Pharaohs* (1964), and C. Desroches-Noblecourt, *Tutankhamen* (1965). Among the best introductions to Egyptian civilization is C. Aldred's *The Egyptians* (1984). Everyday life in the Egyptian village during the New Kingdom is interestingly evoked by J. Romer in *Ancient Lives: Daily Life in Egypt of the Pharaohs* (1984).

---

*Available in paperback.

Studying Effectively—Exercise 1

Learning How to Underline or Highlight the Major Points

Underlining (or highlighting with a felt-tipped pen, as many students prefer) plays an important part in the learning process in college sources. Underlining provides you with a permanent record of what you want to learn. It helps in your efforts to master the material and prepare for exams.

The introductory essay (pp. vii–xi) provides some good guidelines for learning how to underline effectively, and you should review it carefully before continuing.

Further Suggestions

1. In addition to underlining selectively, *consider numbering the main points* to help you remember them. Numbering helps make the main points stand out clearly, which is a major purpose of all underlining or highlighting.

2. *Read an entire section through before you underline or highlight it.* Then, as you read it a second time, you will be better able to pick out and underline key facts, main points, and sentences or paragraphs that summarize and interpret the information.

3. *Avoid false economies.* Some students do not mark their books because they are afraid that the bookstores will not buy them back. This is a foolish way to try to save money for two reasons. First, students must of necessity invest a great deal of time and money in their college education. By refusing to mark their books, they are reducing their chances of doing their best and thus endangering their whole college investment. Probably the only alternative to marking your books is making detailed written notes, which is more difficult and much more time consuming.

   Second, carefully underlined books are *a permanent yet personal record of what you study and learn.* Such books become valuable reference works, helping you recall important learning experiences and forming the core of your library in future years.

Exercise

Read the following passage once as a whole. Read it a second time to underline or highlight it. Consider numbering the points. On completion, compare your underlining with the model on the next page, which is an example of reasonable and useful underlining. Finally, compare the underlined section with the chapter outline in the *Study Guide*. You will see how the outline summary is an aid in learning how to underline major points.

Egypt, The Land of the Pharaohs (3100–1200 B.C.)

The Greek historian and traveler Herodotus in the fifth century B.C. called Egypt the "gift of the Nile." No other single geographical factor had such a fundamental and profound impact on the shaping of Egyptian life, society, and history as the Nile. Unlike the rivers of Mesopotamia it rarely brought death and destruction by devastating entire cities. The river was primarily a creative force. The Egyptians never feared the relatively calm Nile in the way the Mesopotamians feared their rivers. Instead they sang its praises:

> *Hail to thee, O Nile, that issues from the earth and comes to keep Egypt alive! . . .*
> *He that waters the meadows which Re created,*
> *He that makes to drink the desert . . .*
> *He who makes barley and brings emmer [wheat] into being . . .*
> *He who brings grass into being for the cattle.*
> *He who makes every beloved tree to grow . . .*
> *O Nile, verdant art thou, who makest man and cattle to live.*

In the mind of the Egyptians, the Nile was the supreme fertilizer and renewer of the land. Each September the Nile floods its valley, transforming it into a huge area of marsh or lagoon. By the end of November the water retreats, leaving behind a thin covering of fertile mud ready to be planted with crops.

The annual flood made the growing of abundant crops almost effortless, especially in southern Egypt. Herodotus, used to the rigors of Greek agriculture, was amazed by the ease with which the Egyptians raised crops:

> *For indeed without trouble they obtain crops from the land more easily than all other men. . . .*
> *They do not labor to dig furrows with the plough or hoe or do the work which other men do to raise grain. But when the river by itself inundates the fields and the water recedes, then each man, having sown his field, sends pigs into it. When the pigs trample down the seed, he waits for the harvest. Then when the pigs thresh the grain, he gets his crop.*

As late as 1822, John Burckhardt, an English traveler, watched nomads sowing grain by digging large holes in the mud and throwing in seeds. The extraordinary fertility of the Nile valley made it easy to produce an annual agricultural surplus, which in turn sustained a growing and prosperous population.

Whereas the Tigris and Euphrates and their many tributaries carved up Mesopotamia into isolated areas, the Nile unified Egypt. The river was the principal highway, promoting easy communication throughout the valley. As individual bands of settlers moved into the Nile

Valley, they created stable agricultural communities. By about 3100 B.C. there were some forty of these communities in constant contact with one another. This contact, encouraged and facilitated by the Nile, virtually ensured the early political unification of Egypt.

Egypt was fortunate in that it was nearly self-sufficient. Besides the fertility of its soil, Egypt possessed enormous quantities of stone, which served as the raw material of architecture and sculpture. Abundant clay was available for pottery, as was gold for jewelry and ornaments. The raw materials that Egypt lacked were close at hand. The Egyptians could obtain copper from Sinai and timber from Lebanon. They had little cause to look to the outside world for their essential needs, which helps to explain the insular quality of Egyptian life.

Geography further encouraged isolation by closing Egypt off from the outside world. To the east and west of the Nile valley stretch grim deserts. The Nubian Desert and the cataracts of the Nile discouraged penetration from the south. Only in the north did the Mediterranean Sea leave Egypt exposed. Thus, geography shielded Egypt from invasion and from extensive immigration. Unlike the Mesopotamians, the Egyptians enjoyed centuries of peace and tranquility during which they could devote most of their resources to peaceful development of their distinctive civilization.

Yet Egypt was not completely sealed off. As early as 3250 B.C. Mesopotamian influences, notably architectural techniques and materials and perhaps even writing, made themselves felt in Egyptian life. Still later, from 1680 to 1580 B.C., northern Egypt was ruled by foreign invaders, the Hyksos. Infrequent though they were, such periods of foreign influence fertilized Egyptian culture without changing it in any fundamental way.

The God-King of Egypt

The geographical unity of Egypt quickly gave rise to political unification of the country under the authority of a king whom the Egyptians called "pharaoh." The details of this process have been lost. The Egyptians themselves told of a great king, Menes, who united Egypt into a single kingdom around 3100 B.C. Thereafter the Egyptians divided their history into *dynasties*, or families of kings. For modern historical purposes, however, it is more useful to divide Egyptian history into periods. The political unification of Egypt ushered in the period known as the Old Kingdom, an era remarkable for its prosperity, artistic flowering, and the evolution of religious beliefs.

Egypt, The Land of the Pharaohs (3100–1200 B.C.)

Geography

1

The Greek historian and traveler Herodotus in the fifth century B.C. called Egypt the "gift of the Nile." No other single geographical factor had such a fundamental and profound impact on the shaping of Egyptian life, society, and history as the Nile. Unlike the rivers of Mesopotamia it rarely brought death and destruction by devastating entire cities. The river was primarily a creative force. The Egyptians never feared the relatively calm Nile in the way the Mesopotamians feared their rivers. Instead they sang its praises:

> *Hail to thee, O Nile, that issues from the earth and comes to keep Egypt*
> *alive! . . .*
> *He that waters the meadows which Re created,*
> *He that makes to drink the desert . . .*
> *He who makes barley and brings emmer [wheat] into being . . .*
> *He who brings grass into being for the cattle.*
> *He who makes every beloved tree to grow . . .*
> *O Nile, verdant art thou, who makest man and cattle to live.*

1a

In the mind of the Egyptians, the Nile was the supreme fertilizer and renewer of the land. Each September the Nile floods its valley, transforming it into a huge area of marsh or lagoon. By the end of November the water retreats, leaving behind a thin covering of fertile mud ready to be planted with crops. The annual flood made the growing of abundant crops almost effortless, especially in southern Egypt. Herodotus, used to the rigors of Greek agriculture, was amazed by the ease with which the Egyptians raised crops:

> *For indeed without trouble they obtain crops from the land more easily than*
> *all other men. . . . They do not labor to dig furrows with the plough or hoe*
> *or do the work which other men do to raise grain. But when the river by*
> *itself inundates the fields and the water recedes, then each man, having*
> *sown his field, sends pigs into it. When the pigs trample down the seed, he*
> *waits for the harvest. Then when the pigs thresh the grain, he gets his crop.*

2

As late as 1822, John Burckhardt, an English traveler, watched nomads sowing grain by digging large holes in the mud and throwing in seeds. The extraordinary fertility of the Nile valley made it easy to produce an annual agricultural surplus, which in turn sustained a growing and prosperous population.

Whereas the Tigris and Euphrates and their many tributaries carved up Mesopotamia into isolated areas, the Nile unified Egypt. The river was the principal highway, promoting easy communication throughout the valley. As individual bands of settlers moved into the Nile Valley, they created stable agricultural communities. By about 3100 B.C. there were some forty of these communities in constant contact with one another. This contact, encouraged and facilitated by the Nile, virtually ensured the early political unification of Egypt.

3   Egypt was fortunate in that it was nearly self-sufficient. Besides the fertility of its soil, Egypt possessed enormous quantities of stone, which served as the raw material of architecture and sculpture. Abundant clay was available for pottery, as was gold for jewelry and ornaments. The raw materials that Egypt lacked were close at hand. The Egyptians could obtain copper from Sinai and timber from Lebanon. They had little cause to look to the outside world for their essential needs, which helps to explain the insular quality of Egyptian life.

4   Geography further encouraged isolation by closing Egypt off from the outside world. To the east and west of the Nile valley stretch grim deserts. The Nubian Desert and the cataracts of the Nile discouraged penetration from the south. Only in the north did the Mediterranean Sea leave Egypt exposed. Thus, geography shielded Egypt from invasion and from extensive immigration. Unlike the Mesopotamians, the Egyptians enjoyed centuries of peace and tranquility during which they could devote most of their resources to peaceful development of their distinctive civilization.

5   Yet Egypt was not completely sealed off. As early as 3250 B.C., Mesopotamian influences, notably architectural techniques and materials and perhaps even writing, made themselves felt in Egyptian life. Still later, from 1680 to 1580 B.C., northern Egypt was ruled by foreign invaders, the Hyksos.

6 Infrequent though they were, such periods of foreign influence fertilized Egyptian culture without changing it in any fundamental way.

The God-King of Egypt

The geographical unity of Egypt quickly gave rise to political unification of the country under the authority of a king whom the Egyptians called "pharaoh." The details of this process have been lost. The Egyptians themselves told of a great king, Menes, who united Egypt into a single kingdom around 3100 B.C. Thereafter the Egyptians divided their history into *dynasties,* or families of kings. For modern historical purposes, however, it is more useful to divide Egyptian history into periods. The political unification of Egypt ushered in the period known as the Old Kingdom, an era remarkable for its prosperity, artistic flowering, and the evolution of religious beliefs.

Chapter 2
Small Kingdoms and Mighty Empires in the Near East

Chapter Questions

After reading and studying this chapter you should be able to answer the following questions:

How did Egypt pass on its cultural heritage to its African neighbors? How did the Hebrew state evolve, and what are the distinguishing features of Hebrew life and religious thought? What enabled the Assyrians to overrun their neighbors, and how did their cruelty finally cause their undoing? How did Iranian nomads create the Persian Empire?

Chapter Summary

From about the thirteenth century B.C., when the empires of the Hittites and the Egyptians were destroyed by invaders, until the ninth century B.C., when Assyrian rule was imposed on the area, the Near East existed as a patchwork of small, independent kingdoms. This chapter opens with a description of how a weakened Egypt was given a new vibrancy when overrun by its African neighbors, the Nubians and the Libyans, who, at the same time, assimilated Egyptian culture. By 700 B.C., Egypt was reunited, and although it did not re-emerge as an empire, its cultural influence remained paramount, particularly in northern Africa.

The power vacuum that followed the fall of the great empires was significant because it allowed less powerful peoples to settle and prosper independently and, as a result, make particularly important contributions to Western society. Foremost among these peoples were the Phoenicians, who explored the Mediterranean Sea and built a prosperous commercial network, and the Hebrews. Modern archeology confirms the Old Testament account of the Hebrews' move from Mesopotamia into Canaan, their enslavement in Egypt and subsequent liberation, and the establishment of a homeland in Palestine. Important in this process was the Hebrews' vision of their god, Yahweh. A covenant with Yahweh—centering on the Ten Commandments—formed the basis of Hebrew life and law. The kings Saul, David, and Solomon, along with the great prophets, unified the Hebrews into a prosperous society based on high standards of mercy and justice. Their unique monotheism, combined with settled agriculture and urban life, provided the framework for the Hebrews' daily life.

The power vacuum in the Near East evaporated in the ninth century with the rise of the Assyrians, the most warlike peoples the Near East had yet known. For two hundred years the Assyrians ruled an empire that stretched from the Persian Gulf across the Fertile Crescent and westward through northern Egypt. Despite their brutality, the Assyrians owed their success less to calculated terrorism than to efficient military organization. The Assyrian empire fell swiftly in 612 B.C., and had it not been for modern archeological work, may have remained unknown.

The Persian Empire began in 550 B.C. with the first conquests of Cyrus the Great. The next two hundred years of Persian rule in the Near East were marked by efficient administration and respect for the diverse cultures of conquered states. Out of this benevolent rule came an important new religion, Zoroastrianism, which gave to Western society the idea of individual choice in the struggle between goodness and evil.

Study Outline

Use this outline to preview the chapter before you read a particular section in your textbook and then as a self-check to test your reading comprehension after you have read the chapter section.

I. Egypt, a shattered kingdom
   A. The invasions of the thirteenth century B.C. inaugurated an era of weakness and confusion.
      1. The Third Intermediate Period (eleventh to seventh centuries B.C.) was characterized by political fragmentation and loss of power.
      2. From 950 to 730 B.C. northern Egypt was ruled by the Libyans, while southern Egypt came under the control of the Africans of Nubia.
      3. Both the Nubians and the Libyans adopted the Egyptian culture.
   B. In the eighth century B.C., Egypt was reunified by the African Kingdom of Kush.
      1. The king of Kush, Piankhy, brought unity and peace to Egypt, but not a revival of empire.
      2. Egyptian culture had a massive impact on northeastern Africa.
II. The children of Israel
   A. The power vacuum created by the fall of the Hittite and Egyptian states allowed lesser states to thrive.
      1. The Philistines settled along the coast of Palestine and became farmers.
      2. The Phoenicians were outstanding seafarers, merchants, and explorers who developed a new alphabet that related one letter to one sound.
      3. The small, poor kingdom of the Hebrews arose south of Phoenicia.
   B. The rise of Israel
      1. According to the Old Testament, the Hebrews followed Abraham out of Mesopotamia into Canaan, from there migrated into the Nile delta, where they were enslaved.
      2. In he thirteenth century B.C., Moses led the Hebrews out of Egypt and into Canaan, where they built a political confederation.
      3. Under Saul and David, the twelve tribes became united under a monarchy, whose capital was Jerusalem.

4. King Solomon built a great temple and extended Hebrew power.
   a. He replaced the tribal division of Israel with twelve administrative units.
   b. In addition to the temple, he built cities, palaces, fortresses, and roads.
5. At Solomon's death the kingdom was divided in two.
   a. The northern half became Israel, while the southern half was Judah, with its capital still at Jerusalem.
   b. The northern half of the kingdom was eventually destroyed, but the southern half became the center of Judaism.

C. The evolution of Jewish religion
   1. The Hebrew religion was monotheistic, centered on the covenant with the god Yahweh.
   2. Jewish law and ethics, with their stress on justice and mercy, evolved from the Ten Commandments of Yahweh and the words of the prophets.

D. Daily life in Israel
   1. The end of nomadic life and coming of urban life changed family and marriage customs.
      a. Communal landownership gave way to family ownership.
      b. The extended tribal family gave way to the nuclear family, although urbanization weakened family ties and the power of the father.
      c. The end of nomadic life led to monogamous marriages.
      d. Most marriages were legal contracts arranged by the parents.
      e. Divorce was available only to the husband.
   2. Jewish society placed strong emphasis on rearing children.
      a. Children, particularly sons, were important for economic reasons.
      b. Both parents played a role in the child's education.
      c. Children worked in agriculture with their parents.
   3. Peace and prosperity brought about a decline of the small family farm and a rise of large estates and slave labor.
   4. The rise of urban life brought new job opportunities and increased trade.
      a. Craft and trade specialization thrived, often under guilds.
      b. Under Solomon trade and commerce was dominated by the king and/or foreigners.

III. Assyria, the military monarchy
   A. Growth of militarism and political cohesion among the Assyrians
      1. King Shalmaneser unleashed the first of the Assyrian attacks on Syria and Palestine in 859 B.C.
      2. Under Tiglath-pileser III and Sargon II, the Assyrians created an empire that extended from Mesopotamia to central Egypt.
      3. Conquest bred revolt, which in turn led to brutal Assyrian retaliation.
   B. Sources of Assyrian success
      1. An effective military organization and new military techniques and equipment were developed.
      2. The Assyrians set up a flexible system of rule over their conquered land.
      3. The Assyrians organized an empire with provinces and dependent states.
      4. A good communication system was established, and calculated terrorism was practiced.

Multiple-Choice Questions

1. Which one of the following statements about marriage in early Hebrew society is true?
   a. Divorce was not available to the husband.
   b. Restrictions against mixed marriages existed.
   c. Marriages were usually undertaken as a result of affection and physical attraction of the partners.
   d. Marriage was a religious ceremony, not a legal contract.

2. King Solomon is important in Hebrew history for which of the following reasons?
   a. He failed to attend to Hebrew unity and economic growth.
   b. He encouraged the division of Israel into a tribal system.
   c. He removed the religious temple, which stood as the symbol of Hebrew unity.
   d. He imposed far greater taxes than any levied before.

3. The most brutal and militaristic of all the Near Eastern cultures was that of the
   a. Persians.
   b. Assyrians.
   c. Phoenicians.
   d. Hebrews.

4. The Persian king Cyrus the Great carried out a foreign policy based on
   a. torture and submission to Persian traditions.
   b. tolerance of other cultures.
   c. universal acceptance of the Zoroastrian religion.
   d. the tradition of the warrior-king.

5. The Zoroastrian religion stressed which of the following?
   a. The rejection of individual free will
   b. The constant battle between evil and good
   c. The impossibility of eternal life
   d. The absence of a Last Judgment

6. Egypt was reunified in the eighth century by the African Kingdom of
   a. the Nile.
   b. Phoenicia.
   c. Kush.
   d. Ethiopia.

7. The power vacuum following the fall of the Hittite and Egyptian empires in about the thirteenth century B.C. was important because it
   a. resulted in the end of Egypt's cultural influence in the Near East and Africa.
   b. led to the unification of the Near East under Hebrew rule.
   c. allowed less powerful peoples, such as the Phoenicians and the Hebrews, to settle and prosper independently.
   d. led to four centuries of backwardness and cultural regression.

8. The Hebrew family pattern evolved
   a. from an extended family to an urban nuclear family.
   b. from a nuclear family to an extended family.
   c. from a strong emphasis on monogamy to an emphasis on polygamy.
   d. from a matriarchy to a patriarchy.

9. Peace and prosperity in Israel brought about
   a. increased landholding for small farmers.
   b. a breakup of the large estates.
   c. the end of slave labor.
   d. the decline of the small family farm.

10. Zoroastrianism was adopted by
    a. the early Hebrews.
    b. the Egyptians.
    c. Darius, the Persian king.
    d. most of the Mediterranean world.

11. The successors of Cyrus the Great divided his empire into
    a. three separate kingdoms.
    b. twenty satrapies.
    c. an east and a west province.
    d. six military districts.

12. The founder of the Persian empire was
    a. King Darius.
    b. Zoroaster.
    c. Cyrus the Great.
    d. Siyalk.

13. Which of the following statements about marriage in early Hebrew society is *not* true?
    a. Divorce was available to the husband only.
    b. Marriage was most often arranged for family and economic reasons.
    c. Restrictions against mixed marriages existed.
    d. Children were not seen as an important reason for marriage.

14. Iran's chief geographical feature is
    a. a great central plateau between the Tigris-Euphrates and the Indus valleys.
    b. a central mountainous region.
    c. a dense tropical coastal area at its western edge.
    d. the eastern portion of the Fertile Crescent.

15. The wealth of Iran was based on all of the following *except*
    a. iron production.
    b. horse breeding and overland trade.
    c. small-farm agriculture.
    d. the mining and trading of gold.

16. The Persians acquired many of their military and political practices and organizational genius from the
    a. Hebrews.
    b. Sumerians.
    c. Assyrians.
    d. Philistines.

17. As rulers of conquered territory and peoples, the Persians preferred to rely on
    a. diplomacy.
    b. brutal repression.
    c. forced assimilation of Persian ways.
    d. democratic strategies.

18. The Phoenicians are best known as
    a. great militarists.
    b. prosperous urban merchants and sea traders.
    c. religious innovators.
    d. rulers of the entire Near East after the fall of Persia.

19. The Phoenicians
    a. overthrew the Egyptian kingdom.
    b. developed a thriving agricultural community.
    c. waged large-scale wars against the Hebrews.
    d. became merchants and explorers.

20. Which of the following empires of the ancient Near East was the largest?
    a. The Hebrew
    b. The Hittite
    c. The Egyptian
    d. The Persian

21. The priestly class that officiated at sacrifices, chanted prayers, and tended to the sacred flame of early Iranian religion was the
    a. Magi.
    b. *satrapy*.
    c. Medes.
    d. scribes.

22. *Monotheism* means
    a. adherence to the Ten Commandments.
    b. the worship of nature.
    c. marriage within one's race.
    d. worship of one god alone.

23. During the sixth century B.C., Iranian religion was given new life by the religious thinking of
    a. Ahuramazda.
    b. Mithra.
    c. Zarathustra.
    d. Ahriman.

24. The Hebrew god was known as
    a. Moses.
    b. Solomon.
    c. Yahweh.
    d. Zoroaster.

25. Iran's geographical position and topography explains its
    a. isolation from its neighbors.
    b. role as the highway between East and West.
    c. absence of any urban culture.
    d. failure to attract peoples migrating from elsewhere.

Major Political Ideas

Hebrew law grew out of the covenant between the god Yahweh and the Hebrew people. Discuss this covenant in relationship to the Ten Commandments and the law that evolved from it. Explain how Hebrew thought about their god and the law changed through time.

Issues for Essays and Discussion

1. Compare and contrast the ideas and beliefs of Judaism, the monotheism of Akhenaten (see Chapter 1), and Zoroastrianism.

2. What evidence exists to support the claim that the power vacuum resulting from the fall of the Hittite and Egyptian empires encouraged cultural advance among less powerful peoples?

3. The end of nomadic life and the rise of urban living in Israel led to some important changes in Jewish life. Discuss the changes affecting landownership, family life, marriage, the position of children, work, and slavery.

Understanding History Through the Arts

1. What were the accomplishments of the Babylonians, the Assyrians, and the Sumero-Akkadians in the arts? How did the artistic works of these people mirror the environments in which they lived? Begin your inquiry with A. Moortgat, *The Art of Ancient Mesopotamia: The Classical Art of the Near East* (1969).

2. Were the artists of Persia imitators of their neighbors, or did they produce an original art? This and many other aspects of Persian art are explored in R. W. Ferrier, ed., *Arts of Persia* (1989).

Problems for Further Investigation

1. How did monotheism evolve? Students interested in ancient Near Eastern monotheism should start with R. J. Christen and H. E. Hazelton, eds., *Monotheism and Moses** (1969), or the more general work, *A History of Religious Ideas,** 3 vols. (1978–1985), by M. Eliade. For Egyptian beliefs see C. Elmahdy, *Mummies, Myth and Magic* (1989), C. Hobson, *The World of the Pharaohs* (1987), and C. Aldred, *Akhenaten: King of Egypt* (1988).

2. What was life like in the ancient Neat East? Problems of interpretation and investigation in the history of the ancient Near East are set forth, along with an excellent bibliography, in M. Coven Sky, *The Ancient Near Eastern Tradition** (1966). The impact of infectious diseases on ancient civilization is considered in W. McNeill, *Plagues and Peoples* (1976). For insight into the Assyrian character, see H. W. F. Saggs, *The Might That Was Assyria* (1984).

3. What was the position of women in Egyptian society? This and other issues are discussed in B. S. Lesko, ed., *Women's Earliest Records from Ancient Egypt and Western Asia* (1989).

4. Is it true that the biblical flood story did not originate with the Hebrews and that Hammurabi's law code is not the oldest? The sources of the story and the code and other subjects relating to the ancient Near East are considered in S. N. Kramer, *History Begins at Sumer, Twenty-Seven "Firsts" in Man's Recorded History** (1959), and S. Dalley, *Myths from Mesopotamia: Creation, the Flood, Gilgamesh and Others* (1989).

5. How were religion and daily life related in early Hebrew society? The Old Testament is one of the best sources for learning about the history and culture of the Near East. See especially the major history books of the Old Testament: Joshua, Judges, Ruth, I and II Samuel, I and II Kings, Nehemiah, and Esther. Archeological data do not always agree with the biblical accounts. For a good introduction, read K. Kenyon, *Archaeology in the Holy Land** (1979). Also informative is D. J. Wiseman, ed., *Peoples of Old Testament Times* (1973). M. Grant, *The History Of Ancient Israel* (1984), provides an eminently readable discussion of early Hebrew society

---

*Available in paperback.

and the rise of the Hebrew monarchy. A briefer summary is H. M. Orlinsky, *Ancient Israel** (1960). Hebrew law and morality are described in G. Mendenhall, *Law and Covenant in Israel and the Ancient Near East* (1955). J. Goldwin, *The Living Talmud: The Wisdom of the Fathers and Its Classical Commentaries** (1954), offers an interesting essay on Jewish life and religion.

Primary Sources
The Flood Stories of the Ancient Near East

The Old Testament story of Noah's Ark is one of the best known stories of the Judeo-Christian tradition. What are the origins of this famous story? Of the four flood stories below, the first three are from ancient Mesopotamia. The first to have appeared is the *Sumerian King List* in about 2000 B.C., but it is probably based on an earlier version; the second flood story is the account from the *Myth of Atrahasis III* which was written on a tablet in about 1600 B.C., and the third is from the "Standard Version" of the famous *Epic of Gilgamesh* written about 1300 B.C. The *Genesis* story most certainly came last, but there is no way of knowing exactly when this version was first composed and written down. The book of *Genesis* was a part of the Hebrew Torah, which was essentially complete and recognized as authoritative at least as early as the fourth century B.C.

Why did this story appear and acquire significance in several of the Near Eastern cultures? Do these references to a great flood represent some commonly believed myth, or do they reflect an actual event? When reading, consider the point of each story and its significance to the larger story being told. What do all of these stories have in common? In what ways do the narratives differ? How do the stories add to or complement what we know about the ways these societies functioned and in what they believed?

The Flood Story from the *Sumerian King List**

When kingship was lowered from heaven, kingship was (first) in Eridu. (In) Eridu, A-lulim (became) king and ruled 28,800 years. Alalgar ruled 36,000 years. Two kings (thus) ruled it for 64,800 years.

I drop (the topic) Eridu (because) its kingship was brought to Bad-tibira. (In) Bad-tibira, En-men-lu-Anna ruled 43,200 years; En-men-gal-Anna ruled 28,800 years; the god Dumu-zi, a shepherd, ruled 36,000 years. Three kings (thus) ruled it for 108,000 years.

I drop (the topic) Bad-tibira (because) its kingship was brought to Larak. (In) Larak, En-sipa-zi-Anna ruled 28,800 years. One king (thus) ruled it for 28,800 years.

Source: "The Sumerian King List," trans. Thorkild Jacobsen, in *Ancient Near Eastern Texts Relating to the Old Testament*, ed. James B. Pritchard (Princeton, N.J.: Princeton University Press, 1969), 265.

I drop (the topic) Larak (because) its kingship was brought to Sippar. (In) Sippar, En-men-dur-Anna became king and ruled 21,000 years. One king (thus) ruled it for 21,000 years.

I drop (the topic) Sippar (because) its kingship was brought to Shuruppak. (In) Shuruppak, Ubar-Tutu became king and ruled 18,600 years. One king (thus) ruled it for 18,600 years.

These are five cities, eight kings ruled them for 241,000 years. (Then) the Flood swept over (the earth).

After the Flood had swept over (the earth) (and) when kingship was lowered (again) from heaven, kingship was (first) in Kish. In Kish, Ga[. . .]ur became king and ruled 1,200 years—(original) destroyed! legible (only) to heavenly Nidaba (the goddess of writing)—ruled 960 years. [Pala-kinatim ruled 900 years; Nangish-lishma ruled . . . year]; Bah[i]na ruled . . . years; BU.AN. [. .] . [um] ruled [8]40 ye[ars]; Kalibum ruled 960 years; Qalumum ruled 840 years; Zuqaqip ruled 900 years; Atab ruled 600 years; [Mashda, son] of Atab ruled 840 years; Arwi'um, son of Mashda, ruled 720 years; Etana, a shepherd, he who ascended to heaven (and) who consolidated all countries, became king and ruled 1,560 (var.: 1,500) years; Balih, son of Etana, ruled 400 (var.: 410) years; En-me-nunna ruled 660 years; Melam-Kishi, son of En-me-nunna ruled 900 years; Bar-sal-nunna, son of En-me-nunna, ruled 1,200 years; Samug, son of Bar-sal-nunna, ruled 140 years; Tizkar, son of Samug, ruled 305 years; Ilku' ruled 900 years; Ilta-sadum ruled 1,200 years; En-men-barage-si, he who carried away as spoil the "weapon" of Elam, became king and ruled 900 years; Aka, son of En-men-barage-si, ruled 629 years. Twenty-three kings (thus) ruled it for 24,510 years, 3 months, and 3½ days.

The Flood Story from the *Myth of Atrahasis III**

Atrahasis made his voice heard
And spoke to his master,
    'Indicate to me the meaning of the dream,
    [   ] let me find out its portent (?)'
Enki made his voice heard
And spoke to his servant,
    'You say, "I should find out in bed (?)".
    Make sure you attend to the message I shall tell you!
    Wall, listen constantly to me!
    Reed hut, make sure you attend to all my words!
    Dismantle the house, build a boat,
    Reject possessions, and save living things.
    The boat that you build
    [   ]
    [   ]
    Roof it like the Apsu
    So that the Sun cannot see inside it!
    Make upper decks and lower decks.
    The tackle must be very strong,

**Source:* © S. M. Dalley, 1989. Reprinted from *Myths from Mesopotamia,* translated by Stephanie Dalley (1989), by permission of Oxford University Press.

The bitumen strong, to give strength.
I shall make rain fall on you here,
A wealth of birds, a hamper (?) of fish.'
He opened the sand clock and filled it,
He told him the sand (needed) for the Flood was
Seven nights' worth.
Atrahasis received the message.
He gathered the elders at his door.
Atrahasis made his voice heard
And spoke to the elders,
'My god is out of favour with your god.
Enki and [Ellil (?)] have become angry with each other.
They have driven me out of [my house].
Since I always stand in awe of Enki,
He told (me) of this matter.
I can no longer stay in [   ]
I cannot set my foot on Ellil's territory (again).
[I must go down to the Apsu and stay] with (my) god (?).
This is what he told me.'

(*gap of 4 or 5 lines to end of column*)

(*gap of about 9 lines*)

The elders [   ]
The carpenter [brought his axe,]
The reed worker [brought his stone,]
[A child brought] bitumen.
The poor [fetched what was needed.]

(*9 lines very damaged*)

Everything there was [   ]
Everything there was [   ]
Pure ones [   ]
Fat ones [   ]
He selected [and put on board.]
[The birds] that fly in the sky,
Cattle [of Shak]kan,
Wild animals (?) [   ] of open country,
[he] put on board
[   ] . . .
He invited his people [   ]
[   ] to a feast.
[   ] he put his family on board.
They were eating, they were drinking.
But he went in and out,

Could not stay still or rest on his haunches,
His heart was breaking and he was vomiting bile.
The face of the weather changed.
Adad bellowed from the clouds.
When (?) he (Atrahasis) heard his noise,
Bitumen was brought and he sealed his door.
While he was closing up his door
Adad kept bellowing from the clouds.
The winds were raging even as he went up
(And) cut through the rope, he released the boat.

(6 *lines missing at beginning of column*)

Anzu was tearing at the sky with his talons,
[   ] the land,
He broke [   ]
[   ] the Flood [came out (?)].
The *kašūšu*-weapon went against the people like an army.
No one could see anyone else,
They could not be recognized in the catastrophe.
The Flood roared like a bull,
Like a wild ass screaming the winds [howled]
The darkness was total, there was no sun.
[   ] like white sheep.
[   ] of the Flood.
[   ]
[   ]
[   ] the noise of the Flood.
[   ]
[Anu (?)] went berserk,
[The gods (?)] . . . his sons . . . before him
As for Nintu the Great Mistress,
Her lips became encrusted with rime.
The great gods, the Anunna,
Stayed parched and famished.
The goddess watched and wept,
Midwife of the gods, wise Mami:
    'Let daylight (?) . . .
    Let it return and . . . !
    However could I, in the assembly of gods,
    Have ordered such destruction with them?
    Ellil was strong enough (?) to give a wicked order.
    Like Tiruru he ought to have cancelled that wicked order!
    I heard their cry levelled at me,
    Against myself, against my person.
    Beyond my control (?) my offspring have become like white sheep.
    As for me, how am I to live (?) in a house of bereavement?

My noise has turned to silence.
Could I go away, up to the sky
And live as in a cloister (?)?
What was Anu's intention as decision-maker?
It was his command that the gods his sons obeyed,
He who did not deliberate, but sent the Flood,
He who gathered the people to catastrophe
[   ]

(*3 lines missing at beginning of column*)

Nintu was wailing [   ]
    'Would a true father (?) have given birth to the [rolling (?)] sea
    (So that) they could clog the river like dragonflies?
    They are washed up (?) like a raft on [a bank (?)],
    They are washed up like a raft on a bank in open country!
    I have seen, and wept over them!
    Shall I (ever) finish weeping for them?'
She wept, she gave vent to her feelings,
Nintu wept and fuelled her passions.
The gods wept with her for the country.
She was sated with grief, she longed for beer (in vain).
Where she sat weeping, (there the great gods) sat too,
But, like sheep, could only fill their windpipes (with bleating).
Thirsty as they were, their lips
Discharged only the rime of famine.
For seven days and seven nights
The torrent, storm and flood came on.

(*gap of about 58 lines*)

He put down [   ],
Provided food [   ]
[   ]
The gods smelt the fragrance,
Gathered like flies over the offering.
When they had eaten the offering,
Nintu got up and blamed them all,
    'Whatever came over Anu who makes the decisions?
    Did Ellil (dare to) come for the smoke offering?
    (Those two) who did not deliberate, but sent the Flood,
    Gathered the people to catastrophe—
    You agreed the destruction.
    (Now) their bright faces are dark (forever).'
Then she went up to the big flies
Which Anu had made, and (declared) before the gods,
    'His grief is mine! My density goes with his!

He must deliver me from evil, and appease me!
Let me go out in the morning (?) [   ]
[   ]
Let these flies be the lapis lazuli of my necklace
By which I may remember it (?) daily (?) [forever (?)].'
The warrior Ellil spotted the boat
And was furious with the Igigi.
    'We, the great Anunna, all of us,
    Agreed together on an oath!
    No form of life should have escaped!
    How did any man survive the catastrophe?'
Anu made his voice heard
And spoke to the warrior Ellil,
    'Who but Enki would do this?
    He made sure that the [reed hut] disclosed the order.'
Enki made his voice heard
And spoke to the great gods,
    'I did it, in defiance of you!
    I made sure life was preserved [   ]

      (5 *lines missing*)

Exact your punishment from the sinner.
And whoever contradicts your order

      (12 *lines missing*)

    I have given vent to my feelings!'
Ellil made his voice heard
And spoke to far-sighted Enki,
    'Come, summon Nintu the womb-goddess!
    Confer with each other in the assembly.'
Enki made his voice heard
And spoke to the womb-goddess Nintu,
'You are the womb-goddess who decrees destinies.
    [   ] to the people.
[Let one-third of them be   ]
    [   ]
[Let another third of them be   ]
In addition let there be one-third of the people,
Among the people the woman who gives birth yet does
Not give birth (successfully);
Let there be the *pašittu*-demon among the people,
To snatch the baby from its mother's lap.
Establish *ugbabtu*, *entu*, *egisītu*-women:
They shall be taboo, and thus control childbirth.'

(*26 lines missing to end of column*)
(*8 lines missing at beginning of column*)

How we sent the Flood.
But a man survived the catastrophe.
You are the counsellor of the gods;
On your orders I created conflict.
Let the Igigi listen to this song
In order to praise you,
And let them record (?) your greatness.
I shall sing of the Flood to all people:
Listen!
(*Colophon*)
The End.
Third tablet,
'When the gods instead of man'
390 lines,
Total 1245
For the three tablets.
Hand of Nur-Aya, junior scribe.
Month Ayyar [x day],
Year Ammi-saduqa was king.
A statue of himself [   ]
[   ]

The Flood Story from the *Epic of Gilgamesh**

This document begins as a discussion is underway between Gilgamesh and Utanapishtim, a human who attained eternal life. This section begins as the god Ea gives instructions to Utanapishtim.

O man of Shuruppak, son of Ubartutu:
Tear down the house and build a boat!
Abandon wealth and seek living beings!
Spurn possessions and keep alive living beings!
Make all living beings go up into the boat.
The boat which you are to build,
its dimensions must measure equal to each other:
its length must correspond to its width.
Roof it over like the Apsu.'

**Source:* Reprinted from *The Epic of Gilgamesh*, Translated, with an Introduction and Notes, by Maureen Gallery Kovacs with the permission of the publishers, Stanford University Press. © 1985, 1989 by the Board of Trustees of the Leland Stanford Junior University.

I [Utanapishtim] understood and spoke to my lord, Ea:
    'My lord, thus is the command which you have uttered
    I will heed and will do it.
    But what shall I answer the city,[†] the populace, and the
                                 Elders?
Ea spoke, commanding me, his servant:
    'You, well then, this is what you must say to them:
        "It appears that Enlil[‡] is rejecting me
        so I cannot reside in your *city* (?),
        nor set foot on Enlil's earth.
        I will go down to the Apsu to live with my lord, Ea,
        and upon you he will rain down abundance,
        a profusion of fowl, myriad(?) fishes.
        He will bring to you a harvest of wealth,
        in the morning he will let loaves of bread shower down
        and in the evening a rain of wheat!"
Just as dawn began to glow
the land assembled *around me*—
the carpenter carried his hatchet,
the reed worker carried his (flattening) stone,
. . . the men . . .

. . .

The child carried the pitch,
the weak brought whatever else was needed.
On the fifth day I laid out her exterior.
It was a field in area,
its walls were each 10 times 12 cubits in height,
the sides of its top were of equal length, 10 times 12 cubits each.
I laid out its (interior) structure and drew a picture of it (?).
I provided it with six decks,
thus dividing it into seven (levels).
The inside of it I divided into nine (compartments).
I drove plugs (to keep out) water in its middle part.
I saw to the punting poles and laid in what was necessary.
Three times 3,600 (units) of raw bitumen I poured into the
                                 bitumen kiln,
three times 3,600 (units of) pitch . . . into it,
there were three times 3,600 porters of casks who carried (vegetable) oil,
apart from the 3,600 (units of) oil which they consumed (?)
and two times 3,600 (units of) oil which the boatman stored away.
I butchered oxen for *the meat*(?),
and day upon day I slaughtered sheep.
I gave the workmen(?) ale, beer, oil, and wine, as if it were river water,

---

[†]The city of Shuruppak, on the Euphrates River.
[‡]The advisor to the Greek Gods of Shuruppak.

so they could make a party like the New Year's Festival.
. . . and I set my hand to the oiling(?).
The boat was finished by sunset.
The launching was very difficult.
They had to keep carrying a runway of poles front to back,
until two-thirds of it had gone into the water(?).
Whatever I had I loaded on it:
whatever silver I had I loaded on it,
whatever gold I had I loaded on it.
All the living beings that I had I loaded on it,
    I had all my kith and kin go up into the boat,
    all the beasts and animals of the field and the craftsmen I had go up.
    Shamash had set a stated time:
        'In the morning I will let loaves of bread shower down,
        and in the evening a rain of wheat!
        Go inside the boat, seal the entry!'
That stated time had arrived.
In the morning he let loaves of bread shower down,
and in the evening a rain of wheat.
I watched the appearance of the weather—
the weather was frightful to behold!
I went into the boat and sealed the entry.
For the caulking of the boat, to Puzuramurri, the boatman,
I gave the palace together with its contents.
Just as dawn began to glow
there arose from the horizon a black cloud.
Adad rumbled inside of it,
before him went Shullat and Hanish,
heralds going over mountain and land.
Erragal pulled out the mooring poles,
forth went Ninurta and made the dikes overflow.
The Anunnaki lifted up the torches,
setting the land ablaze with their flare.
Stunned shock over Adad's deeds overtook the heavens,
and turned to blackness all that had been light.
The . . . land shattered like a . . . pot.
All day long the South Wind blew . . . ,
blowing fast, *submerging the* mountain *in water*,
overwhelming *the people* like an attack.
No one could see his fellow,
they could not recognize each other in the torrent.
The gods were frightened by the Flood,
and retreated, ascending to the heaven of Anu.
The gods were cowering like dogs, crouching by the outer wall.
Ishtar shrieked like a woman in childbirth,
the sweet-voiced Mistress of the Gods wailed:
    'The olden days have alas turned to clay,

because I said evil things in the Assembly of the Gods!
How could I say evil things in the Assembly of the Gods,
ordering a catastrophe to destroy my people?!
No sooner have I given birth to my dear people
than they fill the sea like so many fish!'
The gods—those of the Anunnaki—were weeping with her,
the gods humbly sat weeping, sobbing with grief(?),
their lips burning, parched with thirst.
Six days and seven nights
came the wind and flood, the storm flattening the land.
When the seventh day arrived, the storm was pounding,
the flood was a war—struggling with itself like a woman writhing (in labor).
The sea calmed, fell still, the whirlwind (and) flood stopped up.
I looked around all day long—quiet had set in
and all the human beings had turned to clay!
The terrain was as flat as a roof.
I opened a vent and fresh air (daylight?) fell upon the side of my nose.
I fell to my knees and sat weeping,
tears streaming down the side of my nose.
I looked around for coastlines in the expanse of the sea,
and at twelve leagues there emerged a region (of land).
On Mt. Nimush the boat lodged firm,
Mt. Nimush held the boat, allowing no sway.
One day and a second Mt. Nimush held the boat, allowing no sway.
A third day, a fourth, Mt. Nimush held the boat, allowing no sway.
A fifth day, a sixth, Mt. Nimush held the boat, allowing no sway.
When a seventh day arrived
I sent forth a dove and released it.
The dove went off, but came back to me;
no perch was visible so it circled back to me.
I sent forth a swallow and released it.
The swallow went off, but came back to me;
no perch was visible so it circled back to me.
I sent forth a raven and released it.
The raven went off, and saw the waters slither back.
It eats, it scratches, it bobs, but does not circle back to me.
Then I sent out everything in all directions and sacrificed (a sheep).
I offered incense in front of the mountain-ziggurat.
Seven and seven cult vessels I put in place,
and (into the fire) underneath (or: into their bowls) I poured reeds, cedar, and myrtle.
The gods smelled the savor,
the gods smelled the sweet savor,
and collected like flies over a (sheep) sacrifice.
Just then Beletili arrived.
She lifted up the large flies (beads*) which Anu had made for his enjoyment(?):

---

*A necklace with carved lapis lazuli fly beads, representing the dead offspring of the mother goddess Beletili/Aruru.

'You gods, as surely as I shall not forget this lapis lazuli around my neck,
may I be mindful of these days, and never forget them!
The gods may come to the incense offering,
but Enlil may not come to the incense offering,
because without considering he brought about the Flood
and consigned my people to annihilation.'
Just then Enlil arrived.
He saw the boat and became furious,
he was filled with rage at the Igigi gods:
'Where did a living being escape?
No man was to survive the annihilation!'
Ninurta spoke to Valiant Enlil, saying:
'Who else but Ea could device such a thing?
It is Ea who knows every machination!'
Ea spoke to Valiant Enlil, saying:
'It is *you*, O Valiant One, who is the Sage of the Gods.
How, how could *you* bring about a Flood without consideration?
Charge the violation to the violator,
charge the offense to the offender,
but be compassionate lest (mankind) be cut off,
be patient lest *they be killed*.
Instead of your bringing on the Flood,
would that a lion had appeared to diminish the people!
Instead of your bringing on the Flood,
would that a wolf had appeared to diminish the people!
Instead of your bringing on the Flood,
would that famine had occurred to slay the land!
Instead of your bringing on the Flood,
would that (Pestilent) Erra had appeared to ravage the land!
It was not I who revealed the secret of the Great Gods,
I (only) made a dream appear to Atrahasis, and (thus) he heard the secret of the gods.
Now then! The deliberation should be about him!'
Enlil went up inside the boat
and, grasping my hand, made me go up.
He had my wife go up and kneel by my side.
He touched our forehead and, standing between us, he blessed us:
'Previously Utanapishtim was a human being.
But now let Utanapishtim and his wife become like us, the gods!
Let Utanapishtim reside far away, at the Mouth of the Rivers.'
They took us far away and settled us at the Mouth of the Rivers."

The Flood Story from the *Book of Genesis**

Wild animals of every kind, cattle of every kind, reptiles of every kind that move upon the ground, and birds of every kind—all came to Noah in the ark, two by two of all creatures that had life in them. Those which came were one male and one female of all living things; they came in as God had commanded Noah, and the LORD closed the door on him. The flood continued upon the earth for forty days, and the waters swelled and lifted up the ark so that it rose high above the ground. They swelled and increased over the earth, and the ark floated on the surface of the waters. More and more the waters increased over the earth until they covered all the high mountains everywhere under heaven. The waters increased and the mountains were covered to a depth of fifteen cubits. Every living creature that moves on earth perished, birds, cattle, wild animals, all reptiles, and all mankind. Everything died that had the breath of life in its nostrils, everything on dry land. God wiped out every living thing that existed on earth, man and beast, reptile and bird; they were all wiped out over the whole earth, and only Noah and his company in the ark survived.

[. . . .]

After forty days Noah opened the trap-door that he had made in the ark, and released a raven to see whether the water had subsided, but the bird continued flying to and fro until the water on the earth had dried up. Noah waited for seven days, and then he released a dove from the ark to see whether the water on the earth had subsided further. But the dove found no place where she could settle, and so she came back to him in the ark, because there was water over the whole surface of the earth. Noah stretched out his hand, caught her and took her into the ark. He waited another seven days and again released the dove from the ark. She came back to him towards evening with a newly plucked olive branch in her beak. Then Noah knew for certain that the water on the earth had subsided still further. He waited yet another seven days and released the dove, but she never came back. And so it came about that, on the first day of the first month of his six hundred and first year, the water had dried up on the earth, and Noah removed the hatch and looked out of the ark. The surface of the ground was dry.

By the twenty-seventh day of the second month the whole earth was dry. And God said to Noah, 'Come out of the ark, you and your wife, your sons and their wives. Bring out every living creature that is with you, live things of every kind, bird and beast and every reptile that moves on the ground, and let them swarm over the earth and be fruitful and increase there.' So Noah came out with his sons, his wife, and his sons' wives. Every wild animal, all cattle, every bird, and every reptile that moves on the ground, came out of the ark by families. Then Noah built an altar to the LORD. He took ritually clean beasts and birds of every kind, and offered whole-offerings on the altar. When the LORD smelt the smoothing odour, he said within himself, 'Never again will I curse the ground because of man, however evil his inclinations may be from his youth upwards. I will never again kill every living creature, as I have just done.

Source: From *The New English Bible.* Copyright © the Delegates of Oxford University Press and the Syndics of the Cambridge University Press, 1961, 1970. Reprinted by permission.

> While the earth lasts
> seedtime and harvest, cold and heat,
> summer and winter, day and night,
> shall never cease.'

God blessed Noah and his sons and said to them, 'Be fruitful and increase, and fill the earth. The fear and dread of you shall fall upon all wild animals on earth, on all birds of heaven, on everything that moves upon the ground and all fish in the sea; they are given into your hands. Every creature that lives and moves shall be food for you; I give you them all, as once I gave you all green plants. But you must not eat the flesh with the life, which is the blood, still in it. And further, for your life-blood I will demand satisfaction; from every animal I will require it, and from a man also I will require satisfaction for the death of his fellow-man.

> He that sheds the blood of a man,
> for that man his blood shall be shed;
> for in the image of God
> has God made man.

But you must be fruitful and increase, swarm throughout the earth and rule over it.'

God spoke to Noah and to his sons with him: 'I now make my covenant with you and with your descendants after you, and with every living creature that is with you, all birds and cattle, all the wild animals with you on earth, all that have come out of the ark. I will make my covenant with you: never again shall all living creatures be destroyed by the waters of the flood, never again shall there be a flood to lay waste the earth.'

God said, 'This is the sign of the covenant which I establish between myself and you and every living creature with you, to endless generations:

> My bow I set in the cloud,
> sign of the covenant
> between myself and earth.
> When I cloud the sky over the earth,
> the bow shall be seen in the cloud.

Then will I remember the covenant which I have made between myself and you and living things of every kind. Never again shall the waters become a flood to destroy all living creatures.

Chapter 3
The Legacy of Greece

Chapter Questions

After reading and studying this chapter you should be able to answer the following questions:

What geographical factors helped to mold the city-states? How and why did the Greeks develop different political forms, such as tyranny and democracy? What did the Greek intellectual triumph entail? How and why did the Greek experiment fail?

Chapter Summary

Ancient Greece made invaluable contributions to human progress and the development of Western civilization. Greek society explored a remarkable range of the problems that beset men and women of all ages: the nature of God and the universe, the dimensions of human sexuality, the challenges of war and imperialism, the proper relationship between the individual and the state. The Greeks were also great thinkers and actors. They have become an example of both human excellence and human frailty, for the Greeks eventually destroyed themselves through war and imperialism. An important question this chapter seeks to answer is why the Greek experiment failed.

The chapter stresses the importance of geographical isolation and proximity to the sea in the political and economic development of the city-state, or polis. It also describes how Greek (Hellenic) religion, art, and life were interwoven. Though the Greek gods were believed to be immortal, they were attributed human qualities. In honoring their gods the Greeks honored the human spirit and sought human excellence. For the Greeks, the search for truth and meaning in life was pursued not only through mythology and religious experience but through rational philosophy—by great thinkers such as Socrates, Plato, and Aristotle—and through the arts as well. The plays of the great dramatists Aeschylus, Sophocles, and Euripides have led generations of people to examine life's basic conflicts. The Greeks saw drama, comedy, sculpture, and philosophy as ways to relate to their gods and discover the truth about life.

The reasons for Greek aggression in the Aegean world are explored, as are the reasons for the war between the two Greek superpowers, Sparta and Athens. These two states represented opposing political systems and different philosophies of life. Daily life in Athens included sophisticated art and great literature, but the economic system was simple and based to a large extent on slavery. Although it was war that saved Greece (and the West) from the oriental monarchy of the Persians, it was also war within Greece—especially among Sparta, Athens, and Thebes—that destroyed the freedom of the Greeks and brought on their conquest by the ambitious Philip II of Macedonia. Only the city-state of Thebes, through its sponsorship of federalism, was able to set forth a resolution to internecine war—a resolution that was adopted by the conqueror Philip II.

Study Outline

Use this outline to preview the chapter before you read a particular section in your textbook and then as a self-check to test your reading comprehension after you have read the chapter section.

I. Hellas: the land
   A. The islands of the Aegean served as stepping stones between the Greek peninsula and Asia Minor.
   B. The mountains both inspired the Greeks and isolated them from one another, hindering unity.
II. The Minoans and Mycenaeans (ca 1650–ca 1100 B.C.)
   A. The Greeks had established themselves in Greece by ca 1650 B.C.
      1. The first Greek-speaking culture was probably at the city of Mycenae.
         a. Archeologists have used Homer's *Iliad* and *Odyssey* to locate this and other sites.
         b. H. Schliemann excavated Mycenae to discover the lost past of the Greek people.
      2. Another early Greek culture, the Minoan, developed on the island of Crete.
         a. The head of Crete was a king; its political-economic centers were a series of palaces.
         b. The Minoan society was wealthy and apparently peaceful.
         c. Like the Mycenaeans, the Minoans used bronze implements.
      3. From their center at Cnossus, the Mycenaeans built cities at Thebes, Athens, Tiryns, and Pylos.
         a. The king and his warrior-aristocracy exercised political and economic control.
         b. Scribes kept records, but little is known of the ordinary people except that an extensive division of labor existed.
      4. Minoan-Mycenaean contacts were originally peaceful but turned to war ca 1450 B.C.
         a. The Minoan capital of Cnossus was destroyed for unknown reasons.
         b. The Mycenaeans grew rich, but eventually were destroyed, probably by internecine war.
      5. The fall of the Mycenaean kingdoms ushered in a "Dark Age" in Greece from 1100–800 B.C.
   B. Homer, Hesiod, and the heroic past (1100–800 B.C.)
      1. The poems of Homer and Hesiod idealized the past.
         a. The *Iliad* recounts an expedition of Mycenaeans to besiege the city of Troy.
         b. The *Odyssey* narrates the adventures of Odysseus during his voyage home from Troy.

      c.   Hesiod's *Theogony* traces the descent of Zeus.

      d.   *Works and Days* offered advice on how to live a good life.

   2. The great poets taught men and women how to live.

III. The polis

   A. By the end of the Dark Age, the polis, or city-state, was common throughout Greece.

     1. Athens, Sparta, and Thebes were the chief city-states.

     2. The acropolis was the religious center of the polis, and the agora was its marketplace and political center.

     3. The polis was both an agricultural and an urban center.

     4. The polis was an intimate community of citizens that tended to exclude outsiders and maintain its independence jealously.

     5. The polis could be governed as a monarchy, aristocracy, oligarchy, democracy, or tyranny.

   B. The exclusiveness and individualism of each polis led to almost constant war, although some Greeks banded together to form leagues of city-states.

IV. The Lyric Age (800–500 B.C.)

   A. Overseas expansion followed the breakdown of the Mycenaean world.

     1. The expansion of Greeks throughout the Mediterranean was due to land shortage and the desire for adventure.

     2. Greek colonies extended from the Black Sea to North Africa and into Spain.

     3. Greek colonization led to greater power for the polis and spread its values far beyond the shores of Greece.

   B. The lyric poets encouraged individualism, energy, and adventure.

     1. Archilochus typifies the restlessness and self-reliance of the era.

     2. Erotic, bisexual love is portrayed in the work of Sappho.

   C. The growth of Sparta into a powerful polis

     1. Sparta's victories in the Messenian wars extended its boundaries and enslaved the Messenians.

     2. The warriors demanded and received political rights.

     3. The Lycurgan regime was a new political, economic, and social system.

        a.   All citizens became legally equal, and oligarchy replaced aristocracy.

        b.   Executive power rested in five elected *ephors*, or overseers.

        c.   Land was divided among all citizens and worked by *helots*, or state serfs.

        d.   Spartan women were more emancipated and independent than women in other Greek states.

     4. The Spartans disdained wealth and luxury, glorified war and patriotism, and suppressed individualism.

   D. The evolution of Athens

     1. Athens moved from aristocracy to democracy.

        a.   Poor peasants demanded legal reforms.

        b.   Draco's code—Athens's first law code—established that the law belonged to all citizens.

     2. Solon became *archon* in ca 594 B.C. and enacted sweeping reforms.

     3. Pisistratus became tyrant in 546 B.C. and reduced the power of the aristocracy.

     4. Beginning in 508 B.C., Cleisthenes reorganized the state and created the Athenian democracy.

        a.   *Demes* were the basis of the political system.

        b. The demes were grouped into tribes.

        c. The central government included an assembly of all citizens and a council of five hundred members.

        d. Ostracism was used to rid the state peacefully of potentially dangerous politicians.

    5. Athenian democracy proved that a large number of people could run the affairs of state.

V. The Classical period (500–338 B.C.)

    A. The deadly conflicts—war between the Greeks and the Persians

        1. Greek victory in war guaranteed the flowering of Greek culture and freedom.

        2. The Greeks won at Marathon (490 B.C.), but the Persian king Xerxes invaded Greece in 480 B.C.

        3. The Persians were defeated at Salamis (480 B.C.) and Plataea (479 B.C.).

    B. The growth of the Athenian Empire (478–431 B.C.)

        1. The Athenians established the Delian League (478 B.C.) as a naval alliance to continue the fight against Persia.

            a. Led by Cimon, the Athenians drove the Persians out of the Aegean.

            b. The Athenians turned the league into a tool of their own empire.

            c. Athenian aggressiveness alarmed Sparta and its allies.

        2. Athens's conflict with Corinth led to war with Sparta.

    C. The Peloponnesian War (431–404 B.C.)

        1. The long war brought death, destruction, stalemate, and a new breed of self-serving Athenian politicians.

        2. The Peace of Nicias (421 B.C.) led to a cold war.

        3. The opportunist Alcibiades led Athens in an invasion of Syracuse in Sicily, only to be defeated (413 B.C.).

        4. A final phase was marked by renewed war between Athens and Sparta, Persian intervention, and revolt by many Athenian subjects.

        5. Under Lysander, the Spartans defeated Athens in 405 B.C.

    D. The birth of historical awareness

        1. Herodotus, the "father of history," covered the major events of the Near East and Greece in *The Histories*.

        2. Thucydides chronicled the history of the Peloponnesian War.

    E. Athenian arts in the age of Pericles

        1. In the last half of the fifth century B.C., Pericles turned Athens into the showplace of Greece.

        2. The Athenian Acropolis became the center of Greek religion and art.

            a. The entrance building (the Propylaea) led to small temples that honored the goddess Athena and Athenian victories.

            b. The Parthenon, a Doric temple, was an architectural masterpiece and the epitome of Greek art and its spirit.

        3. The development of drama was tied to the religious festivals of the city.

        4. Aeschylus, Sophocles, and Euripides were the three greatest dramatists of Athens.

            a. Aeschylus wrote a trilogy of plays about humans in conflict, stressing the themes of betrayal, reconciliation, reason, and justice.

            b. Sophocles' masterpieces (the three *Oedipus* plays) deal with the interplay of human actions, justice, and the will of the gods.

      c. Euripides' plays focus on humans who face disaster because they allow their passions to overwhelm them.

F. Daily life in Periclean Athens
1. Material life was simple, and most goods were produced at home.
2. Slavery was common.
3. Agriculture and small crafts were the major types of labor.
4. Women were protected by law but did not have equal rights with men.
    a. Because the historical evidence is largely military or political, women's role is often underestimated.
    b. Women held a *liminal* position—that is, one of considerable unofficial power.
    c. Women's main functions were to raise the children, oversee the slaves, and work wool into cloth.
5. Acceptance of homosexuality was a distinctive feature of Athenian life.
6. Greek religion was individual and lacked organized creeds and sacred books.
    a. Religion was a matter of ritual and a way to honor the polis.
    b. The Olympic games were held for the glory of Zeus and were a unifying factor in Greek life.

G. The flowering of philosophy
1. The Greeks of the Classical period viewed the universe in terms of natural law, not mythology.
2. Thales, Anaximander, and Heraclitus made important contributions to the sciences.
3. Hippocrates was the founder of modern medicine.
4. The Sophists taught excellence and believed that nothing is absolute.
5. Socrates attempted to discover truth and happiness by continuous questioning; he believed that true happiness could be found in the pursuit of excellence.
6. Plato's philosophy is based on the idea that reality exists only in the immaterial world.
    a. He founded a philosophical school, the Academy.
    b. In *The Republic*, Plato sought to define the ideal polis.
7. Aristotle's range of philosophical inquiry was staggering.
    a. He wrote about the polis in *Politics*.
    b. In *Physics* and *Metaphysics* he developed a theory of nature.
    c. *On the Heaven* expresses his theory of cosmology.

H. The final act (404–338 B.C.)
1. The Spartan defeat of Athens (404 B.C.) set the stage for the Macedonian conquest of Greece.
2. This was a turbulent political period, but also one of cultural vibrancy.
3. The Common Peace was the Greeks' attempt to live in harmony with one another and with Persia.
4. Federalism was another attempt to prevent war and to allow independence.

I. The struggle for hegemony
1. Attempted hegemony (political domination) by the chief states caused both federalism and the Common Peace to fail.
2. Lysander persuaded Sparta to become the head of a new empire.
3. This decision led to the Corinthian War, which ended in Sparta's loss and the first formal Common Peace, the King's Peace (386 B.C.).

7. The polis can be best described as
   a. a community of citizens.
   b. a religious community.
   c. a community of merchants.
   d. a community of warriors.

8. The Acropolis and the Parthenon are two buildings still standing that were built during the Age of
   a. Solon.
   b. Pericles.
   c. Alcibiades.
   d. Aristophanes.

9. The *Iliad* and *Odyssey* were
   a. sacred writings.
   b. collections of laws.
   c. historical records.
   d. epic poems.

10. A woman best known for her erotic poetry was
    a. Tyrtaeus.
    b. Archilochus.
    c. Lesbos.
    d. Sappho.

11. Solon was an Athenian
    a. tyrant.
    b. reformer.
    c. king.
    d. priest.

12. Greeks at first used the word *tyrant* to denote a
    a. leader who ruled without legal right.
    b. cruel leader who oppressed the poor.
    c. champion of the commercial classes.
    d. leader whose efforts destroyed all forms of democracy.

13. Cleisthenes was famous because he
    a. made Athens a major commercial center.
    b. suppressed popular unrest.
    c. was the most successful Athenian tyrant.
    d. created the Athenian democracy.

14. Athens used the Delian League
    a. to colonize the Mediterranean.
    b. to fight the Persians.
    c. to promote Mediterranean trade.
    d. to spread Greek culture.

15. Thucydides wrote in order to
    a. analyze the Peloponnesian War.
    b. describe the Athenian democracy.
    c. record events in the Persian wars.
    d. defend Athenian foreign policy.

16. Which of the following statements does *not* describe the drama *Oresteia* by Aeschylus?
    a. The trilogy deals with the themes of betrayal, murder, and reconciliation.
    b. The use of reason and justice is urged to reconcile fundamental conflicts.
    c. The trilogy ends with a plea that civil dissension not be allowed to destroy societal stability.
    d. The trilogy's major theme is the societal taboo of incest.

17. Aristophanes was popular because
    a. the government tried to censure his plays.
    b. he was the most religious Athenian poet.
    c. he justified Athenian imperialism.
    d. he was a critic of political and social life.

18. Most Greeks supported themselves by
    a. fishing.
    b. trading.
    c. warfare.
    d. farming.

19. Athenian women
    a. had the status of slaves.
    b. had full citizens' rights.
    c. had protection under the law.
    d. had greater rights than men.

20. Greek homosexuality was considered
    a. the curse of the lower classes.
    b. a threat to family life.
    c. an insult to religion.
    d. for many a normal practice.

21. First and foremost the Athenian Acropolis was
    a. an economic and trade center.
    b. a series of temples in honor of Athena.
    c. the monumental gateway to the Athenian harbor.
    d. the center of Greek political activity.

22. The aristocrat and writer Thucydides believed that the fate of men and women was
    a. left to the gods.
    b. entirely in their own hands.
    c. determined by nature.
    d. not to be understood or determined.

23. The power of free women in Greek society is defined as *liminal,* which means that
    a. women had limited power in society.
    b. they had considerable political power through office holding.
    c. they had significant unofficial power.
    d. their influence began only after their husbands died.

24. The city-state that sponsored Greek federalism and successfully blended the three concepts of hegemony, federalism, and the Common Peace was
    a. Thebes.
    b. Athens.
    c. Sparta.
    d. Cornith.

25. The Macedonian king who took advantage of the internecine Greek struggle and thereby conquered Greece was
    a. Alexander the Great.
    b. Philip II.
    c. Cleon.
    d. Cleisthenes.

Major Political Ideas

Define the terms *monarchy, aristocracy, oligarchy, tyranny,* and *democracy.* How does each differ in terms of the placement of authority within society? Describe the transition from aristocracy to tyranny to democracy in Athens. How did the system of democracy evolve and what were its principal features? In what sense was Athenian democracy similar to or different from modern democracy?

Issues for Essays and Discussion

1. The Greek polis was a dramatic break from the past. Explain this by discussing what the polis was and what its major political and cultural achievements were. Was the polis, in your view, a failure?

2. Compare and contrast Pre-Socratic and Socratic philosophy. In your discussion make reference to specific thinkers, their method of acquiring knowledge, and how they explained human experience and the origins of the universe.

3. What characteristics of Athenian daily life made it distinctive? Discuss this by referring to such things as Athenian religion, sport, sexual attitudes, drama, and the role of women. Include examples.

Interpretation of Visual Sources

Study the painting on the Greek vase in the photograph on page 90 of the text. Describe the scene and its participants. How does this scene help explain the relationship between Greek life and Greek religion?

Geography

1. On Outline Map 3.1 provided, mark the approximate location of the following: Athens, Crete, Asia Minor, Mount Olympus, Sparta, the Mediterranean Sea, Lesbos, Marathon, Thebes, the Aegean Sea, Peloponnesus, Mycenae, Troy, the Ionian Sea, Ionia.

2. The geography of Greece encouraged political fragmentation. Explain.

3. Using Map 3.2 as a reference, describe the area that came under Greek control as a result of its overseas expansion. What were the causes of this expansion?

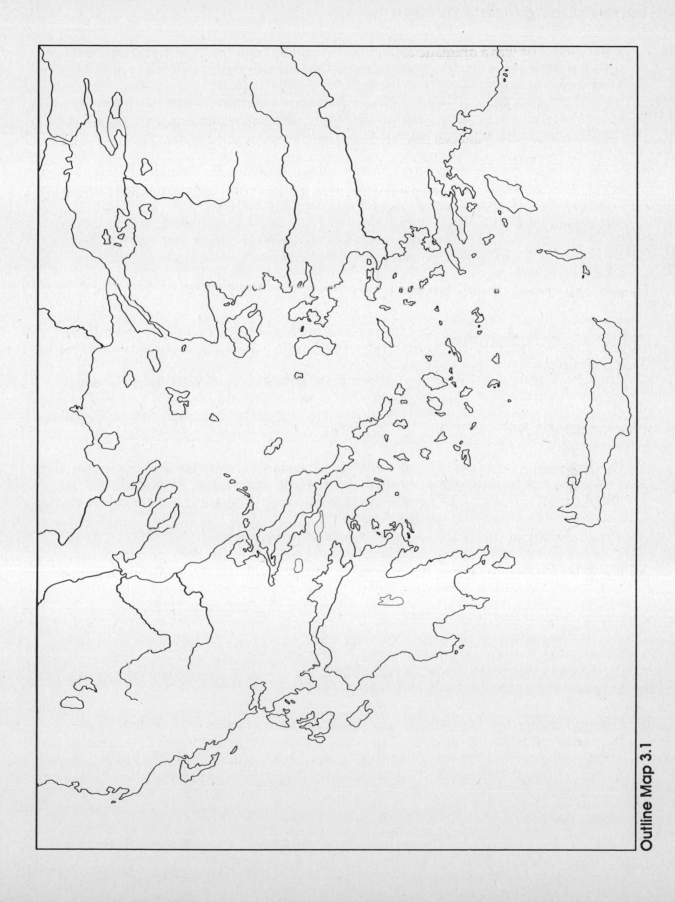

Understanding History Through the Arts

1. What can we discover about Greek life and thought by reading Greek literature? Nothing can be of more value in understanding the Greeks than to go directly to their great literature. The two dialogues of Plato, *Protagoras and Meno*,* W. K. C. Guthrie, trans. 1956, are among the best of Greek prose. *Protagoras*, Plato's dramatic masterpiece, deals with the problem of teaching the art of successful living, while *Meno* considers the immortality of the soul and the idea that learning is knowledge acquired before birth.

2. What motivated Greek society to produce what is regarded as the finest in architecture and sculpture? The elegance and excellence of Greek sculpture and architecture are explored in J. Charbonneaux, R. Martin, and F. Villard, *Classical Greek Art, 480–330 B.C.* (1972), and P. Demargne, *The Birth of Greek Art*, S. Gilbert and J. Emmons, trans. (1964). Both of these are richly illustrated. An excellent introduction to the subject is "Greek Art," in H. W. Jansen, *History of Art*, Chap. 5 (1962). Greek mythology is interestingly told in E. Hamilton, *Mythology* (1942).

Problems for Further Investigation

1. What was Greek society like? The Greek mind? The best short introduction to Greek society—including the polis, religion, war, and the Greek mind—is H. D. F. Kitto, *The Greeks** (1951). Students interested in the development of Greek thought and the Greek way of thinking should read W. K. C. Guthrie, *The Greek Philosophers** (1950, 1960).

2. In what ways did the Greeks define childhood and sexuality differently from society today? Two of the best books on Greek sexuality are H. Licht, *Sexual Life in Ancient Greece*, J. H. Freese, trans. (1932), and K. Dover, *Greek Homosexuality* (1978). On childhood see M. Golden, *Children and Childhood in Classical Athens* (1990).

3. Why did Greek democracy eventually fail? Was Greek society truly democratic? Students interested in pursuing the subject of Greek politics and political theory should begin with J. N. Claster, ed., *Athenian Democracy** (1967), which is a collection of interpretations by various historians, and B. Tierney et al., *Periclean Athens: Was It a Democracy?** (1967).

4. Did the Trojan War, as set forth in the *Iliad*, actually take place? If so, when? What did Heinrich Schliemann actually find at Troy? All these problems are taken up in an engaging work by M. Wood, *In Search of the Trojan War* (1985), a well-illustrated companion volume to a six-part PBS television series with the same title.

5. How did change in society affect the position of women in the ancient world? For a view that sees a reduction in women's role, read M. Arthur, "From Medusa to Cleopatra: Women in the Ancient World," in R. Bridenthal, C. Koonz, and S. Stuard, *Becoming Visible, Women in European History** (2nd ed., 1987). An excellent bibliography is included.

---

*Available in paperback.

Chapter 4
Hellenistic Diffusion

Chapter Questions

After reading and studying this chapter you should be able to answer the following questions:

How was the development of philosophy, religion, science, medicine, and economics affected by the meeting of the Eastern and Western worlds? What did the spread of Hellenism mean to the Greeks and the peoples of the Near East? Did the spread of Greek culture by Philip and Alexander lay the groundwork for later cultures?

Chapter Summary

This chapter describes how the ancient Near Eastern cultures and the Greek, or Hellenic, culture came together to form a new, Hellenistic culture during the time of Alexander the Great, the son of Philip II. This Hellenistic age was a period of both political confusion and cultural unity that lay the groundwork for the triumph of Roman imperialism.

Alexander the Great, who was given a Greek education by Aristotle, conquered most of the known world by 324 B.C. He defeated and conquered Persia and then marched on to India, part of which was incorporated into his Macedonian state. Along the way he founded new cities and military colonies, all of which became agencies by which Hellenistic culture spread throughout most of the Mediterranean and Near Eastern world. When he died, his empire was divided into four kingdoms, which became frontiers of opportunity for large numbers of Greeks in search of jobs, wealth, and power. Thus, Greek men and women settled throughout the East, forming an elite class of professionals and administrators. These Greek settlers also carried Greek literature, law, engineering, architecture, and philosophy into every corner of the Near East and the Mediterranean.

Important new discoveries in science and medicine were made in the Hellenistic period. Philosophy became extremely creative, led by the competing doctrines of the Cynics, the Epicureans, and the Stoics. There were also important advances in food production, trade, and mining. Thus, the Hellenistic age was a time of change and creativity.

Study Outline

Use this outline to preview the chapter before you read a particular section in your textbook and then as a self-check to test your reading comprehension after you have read the chapter section.

I. Alexander and the crusade to conquer Asia Minor
   A. Alexander the King
      1. The son of King Philip, Alexander was tutored by Aristotle.
      2. Alexander became king in 336 B.C. and invaded Asia in 334 B.C.
      3. By 330 B.C., he had defeated the Persians to avenge the Persian invasion of Greece.
      4. He then set out to conquer the rest of Asia.
   B. Alexander's political legacy
      1. After his death in 323 B.C., Alexander's empire was divided among four dynasties: the Antigonids, the Ptolemies, the Seleucids, and the Pergamenes; a kingdom of Bactria was founded in the far northeast.
      2. In Greece the polis system was replaced by leagues of city-states.
      3. The Hellenistic world was politically fragmented and constantly at war.
   C. The cultural legacy
      1. The colonies founded by Alexander and his successors brought many Greeks into Asia, thereby bringing East and West together.
      2. Alexander's empire spread Greek culture as far east as India.
      3. Hellenism became a common bond among the East, peninsular Greece, and the western Mediterranean.
II. The spread of Hellenism
   A. Cities and kingdoms of the Hellenistic age
      1. The new polis was not politically independent but rather a part of a kingdom.
         a. The polis was not self-governing, but rather subject to interference from the king.
         b. Legal and social inequality existed in the Hellenistic polis; Greeks had greater rights.
      2. The Hellenistic kings were frequently at war as they attempted to solidify their kingdoms and gain the loyalty of subjects.
      3. Hellenistic cities formed the cultural foundation on which Roman and Christian cultures were to spread and flourish.
   B. The Greeks and the opening of the East
      1. The Hellenistic kingdoms in Asia and Egypt provided Greeks with lucrative jobs.
      2. Greeks dominated the administrative and military branches of the kingdoms.
      3. They also dominated the other professions—the arts, engineering, architecture, etc.
      4. However, the Hellenistic kings could not gain the complete loyalty of their soldiers and professionals, and thus their kingdoms were weakened.
III. Greeks and Easterners: the spread of Hellenism
   A. The uneven spread of Greek culture
      1. A Greco-Egyptian culture evolved slowly in Egypt.
      2. Under the Seleucid kings, Greek and Eastern culture merged in Asia Minor.
      3. Most Easterners took only the external trappings of Greek culture, such as the Greek dialect called *koine*, while retaining their own way of life.

B. Hellenism and the Jews
1. The Greeks allowed the Jews political and religious freedom.
2. Despite adoption of some Hellenistic culture, Jews remained Hebrew at heart.
IV. The economic scope of Hellenism
A. Commerce
1. Alexander's conquests brought the East and the West together for trade.
2. Overland trade to India and a sea route to Italy were established.
3. Eastern grain was essential to Greece and the Aegean area; in return Greece exported oil, wine, and fish.
4. The slave trade flourished because slavery was important to the Hellenistic economy.
B. Industry
1. Cheap labor left no incentive to invent machinery.
2. The only change in mining was the introduction of the Archimedean screw for pumping water into irrigation ditches and out of the mines.
3. Labor in the gold, silver, and iron mines was harsh; many of the workers were political prisoners and slaves.
4. Important changes in pottery style took place, but production methods remained unchanged.
C. Agriculture
1. The Ptolemies made advances in seed development and produced handbooks on farming.
2. The Ptolemies also made great strides in irrigating the land, partly because of their strong central government.
V. Religion and philosophy in the Hellenistic world
A. Religion in the Hellenistic world
1. The Greek religious cults centered on the Olympian gods.
2. The cults, consisting mainly of rituals, did not fill the religious needs of the people.
3. Many people turned to a belief in *Tyche* (fate or chance).
4. There was a growth in mystery religions to fill emotional and ethical needs.
   a. These religions promised life for the soul after death and union with a god who had himself risen from the dead.
   b. Isis was the most important goddess of the new mystery cults.
B. Philosophy and the common man
1. Common people became interested in philosophy.
2. The new philosophies taught that people could be truly happy only when they rejected the world and focused their attention on enduring things.
3. The Cynics believed in the rejection of the material life.
   a. Diogenes, the greatest of the Cynics, stressed living according to nature and without allegiance to a particular city or monarchy.
   b. The Cynics influenced all the other major schools of philosophy.
4. The Epicureans taught that pleasure was the chief good and advocated political passivity.
5. The Stoics stressed the unity of man and universe and resignation to one's duty.
   a. Zeno made Stoicism the most popular Hellenistic philosophy.
   b. Participation in worldly affairs was encouraged, but leading a virtuous life was most important.

    c. The Stoic concept of natural law—one law for all people—was of great importance, particularly later in Rome.

VI. Hellenistic women
    A. The Hellenistic period brought royal women back into politics.
    B. Women became important in art, literature, and medicine.
    C. Although the Stoics regarded women as inferior, the Cynics treated them as equals.
    D. Women became economically more important and as a result had more opportunities than in Hellenic times.

VII. Hellenistic science and medicine
    A. Aristarchus developed the heliocentric theory of the universe, although Aristotle's earth-centered view remained dominant.
    B. Euclid compiled a textbook on geometry.
    C. Archimedes, an inventor and theoretician, sketched out basic principles of mechanics.
    D. Eratosthenes made advances in mathematics and geography.
    E. Theophrastos founded the study of botany.
    F. The Dogmatic school of medicine, under Herophilus and Erasistratus, used vivisection and dissection to gain knowledge of the body, including the nervous system.
    G. The Empiric school stressed observation and the use of medicine and drugs, including opium.
    H. Many quacks did untold harm, but they were popular.

Review Questions

Check your understanding of this chapter by answering the following questions.

1. What were Alexander's major achievements? Does he deserve to be called "the Great"?
2. Trace the expansion of the Macedonian kingdom into Asia. What were the reasons for this movement?
3. Explain why Alexander's empire began disintegrating at the time of his death. Why could the empire not remain intact?
4. How did the Hellenistic polis differ from the earlier Greek polis? Why?
5. What did the new Hellenistic kingdoms offer the Greeks? Why couldn't these kingdoms gain the loyalty of the Greek immigrants?
6. How successful was Greek culture in penetrating Egypt and the East?
7. What was the impact of Hellenistic policies and culture on the Jews who resided in Hellenic areas?
8. Trace the developments in agriculture and industry in Hellenistic society. Why was there so little technological innovation?
9. Explain the interregional trade patterns of the Hellenistic world. What products did the various parts of the Hellenistic world specialize in?
10. What kinds of commodities made up the caravan trade?
11. How did the position and power of women in Hellenistic society change from those of earlier periods?

12. Discuss the religious and philosophical trends in the Hellenistic world. Why did the common person become interested in philosophy?
13. Trace the development of medical science in the Hellenistic era. What advances were made over the Hellenic period?

Study-Review Exercises

Define the following key concepts and terms.

Hellenism

politeuma

Tyche

natural law

heliocentric theory

empirical tradition

Explain the major ideas and accomplishments of the following people.

Aristarchus of Samos

Euclid

Archimedes

Eratosthenes

Theophrastos

Herophilus

Explain the principal ideas and beliefs of the following Hellenistic philosophers.
Cynics

Epicureans

Stoics

Identify and explain the significance of the following people and terms.
Hellenistic period

Aetolian League

Ptolemy

koine

Alexander the Great

Zeno

Isis

Dogmatic school of medicine

Empiric school of medicine

Test your understanding of the chapter by providing the correct answers.
1. Epicurus taught that the gods had *no/great* effect on human life.

2. The most popular philosophy of the Hellenistic world was _____.

3. The Cynics advised men and women to *accept/discard* traditional customs and conventions.

4. The founder of the Cynics was _____ , who believed that nothing natural was dirty or shameful.

5. The Hellenistic world *did/did not* see much trade in manufactured goods.

6. Alexander the Great's conquest of Persia was completed by about the year

   _____ .

7. The Greek immigrants in the Hellenistic kingdoms generally *did/did not* develop a strong loyalty to the state.

8. After Alexander's death the empire was broken into four parts, the _____ ,

   _____ , _____ , and _____ kingdoms.

9. The political and economic power of women tended to *increase/decrease* during the Hellenistic period.

10. To the Hellenists, *Tyche* meant _____ .

11. Generally, the Greeks tended to be *tolerant/intolerant* toward other religions.

12. _____ was the goddess of marriage, conception, and childbirth.

Multiple-Choice Questions

1. The Epicureans believed that one could find happiness
   a. by becoming involved in politics.
   b. through pain.
   c. by retiring within oneself.
   d. by pleasing the gods.

2. The most important achievement of the Stoics was the
   a. idea of rejecting the state.
   b. cult of Isis.
   c. education of Alexander.
   d. concept of natural law.

3. Which of the following statements about Hellenized Easterners is true?
   a. They rejected everything Greek except Greek religion.
   b. They adopted much but retained the essentials of their own culture.
   c. They became thoroughly assimilated into Greek culture.
   d. They had no culture of their own.

4. Within the Hellenistic world Greeks formed the
   a. middle class of merchants.
   b. favored class.
   c. slave class.
   d. priest class.

5. Alexander's troops refused to proceed farther after they reached
   a. Persia.
   b. India.
   c. Bactria.
   d. China.

6. Alexander made his greatest contribution toward understanding between West and East when he
   a. forced Greeks to marry barbarians.
   b. established the Greek church in India.
   c. established colonies for Greek emigration.
   d. encouraged the adoption of barbarian food and dress.

7. Women's position improved during the Hellenistic age because of
   a. the Greeks' belief that women were equal.
   b. full citizenship rights conferred by law.
   c. their increased activity in economic affairs.
   d. their noble and self-sacrificing deeds.

8. During the Hellenistic period, the greatest strides in agriculture were made by the
   a. Ptolemies in Egypt.
   b. Macedonians.
   c. Seleucids.
   d. Athenians.

9. The Greek word *Tyche* means
   a. revelation.
   b. honor.
   c. to be strong.
   d. fate.

10. The author of *The Elements of Geometry* was
    a. Euclid.
    b. Archimedes.
    c. Aristarchus of Samos.
    d. Eratosthenes.

11. After Alexander's death, his empire was divided into all of the following dynasties except the
    a. Seleucid dynasty.
    b. Ptolemaic dynasty.
    c. Antigonid dynasty.
    d. Athenian dynasty.

12. In the Hellenistic period philosophy was
    a. the pastime of the wealthy.
    b. the profession of specialists.
    c. a propaganda tool of kings.
    d. an outlet for common people.

13. The Cynics thought that
    a. people should avoid pain.
    b. people should live according to nature.
    c. people should uphold the norms of society.
    d. people should enjoy luxury in moderation.

14. Epicurean philosophy taught
    a. the overthrow of monarchies.
    b. the virtue of self-discipline.
    c. the value of religion.
    d. the value of pleasure.

15. The Stoics evolved the idea of
    a. might makes right.
    b. pain against pleasure.
    c. the unity of mankind and the universe.
    d. the unity of mankind and the state.

16. Aristarchus of Samos is important because he thought that
    a. the sun revolved around the earth.
    b. the moon revolved around the earth.
    c. the earth revolved around the sun.
    d. the sun and moon were fixed bodies.

17. Which of the following sciences got its start in the Hellenistic period?
    a. Economics
    b. Physics
    c. Botany
    d. Geology

18. The discoverer of the nervous system was
    a. Herophilus.
    b. Erasistratus.
    c. Heraclides.
    d. Serapion.

19. The Empiric school of medicine emphasized
    a. the study of anatomy.
    b. the study of physiology.
    c. the use of vivisection and dissection.
    d. the cure of sickness through observation and drugs.

20. Hellenistic industry relied chiefly on
    a. labor-saving machines.
    b. new techniques of production.
    c. increased use of animal power.
    d. use of manual labor.

21. In the Hellenistic period, for the most part, the polis
    a. was totally abandoned.
    b. remained unchanged.
    c. became more independent.
    d. were less independent and active than in earlier time.

22. Jews living in Hellenistic cities
    a. often embraced a good deal of Hellenism.
    b. rejected Hellenism.
    c. adopted only the Greek gods.
    d. usually abandoned their religion in favor of Stoicism.

23. The real achievement of Alexander and his successors in the economic realm was
    a. an industrial revolution.
    b. a switch to a sophisticated consumer society.
    c. blocking the overland trade with India and Arabia.
    d. the creation of a broad commercial network linking East and West.

24. After Alexander's conquest of the Persian Empire, the only commodity listed below that did not increase in economic importance because of stimulated trade was
    a. luxury items.
    b. slaves.
    c. raw materials, grain, and industrial products.
    d. manufactured goods.

25. Which of the following statements about the relationship between industrial growth and the labor supply in Hellenistic Greece is true?
    a. The demand for products fell, therefore unemployment rose.
    b. A limited supply of labor led to technological innovation.
    c. An abundance of labor caused many technological advances.
    d. Human labor was cheap, therefore there was little incentive to invent machinery.

Major Political Ideas

1. What is the relationship between political and philosophical thought? The Hellenistic period is particularly interesting because it stressed philosophy for the common people. What did Cynicism, Epicureanism, and Stoicism have to say about the relationship between the individual and the state?

2. Define *natural law*. Why is this an important idea? What are its political implications?

Issues for Essays and Discussion

During the Hellenistic period, much of the Near East was transformed by new ideas. What was the process of Hellenism and what did it mean for society? Describe Hellenism in terms of the exchange of ideas in the fields of culture, political administration, philosophy, science, medicine, and architecture. Was this process entirely successful in creating a unified society?

Interpretation of Visual Sources

Study the picture of the city of Priene on page 108 of your textbook. What can a city like this reveal about the ideals as well as the organization of Hellenistic society? What is the architectural style? The type and apparent function of buildings? The layout and plan? List the features of Hellenic Greek life that appear to have been adopted by this Hellenistic city.

Geography

On Outline Map 4.1 provided, and using maps 4.1 and 4.2 in the textbook as a reference, mark the following:

1. The location of India, Mesopotamia, the Mediterranean Sea, Asia Minor, Persia, the Nile River, the Black Sea, Alexandria, Macedonia, Persepolis, Egypt, the Arabian Desert.

2. The area conquered by Alexander the Great.

3. The boundaries of the four kingdoms established after Alexander's death. Label each kingdom.

4. A route by which goods might have moved between Greece, Asia Minor, Egypt, and the Far East.

Outline Map 4.1

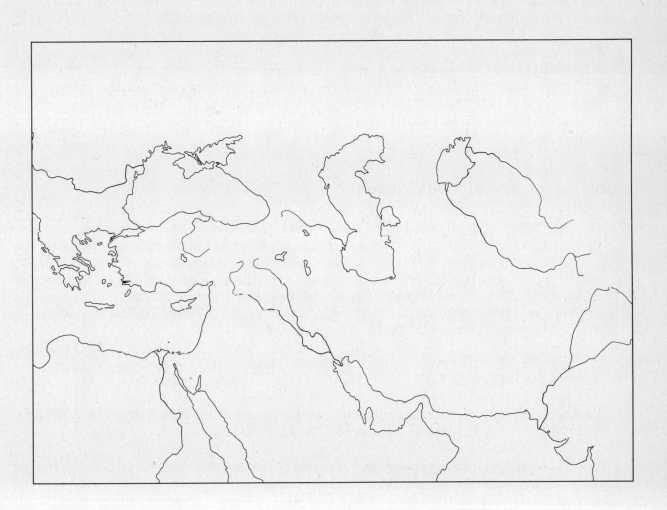

Understanding History Through the Arts

1. What do ancient coins tell us about Hellenistic life? Many of the remarkable personages of the Hellenistic age—including Cleopatra and Ptolemy of Egypt—are featured in N. Davis and C. Kraay, *The Hellenistic Kingdoms: Portrait Coins and History* (1973).

2. What was the social and political function of art in Hellenistic cities? For developments in architecture see J. Charbonneaux, R. Martin, and F. Villard, *Hellenistic Art, 330–50 B.C.* (1973), and T. Fyfe, *Hellenistic Architecture* (1963). For painting and sculpture see C. Havelock, *Hellenistic Art* (1970). The traditions of Hellenistic literature and culture are explored in T. Webster, *Hellenistic Poetry and Art* (1964).

Problems for Further Investigation

1. Has Alexander the Great been turned into a myth by historians? What was the real Alexander like? Alexander the Great is the subject of a number of biographies, including R. L. Fox, *Alexander the Great* (1974), and P. Green, *Alexander of Macedon, 356–323 B.C.** (1973). A fascinating historical novel about life, love, and adventure with Alexander is M. Renault, *The Persian Boy** (1972). The Hebrews' war of liberation against their Hellenistic Syrian overlords is one of a number of subjects dealt with in V. Tcherikover, *Hellenistic Civilization and the Jews,* S. Applebaum, trans. (1959).

2. Did the Hellenists make any significant contributions to science and medicine? To pursue this question begin with E. Hamilton, *The Greek Way to Western Civilization** (1943).

3. What were the reasons for Alexander the Great's conquest of the Near Eastern world? Begin your research with A. R. Burn, *Alexander the Great and the Hellenistic World** (1964).

4. How did Greek philosophy change in this period? What are Stoicism and Cynicism? Those interested in Greek thought should see a book of essays, interpretations, and source material entitled *The Greek Mind** (1957) by W. R. Agard; also A. Long, *Hellenistic Philosophy* (1974).

5. Did women enjoy a new kind of individualism in the Hellenistic city? This is the argument set forth in M. Arthur, "From Medusa to Cleopatra: Women in the Ancient World," in R. Bridenthal, C. Koonz, and S. Stuard, *Becoming Visible: Women in European History** (1987). A bibliography on women in antiquity is included for further study.

---

*Available in paperback.

Chapter 5
The Rise of Rome

Chapter Questions

After reading and studying this chapter you should be able to answer the following questions:

What was the reason Rome succeeded where the Greek polis had failed? How did Rome rise to greatness? What effects did the conquest of the Mediterranean have on the Romans? Why did the Roman Republic collapse?

Chapter Summary

Whereas the Greeks gave the Mediterranean world cultural unity, Rome gave it political unity and a political heritage. This chapter traces the origins of that legacy from the Etruscans in the eighth century B.C. through the troubled but dynamic days of the republic in the first century B.C. Between these two periods the Romans built an enormous empire, gave the world important lessons in politics, and established some new concepts in law.

There are three major themes in this chapter. The first is assimilation. The Romans assimilated many of the customs of the ancient Etruscans and then, like the Macedonians before them, readily adopted the culture of Hellenic Greece. Conquest and imperialism is the second theme. The Romans became empire builders almost by accident. A conflict in southern Italy led to foreign involvement, first in Sicily and then in North Africa during the Punic wars between Rome and Carthage. The third theme is the impact of imperialism on Rome. Did imperialism bring more harm than blessings? The chapter evaluates the economic and political changes that military victory brought, noting how the coming of empire meant a change in lifestyle and, according to some Romans, such as Cato, a general moral deterioration. Certainly, foreign conquests created large standing armies and veterans who played a growing role in Roman politics. Once this happened, government by constitution was doomed.

Study Outline

Use this outline to preview the chapter before you read a particular section in your textbook and then as a self-check to test your reading comprehension after you have read the chapter section.

I. The geography and early settlement of Rome
   A. The land and the sea
      1. Italy's lack of navigable rivers discouraged trade, but the land was fertile and productive and the mountains not as divisive as those of Greece.
      2. The two great fertile plains of Italy are Latium and Campania.
      3. The Romans established their city on seven hills along the Tiber River in Latium.
   B. The Etruscans and Rome (750–509 B.C.)
      1. Between 1200 and 750 B.C., many Indo-European peoples moved into Italy from the north.
      2. Etruscan urban life came to dominate much of Italy.
      3. According to legend, Romulus and Remus founded Rome in 753 B.C.
      4. The Etruscans passed many customs and practices on to the Romans.
      5. The Etruscans turned Rome into an important city and brought it into contact with the Mediterranean world.
   C. The Roman conquest of Italy (509–290 B.C.)
      1. Much of early Roman history is based on legends and tales, brought together by the historian Livy long after the founding of Rome.
      2. According to tradition, the Romans expelled the harsh Etruscan rulers and founded a republic in 509 B.C.
      3. The Romans fought continually against their neighbors and became adept at the arts of war and diplomacy.
      4. In 390 B.C., invading Gauls destroyed Rome but also eliminated the Etruscans, so a rebuilt Rome was able to expand.
      5. Between 390 and 290 B.C., the Romans conquered much of Italy and stood unchallenged.
         a. The Romans frequently granted citizenship to those they conquered, thereby strengthening Rome.
         b. In their willingness to extend citizenship, the political genius of the Romans triumphed where Greece had failed.
   D. The Roman state
      1. In the early republic, power resided in the hands of the members of the aristocracy, called the patricians; commoners were called plebeians.
      2. Rome was ruled by people's assemblies, elected magistrates, and—most important—the senate.
         a. The senate advised the consuls and magistrates, and its advice had the force of law.
         b. The senate gave the republic stability and continuity.
         c. The *comitia centuriata*, which was dominated by the patricians, decided Roman policy.
         d. In 471 B.C. the plebeians gained their own assembly, the *concilium plebis*.
         e. Two elected consuls and the senate ran the state.
         f. In 366 B.C. the office of praetor was created.

3. Rome's greatest achievement was its development of the concept of law.
   a. Civil law developed to protect people and property.
   b. Gradually, the concept of universal law applicable to all societies developed.
E. Social conflict in Rome
   1. The plebeians' desire for equality and justice led to a conflict with the patricians known as the Struggle of the Orders.
   2. A general strike led to concessions being granted to the plebeians—partly because of patrician fears of hostile neighbors.
   3. The plebeians won legal and land reforms.
      a. The *lex Canuleia* allowed for intermarriage between plebeians and patricians.
      b. The Law of the Twelve Tables, a codification of previously unpublished law, was a result of plebeian pressure for legal reform.
      c. Later, the patricians were forced to publish legal procedures, too, so plebeians could enjoy full protection under the law.
   4. Licinius and Sextus brought about further reform for the plebeians, but the struggle did not end until the passage of *lex Hortensia* in 287 B.C.
II. The age of overseas conquest (282–146 B.C.)
A. Roman imperialism
   1. The Romans did not have a pre-existing strategy for world conquest.
   2. Roman imperialism took two forms: aggression in the West and patronage in the East.
   3. Rome's need to control Sicily for its own protection meant it needed to build a navy to control the sea.
B. The Punic wars
   1. The First Punic War, fought over Sicily, was won by Rome in 241 B.C.
   2. The Second Punic War found Carthage attacking Rome by way of Spain, with a major victory at Cannae in 216 B.C.
      a. Hannibal led the Carthaginian forces over the Alps into Italy.
      b. He then spread devastation throughout Italy, yet failed to crush Rome.
   3. Rome's commander, Scipio, took Spain from the Carthaginians in 207 B.C.
   4. A victory by Scipio over Hannibal at Zama in 202 B.C. meant that the western Mediterranean would be Roman.
   5. Fear of Carthage led to the Third Punic War.
      a. In 146 B.C. Carthage was defeated, but Spain was not conquered until 133 B.C.
      b. By 146 B.C. the Mediterranean had become for the Romans *mare nostrum*—"our sea."
III. Old values and Greek culture
A. Consequences of empire
   1. The building of empire brought about the end of traditional values and encouraged a new materialism.
   2. The Romans had to change their institutions, social patterns, and way of thinking to meet their new responsibilities as world rulers.
B. Marcus Cato represented the traditional ideal of a simple and virtuous life.
   1. In traditional Rome the *paterfamilias* held immense power within the family.
   2. The virtues of chastity and modesty among women were valued.
   3. Children began their formal education at the age of seven.
   4. The agricultural year followed the traditional farmer's calendar.

     5. Slavery was common; relations between master and slave were often good.
     6. Religion played an important role in Roman life; Romans believed that if they honored the gods, they could grant them divine favor.

  C. Scipio Aemilianus represented the new spirit of wealth and leisure.
     1. For the new Romans victory in war meant materialism and the pursuit of pleasure.
     2. Greek culture—Hellenism—came to dominate Roman life.
     3. Scipio Aemilianus introduced to Rome the art of personal politics.
     4. He was the center of a circle of Hellenists and helped make the culture of Greece an integral part of Roman life.
     5. Hellenism stimulated the growth of Roman art, literature, and leisure activities such as bathing and dinner parties.
     6. Despite this hedonism, Rome prospered for six more centuries.

IV. The late republic (133–31 B.C.)
  A. War and the demands of the new empire created serious political problems.
     1. The republican constitution no longer suited Rome's needs.
     2. Powerful generals became a threat.
     3. Rome's Italian allies agitated for the rights of citizenship.

  B. War and the new empire also caused economic problems.
     1. Many veterans sold their war-ruined farms to the big landowners and migrated to the cities.
     2. A large number of urban poor emerged.
     3. The Gracchus brothers sought a solution to the problem of the veterans and the urban poor.
       a. Tiberius Gracchus angered aristocrats and the senate by proposing land reform.
       b. The murder of Tiberius Gracchus by the senators initiated an era of political violence.
       c. Gaius Gracchus demanded further land reform and citizenship for all Italians.
       d. Gaius was killed by the senate, but political unrest continued in Rome, while new foreign threats emerged.
     4. Marius reformed the army by recruiting landless men and promising land to the volunteers.
     5. The Social War (91–88 B.C.) began when many Italians revolted against Rome over the issue of full citizenship.

  C. Political struggles led to the end of the republican constitution.
     1. Sulla became dictator of Rome in 82 B.C. and initiated many political and judicial reforms.
     2. Civil war wrecked Rome for the next fifty years.
     3. Cicero urged a balance of political interests—the "concord of the orders."
     4. The First Triumvirate (Pompey, Caesar, and Crassus) controlled Rome after Sulla, but Caesar dominated.
       a. Caesar, a military genius and an intellectual, conquered all of Gaul by 50 B.C.
       b. Conflict between Caesar and Pompey resulted in more civil war.
       c. Caesar defeated Pompey in 45 B.C. and made himself dictator.
       d. Caesar founded colonies to absorb Rome's poor and extended citizenship to many of the provincials.
       e. Caesar was assassinated in 44 B.C., setting off another round of civil war.

2. As a result of the wars of conquest, the small, independent Roman farmers
    a. gained vast new markets for their grain.
    b. found their farms in ruins.
    c. became an important political power.
    d. got rich.

3. Overall, the Romans' greatest achievements were in the field of
    a. empire building.
    b. agriculture.
    c. the arts.
    d. literature.

4. Rome succeeded where Greece had failed because it
    a. conquered peoples and let them govern themselves.
    b. always lived peacefully with its neighbors.
    c. always peacefully incorporated peoples into the Roman system.
    d. conquered peoples and incorporated them into the Roman system.

5. Which of the following was *not* a Roman republican office?
    a. Emperor
    b. Quaestor
    c. Praetor
    d. Consul

6. The Struggle of the Orders resulted in all of the following except
    a. the office of the tribune.
    b. the ascendancy of the patricians.
    c. the Law of the Twelve Tables.
    d. a stronger and more united Rome.

7. The goal of the Gracchi was to
    a. exploit the urban poor and the peasant farmers.
    b. join the patricians.
    c. aid the urban poor and the peasant farmers.
    d. deny citizenship to certain Romans.

8. All but which of the following are principal geographical characteristics of Italy?
    a. Hilly, but not inhospitable, land
    b. The division of the peninsula into northern and southern halves by the Appenine mountains
    c. Few navigable rivers
    d. Two large fertile plains

9. According to Roman legend, the founders of Rome were
   a. the Greeks.
   b. the tribe of Autun.
   c. Livy and his family.
   d. Romulus and Remus.

10. The Roman citizen appointed dictator for fifteen days who returned to his farm after defeating his country's enemy was
    a. Tarquin the Proud.
    b. Cincinnatus.
    c. Servius Tullius.
    d. Pyrrhus.

11. The chief magistrates of republican Rome—the officials who administered the state and commanded the army—were known as
    a. consuls.
    b. quaestors.
    c. praetors.
    d. senators.

12. During the Second Punic War the Carthaginian leader who attempted to conquer Rome was
    a. Philip of Carthage.
    b. Hannibal.
    c. Alexander.
    d. Menenius Agrippa.

13. Most ordinary Roman women
    a. had little influence in family affairs.
    b. spent most of their time performing religious rituals.
    c. had considerable influence and responsibility in the family economy.
    d. exercised total control of their children's upbringing.

14. Which of the following statements best describes the status of Roman slaves?
    a. Slaves were considered to be inferior human beings.
    b. Slaves suffered from racial bias.
    c. Slaves were conscripted into the Roman army.
    d. Slaves were often granted freedom by their masters.

15. The father of Latin poetry was
    a. Gaius Marius.
    b. Ennius.
    c. Scipio Aemilianus.
    d. Cato.

16. The conservative, traditional elements of Rome regarded the public baths as
    a. the only way to encourage reform in public health.
    b. a good way of using Greek culture for the benefit of Rome.
    c. a waste of time and an encouragement to idleness.
    d. important as places for political discussion.

17. The wars during the time of republican Rome
    a. left Rome a strong and prosperous agricultural base.
    b. left Roman farms in a state of decay.
    c. caused Rome to look elsewhere for its food supply.
    d. caused a decentralization of landownership.

18. The Roman leader who was murdered because he proposed that public land be given to the poor in small lots was
    a. Sulla.
    b. Tiberius Gracchus.
    c. Cato.
    d. Caesar.

19. The consul who recruited an army by allowing landless men to serve in the regions was
    a. Cincinnatus.
    b. Tiberius.
    c. Sulla
    d. Marius.

20. By the time of the late republican period in Rome, most industry and small manufacturing was in the hands of
    a. plebeians.
    b. slaves.
    c. Christians.
    d. the army.

21. The Etruscans amassed extensive wealth by
    a. military conquest in Gaul.
    b. moving the center of their community away from Rome.
    c. perfecting agriculture and rural community life.
    d. trading their manufactured goods in Italy and beyond.

22. The status of one who held *civitas sine suffragio* was that of
    a. slavery.
    b. full citizenship, but for Romans only.
    c. citizenship without the right to vote or hold office.
    d. military service.

23. The geographic area described as the "wrestling ground for the Carthaginians and Romans" was
    a. western Greece.
    b. Gaul.
    c. North Africa.
    d. Sicily.

24. Manumission in Roman society was
    a. infrequent.
    b. against all laws.
    c. only common among Christian Romans.
    d. common.

25. The latifundia was
    a. a large farming estate.
    b. a client kingdom of Rome.
    c. a law that provided for equality between plebeians and patricians.
    d. a form of citizenship.

Major Political Ideas

1. How did Roman ideas about the state, citizenship, and participation in the state differ from those of the Greeks?

2. Define *ius civile*, *ius gentium*, and *ius naturae*. Where did political power lie in republican Rome?

Issues for Essays and Discussion

What geographical, political, military, and economic factors contributed to Rome's rise to greatness? Was this rise an inevitable process, or did the Romans exhibit imagination and inventiveness?

Interpretation of Visual Sources

Study the photograph of the decoration for a horse's harness on page 142 of your text. Although this is an idealized depiction of war, what does the picture tell us about the manner of combat, the use of weaponry, and military dress? Does the artist suggest why the Romans are defeating the barbarians? Does the artist of this work make any distinctions between the Romans and the barbarians?

Geography

1. Study Map 5.1 in your textbook and then answer the following questions: how did geography encourage Italy to "look to the Mediterranean"? What geographic features of Italy encouraged the growth and development of Rome? What was special about the area where Rome was established?

2. On Outline Map 5.2 provided, and using Map 5.2 in your textbook as a reference, mark the following: North Africa, Farther and Nearer Spain, Gaul, Cisalpine Gaul, Dalmatia, Germany, Britain, Macedonia, the Mediterranean Sea, Thrace, Phrygia, Cappadocia, Cilicia, Syria, Parthia, Armenia, the Black Sea. Now outline the area held by Rome by 133 B.C. and the territories added to Rome by 44 B.C.

Outline Map 5.2

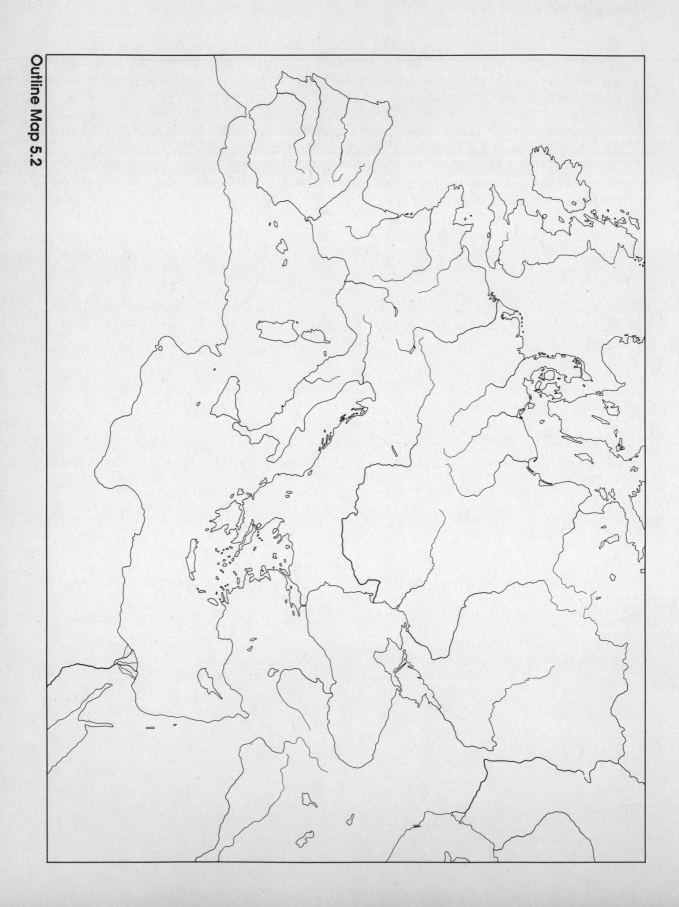

Understanding History Through the Arts

1. How can the culture and beliefs of the peoples of the Italian peninsula be understood through a study of Etruscan and Roman art? For an interestingly written and illustrated beginning source see Chapters 6 and 7 of H. W. Janson, *History of Art* (1962). A richly illustrated and sophisticated study of the subject is the monumental *Rome: the Center of Power, 500 B.C. to A.D. 200*, by R. Bandinelli, P. Green, trans. (1970). A more recent, superbly illustrated book is *The Architecture of the Roman Empire, An Urban Appraisal** by W. MacDonald (1988). See also M. Wheeler, *Roman Art and Architecture** (1985).

2. How does classical literature enable us to better understand Roman politics and military and social history? The best of Roman literature includes Cicero's essay *On Moral Obligation*, J. Higgenbotham, trans., (1967). Other works by Cicero can be found in J. and A. Raubitschek, trans., *Selected Works of Cicero* (1948). A revised and modernized version of Caesar's own story of his conquest of Gaul is found in S. Brady, *Caesar's Gallic Campaigns* (1967).

3. What do its myths reveal about a culture? If you are interested in Roman mythology, see J. Lindsay, *Men and Gods on the Roman Nile* (1968), and M. Grant, *Myths of the Greeks and Romans* (1965).

Problems for Further Investigation

1. What was the role of the family in ancient Rome? How did the Romans define womanhood and childhood? Begin your investigation with B. Rawson, ed., *The Family in Ancient Rome** (1989).

2. How did the Roman Empire emerge? Start your research by reading D. Hood, ed., *The Rise of Rome** (1970).

3. What role did religion play in the life of the Romans? Two good books are M. Grant, *The Jews in the Ancient World* (1973), and T. R. Glover, *The Conflict of Religions in the Early Roman Empire* (1960).

---

*Available in paperback.

Chapter 6
The Pax Romana

Chapter Questions

After reading and studying this chapter you should be able to answer the following questions:

How did the Roman emperors govern the empire and spread Roman influence into northern Europe? What was the effect of the *pax Romana* on the Mediterranean and European world? Why did Christianity sweep across the Roman world to change it fundamentally? How did the empire meet the grim challenges of barbarian invasion and economic decline?

Chapter Summary

This chapter tells the story of Rome in the age of empire and emperors. When Julius Caesar's nephew Augustus became "the First Citizen of the State" in 31 B.C., Rome began a new era of constitutional monarchy called the Augustan Age. This was the "golden age" of Rome in terms of economy, literature, and imperial expansion. Under the Roman Empire the Mediterranean and European peoples enjoyed a long tradition of firmly established personal freedom. The *pax Romana*, or peace of Rome, encouraged the spread of Roman law, justice, and administration as well as the further diffusion of Greek culture, especially into the European world. This era of peace occurred in part because of the constitutional monarchy Augustus established, which lasted until the third century A.D., when once again Rome became wracked by civil war. The emperor's power, however, rested mainly with the army, which he controlled. Indeed, control of the army became a growing problem for Augustus and his successors, many of whom owed their power to some military rebellion in the provinces. Thus, in the long run, Augustus's settlement was not successful. Nevertheless, his contributions were great.

Augustus treated imperial subjects in the conquered provinces justly, and his expansion of the empire north and east into Europe was enormously important for European history. His reign also ushered in a great age of Latin literature. It is through the works of Virgil, Livy, and Horace, all of whom are discussed in this chapter, that we are able to gain a sense of what Roman people were like and what they expected of life.

The development and spread of Christianity also occurred during this era. Paul of Tarsus turned the Jewish cult of Jesus into a universal religion based on the ethics of love and forgiveness. Finally, in the fourth century A.D., Christianity was made the official religion of

Rome. Oddly, what had begun as a Judaean hope for salvation from Rome became Rome's state religion.

In the third century A.D., the breakdown of government and order ushered in an age of civil war and barbarian invasions from which Rome never fully recovered. The reforming emperors Diocletian and Constantine were able to restore the old system only partially. They were not able to turn around the depression and decline in trade and agriculture.

Why did Rome "fall"? Gibbon's famous theory, that Christianity was the primary cause, is flawed, and although economic and political explanations are important, they do not tell the entire story. In a real sense there is no answer because the Roman Empire did not actually fall but slowly merged into a new medieval world. It was Rome and Christianity that provided Europe with the framework for a new age.

Study Outline

Use this outline to preview the chapter before you read a particular section in your textbook and then as a self-check to test your reading comprehension after you have read the chapter section.

I. Augustus's settlement (31 B.C.–A.D. 14)
   A. Augustus's goal was to re-establish the republic after years of civil war, to demobilize the army, and to meet the threat of the barbarians.
   B. The principate and the restored republic
      1. Augustus restored constitutional government but did not give the senate power equal to his own.
      2. Augustus became *princeps civitatis*, "the First Citizen of the State," and held other political, religious, and military titles.
      3. His control of the army was the main source of his power.
         a. Augustus controlled deployment of the soldiers and paid their wages.
         b. He founded colonies of soldiers, which helped unite the Mediterranean world and spread Greco-Roman culture.
      4. Overall, Augustus did not restore the republic but instead created a constitutional monarchy.
   C. Augustus's administration of the provinces
      1. Augustus encouraged self-government and urbanism.
      2. The cult of *Roma et Augustus* gave the empire unity.
   D. Roman expansion into northern and western Europe
      1. Augustus continued Caesar's push into Europe.
         a. In Gaul he founded towns and built roads.
         b. He extended Roman rule into Spain, Germany, and eastern Europe.
      2. The Romans' relations with barbarians varied from cooperation to hostility.
   E. Literary flowering
      1. The Augustan Age was a golden age of Latin literature.
      2. Roman writers celebrated the dignity of humanity and the range of its accomplishments.
         a. Virgil wrote about the greatness and virtue of Rome in his masterpiece, the *Aeneid*.

b. Livy's history of Rome is one of Rome's great legacies to the modern world.
c. Horace praised the simple life and the pax Romana.
F. By sharing power with his son, Augustus created a dynasty.
II. The coming of Christianity
A. The colony of Judaea suffered during the Roman civil wars, and Jewish resentment of Rome increased.
B. Hatred of King Herod and Roman taxes, harsh enforcement of the law, and religious interference led to civil war in Judaea.
C. Two anti-Roman movements existed: Zealot extremists, who fought Rome, and militant believers in the apocalypse, who believed that the coming of the Messiah would end Roman rule.
D. Pagan religious cults were numerous, including the official state cults, the old traditional cults, and the new mystery cults, which met the needs of the people for security and emotional release.
E. Jesus was a teacher who claimed to be the Messiah of a spiritual kingdom.
1. His teachings were in the orthodox Jewish tradition.
2. He taught his followers not to revolt against Rome.
F. Pontius Pilate, the Roman prefect, was worried about maintaining civil order, so he condemned Jesus to death.
G. Peter continued the Jesus cult in accord with Jewish law.
H. Paul of Tarsus transformed the Jesus cult and made it applicable to all people, particularly those who were attracted to the mystery cults.
I. Christianity was attractive for many reasons.
1. It was open to all, including non-Jews, women, and common people.
2. It held out the promise of salvation and forgiveness.
3. It gave each person a role and a sense of importance and community.
III. The Julio-Claudians and the Flavians (27 B.C.–A.D. 96)
A. For fifty years after Augustus's death, the Julio-Claudian dynasty provided the emperors of Rome.
1. Claudius created a system of imperial bureaucracy so he could delegate power.
2. The army, especially the Praetorian Guard, began to interfere in politics.
3. The Year of the Four Emperors proved the Augustan settlement a failure.
B. The Flavian dynasty
1. Vespasian created a monarchy and suppressed rebellions, destroying the state of Judaea in the process.
2. Domitian won additional new territory for the empire.
IV. The Age of the "Five Good Emperors" (A.D. 96–180)
A. The age of the Antonines was one of unparalleled prosperity.
B. The Antonines were emperors in fact as well a theory—the emperor became an indispensable part of the imperial system.
1. The emperors were the source of all authority in the empire.
2. Hadrian reformed the bureaucracy by making it more professional and organized.
C. Changes in the army
1. Under the Flavians the boundaries of the empire became fixed.
2. More and more soldiers came from the provinces closest to the frontiers.

V. Life in the "golden age"
   A. Imperial Rome
      1. The city was huge, and fire and crime were ongoing problems.
      2. The government provided the citizens of Rome with free grain, oil, and wine to prevent riots.
      3. Free, often brutal, entertainment was provided, but the most popular entertainment was chariot racing.
      4. Most Romans worked hard and lived average lives.
   B. The provinces
      1. Agriculture flourished on large tracts of land cultivated by free tenant farmers.
      2. Retired legionaries brought essential skills to new areas.
      3. Trade with Eastern merchants expanded, and grain production in northern Europe increased as the provinces became linked in a vast economic network.
      4. Manufacturing, such as glass and pottery making, tended to move from Italy to the provinces, especially to northern Europe.
      5. Northern and western European cities enjoyed growth and peace under Roman rule.
VI. Civil wars and invasion in the third century
   A. Commodus's reign led to civil war; over twenty emperors ascended the throne between 235 and 284.
   B. Migrating barbarians on the frontiers found gaps in the Roman defenses.
      1. In A.D. 258, the Goths burst into Europe.
      2. The Alamanni, Franks, Saxons, and other tribes invaded the empire.
   C. Invasion brought turmoil and impoverishment to farm and village life.
      1. The breakdown of the system led to crime and corruption.
      2. Much of the damage was done by officials and soldiers.
VII. Reconstruction under Diocletian and Constantine (A.D. 284–337)
   A. The end of political turmoil under Diocletian's reign
      1. Diocletian claimed that God had chosen him to rule; his power became absolute.
      2. Because the empire was too big for one person to govern well, Diocletian reorganized it.
         a. Imperial authority was split between two emperors—Diocletian in the east and an *augustus* in the west.
         b. Each emperor was assisted by a *caesar*.
         c. The power of the provincial governors was reduced.
         d. Diocletian's division between east and west became permanent.
   B. Inflation and taxes
      1. The monetary system was in ruins and highly inflated.
      2. Diocletian attempted to curb inflation through wage and price controls.
      3. The new imperial taxation system led to a loss of freedom as people became locked into their jobs.
   C. The decline of small farms
      1. Worsening conditions fostered the growth of large, self-sufficient villas.
      2. Small farmers turned to big landlords for protection, in exchange for their land.
   D. The legalization of Christianity
      1. Constantine realized that Christianity could serve his empire and so legalized it.
      2. Many Romans misunderstood Christianity.

a. They believed the Christians hated the human race.
b. They distrusted their exclusiveness.
c. They thought that Christians performed immoral rituals.
d. They thought the Christians were atheists because they denied the existence of pagan gods.

3. As time went on, pagan hostility decreased.

E. The construction of Constantinople

1. Constantine built a new capital for the empire at the site of Byzantium.
2. The focus of the empire shifted to the east.

VIII. The "Awful Revolution"

A. Gibbon's book *The Decline and Fall of the Roman Empire* (1910) has dominated historical thought for over two hundred years.

1. His thesis is that after two centuries of existence, the Roman Empire declined in strength, vitality, and prosperity and then fell into ruin.
2. Gibbon blamed Christianity, particularly its emphasis on an afterlife, for the empire's decline.

B. A number of other theories to explain the fall of Rome have been advanced.

1. The racial, lead poisoning, and slavery theories are all unsound.
2. The most accepted theories are the political explanations, particularly those that center on the problem of how to pass on imperial power.

C. In reality, the Roman world survived to influence the medieval world.

Review Questions

Check your understanding of this chapter by answering the following questions.

1. What were the sources of Augustus's power? Was Augustus a "dictator" in the modern sense?
2. What were Augustus's accomplishments with regard to the administration and expansion of the empire?
3. What does the work of the writers during Rome's golden age of literature tell us about Roman life and what the Romans thought important?
4. Why was the relationship between Rome and Judaea so strained in the age of Augustus? What were the motives and responses of both Jews and Romans?
5. Describe the political climate in Judaea during the life of Jesus of Nazareth. Did this climate influence the course of religious history?
6. Did Jesus intend to found a new religion? Explain by evaluating his work.
7. What role did Paul of Tarsus play in the evolution of Christianity, and what might have happened if Peter of Jerusalem had kept control over the cult?
8. Why was Christianity so attractive? How was this religion unlike that of the Greeks and Romans?
9. Under what circumstances did the Flavian dynasty come about and what were its contributions?
10. What features of the Roman army made it a source of both strength and weakness for the empire?
11. What is meant by the term *barracks emperors?*

3. The government that developed under Augustus is best described as a
   a. dictatorship.
   b. constitutional monarchy.
   c. republic.
   d. democracy.

4. The man most responsible for the spread of Christianity to non-Jews was
   a. Emperor Diocletian.
   b. St. Peter.
   c. Livy.
   d. Paul of Tarsus.

5. Which of the following statements about farm and village life during the turmoil of the third century A.D. is true?
   a. Crime decreased.
   b. Corruption increased.
   c. The villas disintegrated.
   d. Small landholdings increased.

6. In the restored republic, Augustus became
   a. *Res Gestae*.
   b. *Sanhedrin*.
   c. *dominus*.
   d. *princeps civitatis*.

7. Augustus's attitude toward the provinces was one of
   a. neglect.
   b. oppression.
   c. prejudice toward minorities.
   d. respect for local customs.

8. Which of the following was an anti-Roman group in Judaea?
   a. Zealots
   b. Baruch
   c. Essenes
   d. Hittites

9. Many people in the Roman era were attracted to Christianity because
   a. Christianity didn't discriminate by class or sex.
   b. Christianity did not share any of the features of mystery religions.
   c. Christianity was passive.
   d. Christianity would not have anything to do with the worldly and the sinner.

10. The backbone of Roman agriculture in the Augustan Age was
    a. slave labor.
    b. imported foods from the empire.
    c. captured barbarian labor.
    d. small free farmers.

11. Before Constantine legalized Christianity, the Romans demanded that the Christians
    a. worship the Roman gods.
    b. observe the ritual of sacrifice to the gods.
    c. deny Christ as a god.
    d. go back to their Jewish beliefs.

12. The city that Constantine made the capital of the eastern Roman Empire was
    a. Kiev.
    b. Constantinople.
    c. Alexandria.
    d. Athens.

13. *The Decline and Fall of the Roman Empire* was written by
    a. Constantine.
    b. Livy.
    c. Gibbon.
    d. Paul of Tarsus.

14. During the reign of Augustus, the direction of Roman conquest was toward
    a. Judaea.
    b. northern Europe.
    c. Britain.
    d. the Black Sea.

15. Above all, Virgil's *Aeneid* is
    a. a plea for Christianity.
    b. an argument against Roman imperialism and war.
    c. a vision of Rome as the protector of good in the world.
    d. the history of the fall of Athens.

16. The Roman-appointed king of Judaea was
    a. Herod.
    b. Jesus.
    c. Philip Augustus.
    d. Cato.

17. All except which of the following were characteristic of the third-century period of the barracks emperors?
    a. Civil war
    b. Barbarian invasions
    c. Severe economic decline
    d. Expansion of the empire into northern and western Europe

18. A villa was
    a. a Jewish military district.
    b. the Roman banking system.
    c. a Roman civil service district.
    d. a large, self-sufficient estate.

19. Rome's greatest pact was
    a. Horace.
    b. Livy.
    c. Caligula.
    d. Virgil.

20. To solve problems resulting from the Empire's vast and unmanageable size, Diocletian
    a. reduced the empirc's size by declaring the frontiers independent.
    b. tripled the number of local rulers to maintain better control.
    c. divided the territory among four emperors.
    d. divided the empire into an eastern and western half, appointing a colleague to rule in the western part.

21. The Flavian period came about largely because of
    a. military interference in the selection of the emperor.
    b. the Flavian control of the banking system.
    c. military defeat of Rome by the Goths.
    d. revolution in Judaea.

22. When the Roman general Decius bid for the emperorship by invading Rome in A.D. 249, the result was
    a. a strengthening of the frontiers.
    b. the expansion of the empire.
    c. greater military attention to imperial defenses.
    d. invasion by the Goths.

23. The Roman solution to the problems of food shortages and the ensuing food riots in the city of Rome was
    a. a free market economy with regard to food.
    b. new and improved crowd-control measures.
    c. land reform in order to improve productivity in the countryside.
    d. free grain for all citizens and cheap grain for noncitizens.

24. Hadrian's major contribution to Roman government was
    a. the merger of the civil service with the military.
    b. the creation of a professional, efficient government bureaucracy.
    c. the establishment of a constitutional monarchy.
    d. the conquest of Gaul.

25. In contrast to the Greek system of colonies, Roman colonies were
    a. independent.
    b. not influenced by the culture of the conqueror.
    c. not linked together by any economic ties.
    d. part of a tightly linked imperial system.

Major Political Ideas

1. Describe the two Jewish responses to Roman rule, the Zealots and the growth of a militant apocalyptic sentiment. Which one was more successful? Was Jesus a revolutionary?

2. What was the *princeps civitatis* and what was the system of picking him after the death of Augustus? Did the system work?

3. What was the source of Augustus's power? Was he a dictator? Explain how the concept and power of the emperor changed under Diocletian and Constantine. Why did these changes occur?

Issues for Essays and Discussion

1. What is meant by the term *pax Romana*? What was the secret of Roman success? Answer these questions by making reference to the particular accomplishments of the Romans in the areas of law, administration, politics, literature, and religion. Did the Romans create anything new, or did they simply build on the accomplishments of others, such as the Greeks?

2. What were the results of the period of civil war between A.D. 235 and 284? Could it have been prevented? What is meant by the claim that it was in this period of disruption that the medieval world had its origin?

3. Was the rise of Christianity simply a reaction on the part of Jews to Roman rule? Describe the life and teachings of Jesus. What was Christianity's appeal to so many people in the Roman world? How did it evolve from an outlawed religion to the state religion of Rome?

Interpretation of Visual Sources

Study the reproduction of the print titled "A Large Roman Villa" on page 182 of your textbook. On what is the economy of this particular villa based? How large and how varied is the labor force? What do you perceive to be the function of the villa? How could your observations substantiate the view that the origins of the medieval world lay in the third century?

Geography

1. On Outline Map 6.1 provided, and using Map 6.1 and Map 6.4 in the textbook as a reference, mark the following: the boundaries of the Roman Empire under Augustus, the empire's division under Diocletian, Rome, Sicily, Britain, the Rhine River, Byzantium, Crete, the Danube River, Carthage, Jerusalem, the Teutoburger forest.

2. Describe the Roman penetration into northern and western Europe. What kinds of problems did the Romans face, and what techniques did they use in their successful conquests?

Outline Map 6.1

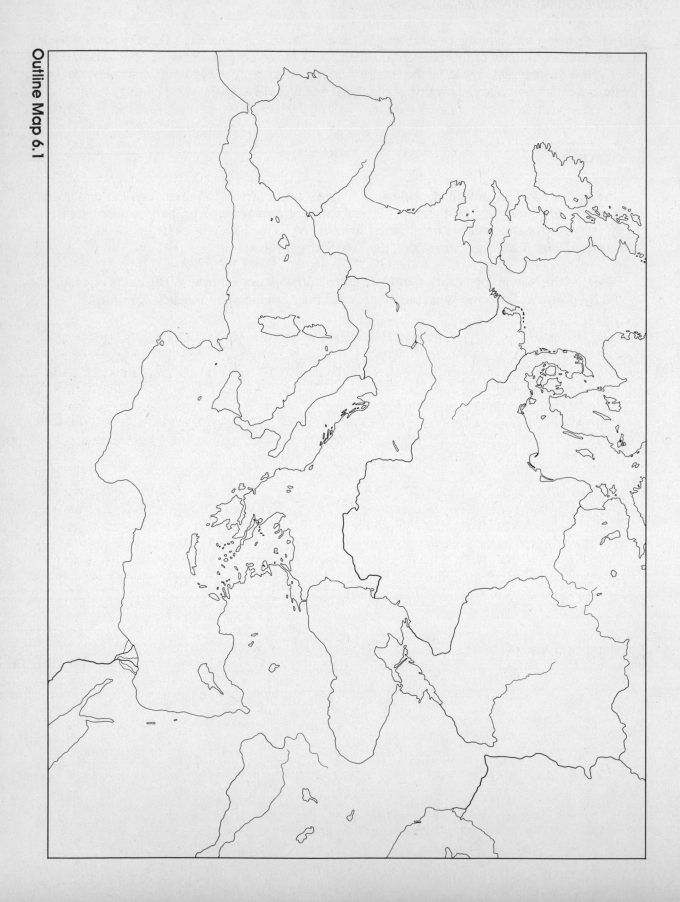

Understanding History Through the Arts

1. Were the Romans innovators or mimics in the realm of art? Since the source of much Roman art was Greece, many argue that there is hardly such a thing as a "Roman" style and that only in architecture were the Romans truly original. The arch and vault and the construction of sewers, bridges, roads, and aqueducts were among Rome's great enterprises. Chapter 7, "Roman Art," in H. W. Janson's *History of Art* (1962) is an excellent review. A more detailed account is G. Rivoira, *Roman Architecture* (1930), and R. Bandinelli, *Rome: The Late Empire. Roman Art*, A.D. *200–400*, P. Green, trans. (1971).

2. Why was Virgil's poetry so popular? For insight into the works of this poetic genius see W. Knight, *Roman Virgil** (1966). Other works of interest include *On the Nature of the Universe,** R. Latham, trans. (1967) by Lucretius, a poet and Epicurean, and Ovid's *The Love Poems of Ovid,** (H. Gregory, trans. (1964).

Problems for Further Investigation

1. Why did Rome "fall"? The reasons for the decline of Roman civilization have interested scholars for hundreds of years. Even the people of Rome were obsessed with the feeling of deterioration. Many prophecies, including the biblical book of Revelation, foretold the end of the empire. The problems of the decline and identification of its causes are the subjects of a scholarly book, *The Awful Revolution* (1969), by F. W. Walbank. The subject is also dealt with in the Problems in European Civilization series' *Decline and Fall of the Roman Empire** (1962) by D. Kagan. These can be supplemented by G. Milner, *The Problem of Decadence* (1931).

2. What was Jesus really like? Reading biography can be an interesting and rewarding way of discovering the past. A. Schweitzer's *The Quest of the Historical Jesus* (1948) is a superb work, and A. D. Nock's *St. Paul* (1938) is an interesting study of one of the most important men in world history. *Rome in the Augustan Age* (1962) by H. Rowell is about Augustus, the man whose imprint on the empire was immense. Also recommended is R. Warner, *The Young Caesar* (1958). R. Graves's *I, Claudius** (1934) is an exciting account of the families, the work, and the loves of the emperors from Augustus to Claudius.

---

*Available in paperback.

Chapter 7
The Making of Europe

Chapter Questions

After reading and studying this chapter you should be able to answer the following questions:

How did the Greco-Roman heritage, the Germanic traditions, and Christianity act upon one another and contribute to the making of a new Europe? What influence did Byzantine and Islamic cultures have on the making of European civilization?

Chapter Summary

Between 400 and 900, a distinctly "European" society evolved. The basic ingredients of this new European civilization were the Greco-Roman culture, the customs and traditions of the Germanic peoples, and Christianity.

Diocletian had divided the Roman Empire into two major parts. The capital of the western half was Rome; the capital of the eastern half was Constantinople. The eastern (Byzantine) empire lasted for nearly a thousand years after the disintegration of the western empire in the fifth century. Imperial administration in the West had, by 476, given way to massive Germanic invasions. Within Europe the strongest power and the only stabilizing force was the Roman church, which, largely by default, came to be the major political as well as spiritual power. In the eastern empire the emperor held supreme authority over the church. In Rome, however, the bishops formulated the theory of the church's ultimate power over the state. The church in the West assimilated much of the Greco-Roman culture and used its intellectual passion and administrative talent to tame and transform the Germanic tribes. Of equal importance in the making of Europe were the monastic orders, which after about 529 were unified under the *Rule* of Saint Benedict.

While Germans were being baptized and were consolidating themselves into great kingdoms, the new threat of Islam pushed into Europe. Founded by Muhammad in the early seventh century, the religion of Islam united the Arabs and in a short period produced one of the most expansionist cultures the world has ever witnessed. By the early eighth century, Muslims had conquered Spain and were pushing into France.

Both the Byzantine and the Islamic empires were important for European development. Both preserved much Greco-Roman knowledge, a great deal of which was not rediscovered in the

West until much later, and they made important contributions to law, science, and medicine. Germanic tradition and custom were also important in that development. But above all, it was Christianity that gave Europe its strength and unity.

Study Outline

Use this outline to preview the chapter before you read a particular section in the textbook and then as a self-check to test your reading comprehension after you have read the chapter section.

I. The growth of the Christian church
  A. The word *church* can mean several things, but at this time it was often applied to the officials, or *papa*, who presided over all Christians
    1. The church adopted the Roman system of organization and succeeded in assimilating many peoples.
    2. The church possessed able administrators and literate, creative thinkers.
  B. The church and the Roman emperors
    1. Constantine supported and legalized Christianity in 312.
      a. He helped settle theological disputes.
      b. He endowed the building of Christian churches.
    2. Theodosius increased the power of the church and made Christianity the official religion of the Roman Empire.
    3. The emperors were important in enforcing theological uniformity in the church.
      a. Constantine summoned the Council of Nicaea in 325 to combat the Arian heresy, which denied that Christ was divine.
      b. The council produced the Nicene Creed—the doctrine that Christ was of the same substance as God, and this became the orthodox position, supported by the state.
    4. Bishop Ambrose formulated the theory that the church was supreme over the state.
  C. Inspired leadership in the early church
    1. Many talented Romans, such as Ambrose, became administrators and workers in the church.
      a. The church adopted the empire's system of dioceses.
      b. Bishops came to preside over dioceses.
    2. The bishop of Rome eventually became the "Patriarch of the West," while other patriarchs sat at Antioch, Alexandria, Jerusalem, and Constantinople.
    3. Because the position of emperor disappeared in the West, the Roman bishop became the chief civil authority in Italy.
      a. It was said that Pope Leo I saved Rome from Attila.
      b. Pope Gregory acted as civil authority.
  D. The missionary activity of the early Christians
    1. The Roman soldier Martin of Tours brought Christianity to Gaul, while Saint Patrick brought Christianity and Roman culture to Ireland.
      a. Under Saint Columbia, Iona in Scotland became an important Christian center.
      b. In 597, Pope Gregory I sent a delegation of monks to Britain, under the leadership of Augustine, to convert the English.

2. Two forms of Christianity—Roman and Celtic—clashed, but the Roman tradition won out at the Synod of Whitby in 664.
3. Between the fifth and tenth centuries, most people living in Europe were baptized.
    a. Religion influenced tribal life.
    b. Participating in religious observances was a social duty.
4. Because of the Germans' warlike customs and different culture, their assimilation into Christianity was slow.
    a. The Christian emphasis on poverty, universal brotherhood, and love of enemies was difficult for German warriors to accept.
    b. The Christian concepts of sin and repentance were also hard for them to understand.

E. Conversion and assimilation
1. The missionaries pursued a policy of preaching and assimilating pagan customs and beliefs into Christianity.
2. Penitentials—manuals used to examine one's conscience—were used by priests to teach people Christian virtue.
    a. The penitentials reveal a lot of information about the ascetic ideals of early Christianity and about the prevalence of crime in Celtic and Germanic cultures.
    b. The penitential system helped religion become a private, personal matter.

II. Christian attitudes toward classical culture
A. The early Christians were hostile toward pagan Roman culture.
1. Early Christians believed that Roman culture was useless and immoral.
2. They hated the Romans because they had crucified Christ and persecuted his followers.

B. Christianity's compromise and adjustment to Roman culture
1. Early Christians encouraged adjustment to the existing social, economic, and political establishment.
2. Christians adopted the views of their contemporary world.
    a. Jesus had regarded women as equal to men but other (often later) influences were to cause Christianity to view women as inferior and sexual intercourse as undesirable.
    b. Early Christians had no objections to homosexuality; objections came later, as Greco-Roman urban culture gave way to rural medieval culture.
3. Saint Paul and Saint Jerome incorporated pagan thought into Christianity.

C. Saint Augustine and the synthesis of pagan and Christian thought
1. Augustine, one of the most brilliant thinkers of Western culture, had a major impact on Christian thought.
    a. *The Confessions* describes Augustine's conflict between his spiritual self and his sensual self.
    b. Contrary to the Donatists, Augustine believed that Christians should live in and transform society.
    c. In *City of God*, Augustine argued that the state is a necessary evil, but it can work for the good by providing the peace, justice, and order that Christians need to learn to live according to their religion.
    d. Augustine believed that the function of the state is to protect people, and that ultimate authority in society lies with the church.
2. Augustine assimilated Roman-pagan history and culture into Christianity.

D. Monasticism and the *Rule* of Saint Benedict
   1. With the legalization of Christianity, monks took the place of martyrs as those who could speak for God.
   2. Early eremitical life was at first viewed as dangerous by the church.
   3. There were many experiments in communal monasticism in the fifth and sixth centuries, which the church encouraged.
      a. The monastery of Lérins encouraged the severely penitential and ascetic behavior of the East and had a direct influence on Irish monastic life.
      b. Cassiodorus started the association of monasticism with scholarship and learning.
   4. Benedict of Nursia's *Rule of Saint Benedict* became the guide for all Christian monastic life.
      a. The *Rule* outlined a life of regularity, discipline, and moderation applicable to varying physical and geographical conditions.
      b. Monks made a vow of stability, conversion of manners, and obedience.
      c. The *Rule* is an expression of the assimilation of the Roman spirit into Western monasticism.
   5. The Benedictine form of monasticism succeeded because it was balanced and suited the social circumstances of early medieval society.
      a. It provided for both intellectual and manual activity.
      b. It generated great wealth.
      c. It provided local young people with education.
III. The migration of the Germanic peoples
   A. The Völkerwanderugen of the Germanic peoples was important in the decline of the Roman Empire and the making of European civilization.
      1. Germanic tribes had been pushing against the Roman Empire's frontiers since about 150.
      2. The Germans migrated into Europe possibly because they were overpopulated, had food shortages, and were attracted to Roman wealth.
   B. Romanization and barbarization
      1. From the third century the Roman army was the chief agent of barbarization.
      2. Barbarian people entered the empire as army recruits, *laeti* (refugees or prisoners of war), or *foederati* (free barbarian units).
      3. The arrival of the Huns in the West in 376 caused the entry of entire peoples, the *gentes*, into the empire.
      4. The Visigoths crushed a Roman army at Adrianople in 376, making further invasions possible.
      5. Except for the Lombards, barbarian conquests on the continent ended about 600.
      6. The Visigoths, Vandals, Burgundians, and other tribes established a number of kingdoms.
         a. Theodoric, an Ostrogoth king, established control over Italy and Sicily and pursued a policy of assimilation between the Germans and the Romans.
         b. The most important new kingdom was the Frankish kingdom established by the chieftain Clovis.

IV. Germanic society
   A. Kinship, custom, and class
      1. The basic Germanic social unit was the tribe, or *folk*.
         a. Law was unwritten custom, handed down orally from generation to generation.
         b. Tribes were bound by shared peace and led by kings or chieftains.
      2. The *comitatus*, or war band, fought with the chieftain; gradually, a warrior-nobility evolved.
   B. Germanic law
      1. In the sixth century, during the process of Christianization, Germanic law began to be written down.
      2. Under Salic Law each person had a *wergeld*, or monetary value, and each offense had a fine.
      3. German law aimed at the reduction of violence; it was not concerned with abstract justice.
   C. German life
      1. Germans lived in small villages.
         a. German males engaged in animal husbandry.
         b. The women raised grain and were responsible for the weaving and spinning.
         c. The number of cattle a man possessed indicated his wealth and determined his social status.
         d. German society was patriarchal.
      2. Ironworking was advanced, but the goods were produced for war and the subsistence economy, not for trade.
      3. Warfare constituted the main characteristic of Germanic society.
      4. The law codes show that women were regarded as family property and could be sold.
      5. Some royal women, such as Clothilde, exercised considerable influence.
   D. Anglo-Saxon England
      1. The native Britons, who were Celtic people, were fully romanized.
      2. When Rome withdrew from Britain, the island was open to plundering Picts and Germans, and the Britons fled to Wales.
         a. The Anglo-Saxon invasion gave rise to the Arthurian legends; Roman culture disappeared.
         b. By the seventh and eighth centuries there were seven Germanic kingdoms, which were united under Alfred of Wessex in the ninth century.
V. The Byzantine East
   A. The western and eastern halves of the empire drifted apart.
      1. In the West, civic functions were performed first by church leaders and then by German chieftains.
      2. In the East, the Byzantines continued the traditions of the Roman Empire.
   B. Differences between the Byzantine East and the Germanic West
      1. In the West there were conflicts between church and state leaders, while in the East the state was supreme over the church.
         a. Religion was seen as a branch of the state in the East.
         b. It was the duty of the emperor to protect the faith.

2. Classical culture was condemned in the West; in the East, apologists, or defenders, of Christianity demanded harmony between classical culture and Christianity.
3. In 1054, a theological dispute led the bishop of Rome and the patriarch of Constantinople to excommunicate each other—the two churches split apart.
4. Despite religious differences, the Byzantine Empire protected the West against invasions from the East.
5. The Byzantines civilized the Slavic people and converted them to Christianity.
   a. The Byzantine missionary Cyril invented a Slavic alphabet using Greek characters (the Cyrillic alphabet).
   b. Byzantine art and architecture became the basis of Russian forms.
C. The law code of Justinian
   1. The law codes of the emperors Theodosius and Justinian are among the most important contributions of the Byzantine Empire.
   2. The *corpus juris civilis*—based on the *Code, Digest,* and *Institutes*—is the foundation of European law.
D. Byzantine intellectual life
   1. The Byzantines kept scholarship alive, especially history.
   2. They passed Greco-Roman culture on to the Arabs.
   3. Although they made no advances in science or mathematics, they did make contributions to medicine and military technology.
VI. The Arabs and Islam
   A. The Arabs
      1. The Hejaz Arabs were urban and commercial, while the Bedouin Arabs were nomadic and rural.
      2. All Arabs, however, were tribal and followed similar religious rules.
   B. Muhammad and the faith of Islam
      1. Muhammad was a merchant who became a preacher-prophet.
         a. He described his visions in verse form—his Qur'an.
         b. After Muhammad's death, scribes organized these revelations into chapters.
      2. The Qur'an outlines the monotheistic theology of Islam.
         a. Islam means "submission to the word of God," and its central idea is the Day of Judgement.
         b. Islam is a strict religion that condemns such things as immorality, alcoholic beverages and gambling, and usury; it insists on regular prayer and alms giving.
         c. Muslims believed that following their religion's basic rules would automatically gain them salvation, as would dying for their faith in battle.
      3. The doctrines of Islam superseded tribal ties and bound all Arabs.
   C. When the caliph Ali (successor to Prophet Muhammad) was assassinated in 661, Islam split into the Shi'ite (or Shi'a) and the Sunni factions.
      1. The Shi'ites claimed to be the blood descendants of Ali and to possess divine knowledge.
      2. The Sunnis, the majority of the faith, claimed that the *Sunna* was a source of truth.
   D. Islam united the Arabs and encouraged expansion and conquest.
      1. Much of the old Roman Mediterranean empire came under Muslim control.
      2. Spain was held until the *reconquista* began in the twelfth century.

3. The Muslims were stopped at Tours in 733, but successfully carried their conquest to India and Africa.
4. In Spain they made great contributions to agriculture and established intellectual centers, such as at Toledo.
   a. They developed algebra and made other contributions to mathematics, such as the concept of zero.
   b. They excelled in medical knowledge and preserved Greek philosophical thought.

Review Questions

Check your understanding of this chapter by answering the following questions.

1. What was the role of the Roman emperors and the empire in the growth of Christianity from an outlawed movement to the most important power in Rome?
2. Why did Rome become the capital of the Christian church in the West?
3. How did Christian missionaries convert the pagans? What devices and techniques did they use in the assimilation of Germanic peoples into Christianity?
4. Why and how did the Christian rejection of paganism turn to compromise?
5. What ideas did Saint Augustine contribute to Christian thought?
6. What was happening to Rome at the time Saint Augustine wrote *City of God*? How could this have influenced his philosophy that the City of God is more important than the city of man?
7. What was the purpose of monasticism? Why is Benedict of Nursia one of the most important figures in the history of Christian monasticism?
8. Describe the Benedictine *Rule*. Why was it successful?
9. What role did the monasteries play in European society?
10. Why was the defeat of the Roman army by the Visigoths in 378 a turning point in European history?
11. What patterns of social and political life existed in German society and what was the economy like?
12. How and why did Germanic law evolve and how did it work?
13. Name the kingdoms of the English Heptarchy. What were their origins and what role did King Alfred of Wessex play in this development?
14. Why was there no church-state conflict in the eastern part of the empire?
15. How did the Byzantine Empire serve the West as both a protector from the East and as a preserver of ancient culture?
16. Describe the historical evolution of Islam and its major beliefs. What kind of lifestyle does it demand of its followers?
17. What are the similarities among Judaism, Christianity, and Islam?
18. What was Muhammad's message?
19. What impact did the Muslims have on the politics and culture of the Mediterranean world?

8. Saint Augustine is important in European history because he
   a. worked out the theory of papal supremacy.
   b. compiled the writings of Jesus into a new testament.
   c. assimilated Greco-Roman thought into Christianity.
   d. was the first bishop of Rome.

9. The Benedictine *Rule* was primarily designed to
   a. spread Christianity to the Germans.
   b. draw the individual away from love of self.
   c. encourage new economic ventures.
   d. train officials for government.

10. The Qur'an is the
    a. sacred book of Islam.
    b. Germanic practice of infanticide.
    c. Islamic religious center at Mecca.
    d. leading Muslim official.

11. Collections of early Germanic laws dealt primarily with
    a. sex.
    b. civil rights.
    c. property rights.
    d. fines for criminal offenses, such as theft, murder, rape, and so forth.

12. The basic Germanic social unit was the
    a. laeti.
    b. comitatus.
    c. foederati.
    d. folk.

13. The most important ecclesiastical statement about church-state relations was formulated by
    a. Arius of Alexandria.
    b. the emperor Theodosius.
    c. the emperor Diocletian.
    d. Ambrose of Milan.

14. Which of the following did *not* provide political and social leadership in the early Christian era?
    a. Giaseric
    b. St. Paul
    c. Leo I (440–461)
    d. Gregory 1 (590–604)

15. Religious conversion means
    a. baptism.
    b. a turning of the heart and mind to God.
    c. confession.
    d. confirmation.

16. Missionaries used all of the following methods to get pagan peoples to accept Christianity except
    a. preaching.
    b. edification through stories about Christ.
    c. the adaptation of pagan places and practices to Christian use.
    d. group penintentials and baptisms.

17. Church organization was closely associated with local monastic life in
    a. Germany.
    b. Scotland.
    c. Ireland.
    d. Italy.

18. Cassiodorus identified monasticism entirely with
    a. prayer and mortification.
    b. study and learning.
    c. manual labor.
    d. service to the poor and orphaned.

19. The monastic vows in the *Rule* of St. Benedict were
    a. poverty, chastity, and obedience.
    b. the Work of God.
    c. stability, conversion of manners, and obedience.
    d. designed to spread the Gospel through missionary activity.

20. Benedictine monasticism replaced other forms of early Christian monasticism largely because
    a. of its moderation, flexibility, and balanced life.
    b. the emperors encouraged it.
    c. Benedictine monks were clever.
    d. Europeans were especially suited to the eremitical life.

21. The Byzantine emperor Justinian secured a permanent place in European history for his
    a. defeat of the Slavs and Turks.
    b. production of the *corpus juris civilis*.
    c. marriage to Theodora.
    d. invention of the Cyrillic alphabet.

22. The *corpus juris civilis* was
    a. snippets of the works of Herodotus, Procopius, and Aristotle.
    b. Russian, Roman, and Greek laws.
    c. Roman law and Greek practices.
    d. the body of civil law of Justinian.

23. *Islam* literally means
    a. "the Day of Judgment is at hand."
    b. "submission to the word of God."
    c. "the Qur'an is a sacred book."
    d. "Muhammad is Allah's prophet."

24. Which of the following statements about Islam, Christianity, and Judaism is false?
    a. All three religions teach predestination.
    b. Members are called People of the Book by Muslims.
    c. All three religions and monotheistic.
    d. Members of all three religions worship the same God.

25. The center of Spanish learning was
    a. Mecca.
    b. Madrid.
    c. Iona.
    d. Toledo.

Major Political Ideas

1. According to St. Augustine, what is the origin of the state and the purpose of government? How does this view fit into his philosophy of history?

2. What was St. Ambrose's position with regard to authority within society? Which was, in his view, the ultimate power—the church or the state?

Issues for Essays and Discussion

By 476 the western Roman Empire had given way to massive invasions. What sort of new culture grew out of this disruption? Discuss this by making reference to the role of the Christian church and the role of the Germanic peoples. what were the strengths and contributions of each?

Interpretation of Visual Sources

Study the photograph on page 199 of your textbook that shows the interior of the Pantheon in Rome. What is the function of this building? What cultural influences can you detect in it? In what way does this building reflect the adaptability and flexibility of early Christianity?

Geography

1. On Outline Map 7.3 provided, and using maps 6.1, 7.3, and 7.4 in the textbook as guides, mark the following: the boundaries of the Roman Empire at the time of Hadrian, the invasion routes of the seven Germanic invasion groups, the battle site of Tours, Constantinople, the Red Sea, Paris, Rome, Jerusalem, the Black Sea, Egypt.

2. Using Map 7.4 in the text as a guide, (a) show the extent of Muslim expansion by 733, and (b) locate and explain the significance of the following Muslim cities: Mecca, Damascus, Cordova, Toledo.

Studying Effectively—Exercise 2

Learning to Improve Your Underlining Skills

Read the following paragraphs, in which some words are printed in italic type to help you find the major points. Read the passage a second time and underline or highlight one or two sentences in each paragraph that best summarize the paragraph's major point. Now study and review these points. Finally, close the book and on a piece of notepaper summarize the major points *with a few words* under the heading "The Success of Benedictine Monasticism." Compare your summary with that found at the end of the exercise.

The Success of Benedictine Monasticism

Why was the Benedictine form of monasticism so successful? Why did it eventually replace other forms of Western monasticism? The answer lies partly in its *spirit of flexibility and moderation*, and partly in the *balanced life* it provided. Early Benedictine monks and nuns spent part of the day in prayer, part in study or some other form of intellectual activity, and part in manual labor. The monastic life as conceived by Saint Benedict did not lean too heavily in any one direction; it struck a balance between asceticism and idleness. It thus provided opportunities for persons of entirely different abilities and talents—from mechanics to gardeners to literary scholars. Benedict's *Rule* contrasts sharply with Cassiodorus's narrow concept of the monastery as a place for aristocratic scholars and bibliophiles.

Benedictine monasticism also *suited the social circumstances of early medieval society*. The German invasions had fragmented European life: the self-sufficient rural estate replaced the city as the basic unit of civilization. A monastery, too, had to be *economically self-sufficient*. It was supposed to produce from its lands and properties all that was needed for food, clothing, buildings, and the liturgical service of the altar. The monastery fitted in—indeed, represented—the trend toward localism.

Benedict monasticism also succeeded partly because it was so *materially successful*. In the seventh and eighth centuries, monasteries pushed back forest and wasteland, drained swamps, and experimented with crop rotation. For example, the abbey of Saint Wandrille, founded in 645 near Rouen in northwestern Gaul, sent squads of monks to clear the forests that surrounded it. Within seventy-five years, the abbey was immensely wealthy. The abbey of Jumièges, also in the diocese of Rouen, followed much the same pattern. Such Benedictine houses made *a significant contribution to the agricultural development* of Europe. The communal nature of their organization, whereby property was held in common and profits pooled and reinvested, made this contribution possible.

Finally, *monasteries conducted schools* for local young people. Some learned about prescriptions and herbal remedies and went on to provide medical treatment for their localities. A few copied manuscripts and wrote books. This training did not go unappreciated in a society desperately in need of it. Local and royal governments drew on the services of *the literate men and able administrators* the monasteries produced. This was not what Saint Benedict had intended, but the effectiveness of the institution he designed made it perhaps inevitable.

Answer

The Success of Benedictine Monasticism

1. A flexible and balanced life
2. Economically self-sufficient
3. Economically successful, especially in agriculture
4. Provided education for young and able administrators for governments

Chapter 8
The Carolingian World: Europe in the Early Middle Ages

Chapter Questions

After reading and studying this chapter you should be able to answer the following questions:

How did Charlemagne acquire and govern his empire? What were the relations between Carolingian rulers and the church? What was the Carolingian Renaissance and in what sense was it the first European civilization? What was feudalism and how did it come about? What factors contributed to the disintegration of the Carolingian Empire?

Chapter Summary

For about a century after the Franks defeated the Muslims at the Battle of Tours in 733, Europe enjoyed a period of political and economic regeneration and unity. The chief benefactor of this regeneration was the Frankish Carolingian family. It was the Carolingian Charles Martel who won at Tours, and it was his son, Pippin III, and grandson, Charlemagne, who molded western Europe into a unified Christian empire—the Carolingian Empire.

The Carolingian era was a high point of stability and creativity in the early Middle Ages, which was generally a precarious time. The Carolingians struck up a mutually beneficial relationship with the church. They supported church missionaries and enforced Christian moral codes. In return, the pope recognized and strengthened Carolingian political authority. Charlemagne extended the boundaries of his empire and brought peace to Europe. Within this climate of peace a meaningful renaissance in learning and the arts took place. The center for both the intellectual renaissance and the Carolingian Empire was northern Europe. The very fact that this Carolingian Empire and culture developed in the north, or even at all, was due to the forced isolation of Europe from the Islamic-Mediterranean world, as the great historian Henri Pirenne first argued.

While these changes related to the Carolingian era were taking place, Europe continued to experience the economic-political transformation that historians call feudalism. Beginning as a natural response of insecure people to the disappearance of the protection the strong Roman government had provided, feudalism became a means for communities to defend themselves.

Over time, as discussed in Chapter 6, freemen gave up their personal rights and their property to local lords. These lords provided protection, in return, and built their own little empires. Essential to the feudal system was the fief—the land a lord received from the monarch. Charlemagne was able to manage the feudal lords, but his grandsons could not keep control of the feudal system. When they divided Charlemagne's empire into three parts in 843, it was already soaked in blood because of the ambitions of petty lords. The division was an invitation to invasion from the outside. The Vikings, Magyars, and Muslims then threw Europe back into a period of violence and fear.

Study Outline

Use this outline to preview the chapter before you read a particular section in the textbook and then as a self-check to test your reading comprehension after you have read the chapter section.

I. The Frankish aristocracy and the rise of the Carolingian dynasty
   A. The Franks, under Clovis, emerged as the most powerful people in Europe in the sixth century.
      1. The Frankish kingdom included most of France and southwestern Germany.
      2. Clovis had the support of the church.
   B. After Clovis's death in 511, the Merovingians fell into a long period of civil war in which Queen Brunhilda played an important role.
      1. Civil war was accompanied by the rise of a wealthy and powerful aristocracy.
      2. Reconstruction of the Frankish kingdom began with Pippin of Landen, mayor of the East Frankland palace.
   C. The rise of the Carolingian dynasty
      1. The Carolingian family under Martel and Pippin III built a vast power base in France, aided by the church.
      2. Bishop Boniface organized the church and spread Christianity in central Europe.
         a. He established *The Rule of Saint Benedict* in all monasteries he founded or reformed.
         b. He reformed the Frankish church.
      3. Boniface and the Carolingians attacked Germanic sexual customs.
         a. German custom had encouraged incest but Boniface disagreed.
         b. Polygamy was attacked.
   D. Monarchy and papacy
      1. Pippin III's acquisition of the kingship was aided by the pope.
      2. Pippin created strong ties between the church and the Carolingian dynasty.
II. The empire of Charlemagne
   A. The warrior-ruler Charlemagne is described in Einhard's biography as both an intellectual and a strong, brutal man.
   B. Territorial expansion
      1. Charlemagne continued the Carolingian tradition by building a large European kingdom.
      2. He checked Muslim expansion by establishing *marches* (strongly fortified areas) and conquered the Saxon German tribes.

3. He incorporated Lombardy into the Frankish kingdom.
4. He added northern Italy to his kingdom, but his Spanish campaign failed, inspiring the *Song of Roland*.

C. The government of the Carolingian Empire
1. The empire of Charlemagne was mainly a collection of agricultural estates.
2. The political power of the Carolingians depended on the cooperation of the Frankish aristocracy.
3. Charlemagne appointed *missi dominici* as links between local authorities and the central government.

D. The imperial coronation of Charlemagne in 800
1. The church supported Charlemagne, and in 800 the pope crowned him the emperor.
2. Charlemagne consciously perpetuated old Roman imperial notions while at the same time identifying with the new Rome of the Christian church.
3. The coronation gave rise to theories of both imperial and papal supremacy.

III. The Carolingian intellectual revival
A. The revival of learning began with Irish-Celtic influence in Anglo-Saxon Britain.
B. Northumbrian culture in Britain
1. Under Saint Benet Biscop and others, Irish-Celtic culture permeated Roman Britain and Europe, partly by way of monastic missals and other books.
2. The Lindisfarne book, in a Celtic script, is a high point in the Northumbrian artistic renaissance.
3. The noblewoman Hilda and others established "double monasteries" that were governed by women and were intellectual centers.
4. The venerable Bede wrote a history—*The Ecclesiastical History of the English Nation*—that is the chief source of information about early Britain.
5. The epic poem *Beowulf* illustrates the complexities and contradictions within people and society and the importance of loyalty, fame, and warfare in medieval society.

C. The Carolingian Renaissance
1. Charlemagne fostered an intellectual revival which centered on his court at Aachen.
2. His scholars (the most important being Alcuin) encouraged interest in the classics and preserved Greek and Roman knowledge.
3. Basic literacy was established among the clergy, and Christianity was spread.

D. Health and medical care in the early Middle Ages
1. No rational understanding of disease existed among the Germanic peoples.
2. Drug and prescription therapy was common.
3. Physicians knew little about disease, and their treatments were primitive and often harmful.
4. Christianity contributed to a better understanding of medicine.
   a. In the sixth and seventh centuries, medical treatment was provided by monasteries.
   b. The Italian school at Salerno was an important medical center, and several female physicians played a key role in medical writings.

IV. Division and disintegration of the Carolingian Empire (814–987)
   A. Charlemagne left his empire to his son, Louis the Pious.
   B. Louis could not retain the loyalty of the warrior-aristocracy, and disintegration began almost immediately.
      1. The huge empire lacked an efficient bureaucracy.
      2. The Frankish custom of dividing estates among male heirs also contributed to the breakup of the empire.
         a. Dissatisfied with their portions, Louis's sons—Lothair, Louis the German, and Charles the Bald—fought bitterly.
         b. Finally, in the Treaty of Verdun in 843, they agreed to divide up the empire.
   C. Fratricidal warfare among Charlemagne's descendants hastened the spread of feudalism in the tenth century.
V. Feudalism
   A. Feudalism was a type of government in which power was considered private and was divided among many lords.
   B. Feudalism existed at two social levels, that of armed retainers (knights) and of royal officials such as counts.
      1. The adoption of the stirrup made the cavalry a potent weapon, and armed retainers became very valuable.
      2. Retainers took an oath of fealty, and some, called vassals, were given estates by their lords.
      3. Counts held power at the local level and came to rule independently.
   C. Because of the premium placed on physical strength, women were subordinate to men, although they occasionally held positions of power.
   D. Manorialism, which was the economic and social side of feudalism, centered on the relationship between peasant (or serf) and the lord's estate.
      1. Peasants exchanged their labor and land for protection from the lord.
      2. The free farmers became serfs—bound to the land and to the lord.
VI. The great invasions of the ninth century
   A. Disunity in Europe after Charlemagne's death was an invitation to aggression from the outside.
      1. Beginning around 787, the Vikings from the north overran northwest France, Britain, parts of Russia, and elsewhere.
         a. Their superb seamanship gave them an overwhelming advantage.
         b. Reasons for their attacks include overpopulation, crop failures, and trade.
      2. The Magyars, or Hungarians, pushed into Europe from the east, and the Muslims pushed up from the south.
   B. These invasions accelerated the growth of feudalism.
   C. The invaders brought with them some important advances in agriculture, law, and industry.

Review Questions

Check your understanding of this chapter by answering the following questions.

1. What was the relationship between the Carolingians and the pope? How did both sides benefit from the relationship?
2. How successful was Charlemagne in expanding the power of the Frankish state?
3. What techniques and methods did Charlemagne use to govern his vast empire? How well did his empire function?
4. What was the church's attitude toward Charlemagne and the political value of the "state"?
5. What were the probable reasons for Charlemagne's quest for the title of emperor? The results?
6. Describe the Northumbrian cultural revival. What were its sources of inspiration and its goals?
7. What was the "Carolingian Renaissance"? Who were its participants and what did they accomplish?
8. In the early medieval period, a person of forty was considered old. Why did people die so young? How much did people understand about disease, and what kind of health care existed?
9. Define feudalism and describe its origins. What impact did it have on the peasants?
10. Who were the Vikings? What were their motives and why were they able to terrorize Europe so well after 814?
11. Describe the Magyar and Muslim invasions in terms of motives, areas terrorized, methods, and impact.

Study-Review Exercises

Define the following key concepts and terms.

fief

feud

missi dominici

vassal

polygamy

Carolingian Renaissance

Pirenne thesis

Charlemagne's marches

Identify and explain the significance of each of the following people.
Saint Hilda

Queen Brunhilda

The Venerable Bede

Pippin of Landen

Pippin III

Saint Boniface

Charles Martel

Charlemagne

Alcuin

Louis the Pious

Pope Leo

Benet Biscop

Louis the German

Charles the Bald

Lothair

Explain what the following events were, who participated in them, and why they were important.
Northumbrian cultural renaissance

coronation of Charlemagne

Battle of Tours

Treaty of Verdun

Explain the subject matter and historical significance of the following works.
The Ecclesiastical History of the English Nation

On the Physical Elements

Beowulf

The Song of Roland

Test your understanding of the chapter by providing the correct answers.

1. Charlemagne's biographer. _____

2. In general, the economic and political power and status of aristocratic women in the early Middle Ages tended to *increase/decrease.*

3. In the eighth and ninth centuries, the population of western Europe tended to become *more/less* free.

4. In general, the relationship between the Carolingian emperor Charles and the Christian church was *good/warlike.*

5. This Northumbrian was an important scholar and educator and the major adviser to

    Charlemagne. _____

6. The foundation of a medical school at _____ in the ninth century gave
    tremendous impetus to medical study.

Place the following events in correct chronological order.

Beginning of Magyar tribal invasions across the Danube
Battle of Tours
Coronation of Charlemagne
Founding of Wearmouth and Jarrow monasteries by Biscop
Charlemagne's Spanish campaign
Life of the Venerable Bede
Death of Louis the Pious
Pope Zacharias confirms that Pippin III is king of the Franks

1.

2.

3.

4

5.

6.

7.

8.

Multiple-Choice Questions

1. Saint Boniface, the missionary monk
    a. refused to support the Carolingian kings.
    b. encouraged monasteries to develop their own religious rule.
    c. attacked Germanic sexual and marriage customs.
    d. was a staunch enemy of Roman ideas and Roman traditions.

2. The most important source of Northumbrian (and Carolingian) cultural revival was
   a. Muslim society.
   b. Jewish society.
   c. Irish-Celtic society.
   d. Frankish society.

3. The *missi dominici* of Charlemagne were
   a. missionaries.
   b. peasant farmers.
   c. royal legal officials.
   d. military outposts.

4. Charlemagne was crowned emperor by
   a. himself.
   b. his father Pippin.
   c. the pope.
   d. the Frankish council.

5. Which of the following peoples was *not* part of the great invasions of the ninth century?
   a. The Vikings
   b. The Franks
   c. The Magyars
   d. The Muslims

6. Which of the following was *not* one of Charlemagne's accomplishments?
   a. The establishment of the missi dominici
   b. The creation of marches
   c. The encouragement of literature and art
   d. The destruction of papal power

7. The Northumbrian period of creativity was centered in
   a. Charlemagne's court.
   b. the monasteries of Britain.
   c. the courts of feudal lords.
   d. Pavia in Lombardy.

8. When Charlemagne's son, Louis the Pious, died, the empire
   a. was divided into three parts.
   b. remained intact under Charles Martel.
   c. was united with the Anglo-Saxon kingdoms.
   d. remained a unified but weak state.

9. The monk-historian who wrote *The Ecclesiastical History of the English Nation* was
   a. Louis the German.
   b. Pippin III.
   c. Bede.
   d. Augustine.

10. The Battle of Tours (733)
    a. aided the spread of Christianity in the Frankish kingdom.
    b. checked the advance of the Muslims in Europe.
    c. made Pippin II mayor of the palace.
    d. ended the Viking attacks.

11. Saint Boniface is famous as
    a. the biographer of Charlemagne.
    b. the author of *Beowulf*.
    c. the apostle of Germany.
    d. the author of a great medical treatise.

12. Historians consider the narrative poem *Beowulf* useful for
    a. an illustration of early Germanic marriage laws.
    b. its information on eighth-century monastic life.
    c. an early example of Germanic fairy tales.
    d. the picture it provides of Anglo-Saxon society and ideals.

13. The Carolingian Empire collapsed because
    a. it was too large and lacked an effective bureaucracy.
    b. it was overrun by Arabs and Turks.
    c. Charlemagne's grandsons were lazy and incompetent.
    d. Charlemagne failed to make a will.

14. The first major medical center in Europe was at
    a. Aix-la-Chapelle.
    b. Bologna.
    c. Salerno.
    d. Strasbourg.

15. Constantine the African advanced medical knowledge by
    a. founding hospitals.
    b. researching gynecological problems.
    c. recommending heroin as an anesthetic.
    d. translating Arabic medical treatises.

16. Viking expansion in the eighth century was probably due to
    a. underpopulation.
    b. the search for a colder climate.
    c. the search for new trade and commercial outlets.
    d. their desire to learn Carolingian shipbuilding techniques.

17. Feudalism was a form of government concerned with the rights and powers of
    a. the church.
    b. peasants.
    c. the military elite.
    d. absolute monarchs.

18. A feudal lord exercised all of the following rights *except*
    a. judicial.
    b. religious.
    c. political.
    d. economic.

19. The famous noblewoman who ruled the double monastery of Whitby was
    a. Queen Brunhilda.
    b. Martha of Aachen.
    c. Saint Hilda.
    d. Abbess Marie.

20. The medieval rebirth of interest in and preservation of achievements of classical Greece and Rome was
    a. the Carolingian Renaissance.
    b. feudalism.
    c. the Danelaw.
    d. *rex et sacerdos*.

21. Charlemagne's fortified areas in northeastern Spain were known as
    a. missi.
    b. villas.
    c. courts.
    d. marches.

22. *The Song of Roland* was based on Charlemagne's crusade in
    a. Spain.
    b. Greece.
    c. England.
    d. Germany.

23. "On the very day of the most holy nativity of the Lord, when the king at Mass had risen from prayer . . . Pope Leo placed the crown on his head . . ." The person who was crowned in this event was
    a. King Leopold.
    b. Charlemagne.
    c. Charles Martel.
    d. Boniface.

24. The Norse word *vik* means
    a. "boat."
    b. "feudalism."
    c. "creek."
    d. "red."

25. Manorialism is concerned with
    a. the economic side of feudalism.
    b. the way the military was organized.
    c. the spread of ancient texts.
    d. the conversion of manors to centers of learning.

Major Political Ideas

1. Define *feudalism*. Was it primarily a political, military, or social system? What were the reasons for its emergence? Was it, in your analysis, a source of order or a source of instability in Europe? What impact did it have on the peasants?

2. What is an aristocracy? What was the aristocrats' source of wealth and power, and why were they looked upon as dangerous by the Merovingian kings?

Issues for Essays and Discussion

1. It is said that between 733, when the Muslims were defeated at Tours, and the division of Charlemagne's empire in 843, a distinctly European society emerged. Three of the main developments of this new society were Charlemagne's empire, the rise of feudalism, and an intellectual revival. Discuss this new Europe by describing each of these developments. Was this a unique new society? In what ways was this society different from that of Roman times?

2. Who or what was more important in the development of European society in the Carolingian era, the warrior-rulers or the men and women of the church? Support your argument with historical evidence.

Interpretation of Visual Sources

Study the "Plan for an Ideal Monastery" on page 243 of your textbook. What were the different classes or groups of residents at the monastery? What was the diet of the community? What seems to have occupied most of the time of the residents? Compare this ninth-century design to the eleventh-century monastery of Cluny, which is pictured on page 306 of your textbook.

Geography

On Outline Map 8.1 provided, and using maps 8.1, 8.2, and 8.3 in the textbook as a reference, mark the following: the geographic boundaries of Charlemagne's empire, the location of the Spanish and Danish marches, Aachen, Rouen, Strasbourg, Paris, the Rhine, and the Elbe, the division of Charlemagne's empire in 843, and the invasionary routes of the Vikings, the Magyars, and the Muslims.

Outline Map 8.1

Understanding History Through the Arts

What were the architectural and artistic achievements of this age? For architecture, see K. Conant, *Carolingian and Romanesque Architecture, 800–1200** (1978). A good general introduction to the illuminated manuscripts and religious treasures of the period is J. Beckwith, *Early Medieval Art** (1979).

Problems for Further Investigation

1. What can be learned about early medieval life from works like *Beowulf*? Paperback editions of several early medieval works are available: L. Sherley-Price, trans., *Bede: A History of the English Church and Peoples** (1962); M. Alexander, trans., *The Earliest English Poems** (1972); D. L. Sayers, trans., *The Song of Roland**; and D. Wright, trans., *Beowulf** (1957). Einhard's biography of Charlemagne is available in a 1960 edition with a foreword by Sidney Painter.

2. How did Merovingian and Carolingian government work? How did the concept of kingship evolve? Was Christianity as important as claimed? These and other questions are answered in P. Wormald et al., *Ideal and Reality in Frankish and Anglo-Saxon Society* (1984).

3. What were the contributions of women in medieval society? Begin your inquiry with D. Baker, ed., *Medieval Women** (1981), and S. F. Wemple, *Women in Frankish Society: Marriage and the Cloister, 500 to 900* (1981). See also the chapter bibliography for additional important works on women in this period.

4. What were the motives of the pope and Charlemagne at the time of the coronation on Christmas Day in 800? Of what significance is it that the church gave the title to the king? These and other questions are considered in a collection of interpretations entitled *The Coronation of Charlemagne** (1959), edited by R. E. Sullivan.

5. How much did the Islamic movement shape the course of European history? The classic statement on this is Henri Pirenne, *Mohammed and Charlemagne** (1958).

---

*Available in paperback.

Chapter 9
Revival, Recovery, and Reform

Chapter Questions

After reading and studying this chapter you should be able to answer the following questions:

How did the revival of Europe come about? What was the social and political impact of the recovery of Europe? How did the reform of the Christian church affect relations between church and civil authorities? What were the Crusades and how did they manifest the influence of the church and the ideals of society?

Chapter Summary

When Charlemagne died in 814, Europe was thrown into a century and a half of disorder. Then, around the year 1000, Europe began to recover from this long, bitter winter of violence. This chapter deals with two of the most important signs of that European springtime: political recovery and the spiritual and political revival of the church. These two revivals were of great importance for the evolution of individual freedom and for the political and intellectual growth of Europe.

One of the earliest signs of revival was the success of feudalism in bringing peace and unity to Europe in the tenth and eleventh centuries. The reduced level of warfare in this period, together with favorable changes in climate, resulted in both population expansion and agricultural improvement, and medieval engineers made significant advances in harnessing both waterpower and windpower. More forceful testimony to the dynamism of the age was the Crusades. Growing out of the influence of the papacy and religion in medieval society, and the efforts of the *reconquista* in Spain, the Crusades provided an outlet for the spiritual and political energy of Europe, although their cultural and economic effects remain debatable.

The religious revival also began, with monastic reform at the abbey of Cluny in the eleventh century, and spread across Europe. When monastic life was subsequently threatened by materialism and lay interference, there were fresh demands for reform by the Cistercians at the abbey of Citeaux. At the same time, and partly as a result of the Cistercian reforms, the papacy set out to purify itself and to redefine its relationship with the emperors, kings, and other lay political authorities of Europe. This led to the investiture controversy, which reached its height in the conflict between Pope Gregory VII and the German emperor Henry IV. The struggle

149

between the popes and the emperors turned out to be one of the most important and long-lasting political conflicts in European history.

Study Outline

Use this outline to review the chapter before you read a particular section in your textbook and then as a self-check to test your reading comprehension after you have read the chapter section.

I. Political revival in western Europe in the tenth and eleventh centuries
    A. The decline of invasions and civil disorder
        1. Rollo and William made Normandy a strong territory.
            a. The Vikings became Christianized.
            b. The Vikings and the French became assimilated, and major attacks on France ended.
        2. The nobles elected Hugh Capet king in 987, laying the foundation for future political stability.
        3. In England, the victory of Alfred of Wessex over the Danes in 878 slowly led to English unity.
        4. The Danish king Canute made England part of a large Scandinavian empire.
        5. The German king Otto halted the Magyars in 955.
            a. The base of Otto's power was his alliance with the church, which he used to weaken the feudal lords.
            b. Otto's coronation in 962 laid the foundation for the future Holy Roman Empire.
        6. The Italian cities of Venice, Genoa, and Pisa broke Muslim control of Mediterranean trade.
    B. Population, climate, and mechanization
        1. The decline in war and disease meant a rise in population.
        2. The warmer climate meant better agricultural production.
        3. An ancient energy system, the water mill, was used on a more widespread basis for food production and industry.
        4. Windmills also came into use.
II. Revival and reform in the Christian church in the eleventh century
    A. The monastic revival
        1. Monastic activity had declined as the Carolingian Empire disintegrated.
        2. The abbey of Cluny led the way in a tenth-century monastic revival.
            a. Cluny provided strong leadership for reform of abuses such as simony, for high religious standards, and for sound economic management.
            b. The Cluniac reform spread throughout Europe.
        3. The monastic reform led by abby of Gorze emphasized literary culture, simple lifestyle, and lay authority.
        4. By the eleventh century, wealth and lay interference caused corruption.
        5. The Cistercians (beginning in 1098) isolated themselves from laymen and elaborate ritual.
            a. Their reform movement centered on farming and a simple communal life.
            b. The Cistercians founded 525 new monasteries in the twelfth century and had a profound influence on European society.

B. The reform of the papacy
1. The tenth-century papacy was corrupt and materialistic and provided little leadership to the people of Europe.
   a. Factions in Rome sought to control the papacy for their own gain.
   b. The office of pope was frequently bought and sold.
   c. There were many married priests.
2. Leo IX made the first sweeping reforms.
3. Later reforms stipulated that the college of cardinals would henceforth elect the pope.
III. The Gregorian revolution in church reform
A. Pope Gregory VII's ideas for reform of the church
1. Gregory believed that the pope could hold kings accountable.
2. He wanted the church to be free from lay control.
B. The controversy over lay investiture
1. The church outlawed the widespread practice of lay investiture (the appointment of church officials by secular authority) in 1075.
2. Emperor Henry IV of the Holy Roman Empire protested Pope Gregory's stand on investiture.
   a. The decree raised the question of who had the ultimate authority in a Christian society, the king or the pope.
   b. In 1076, Gregory excommunicated Henry.
3. Their conflict was resolved by Henry's submission to the pope at Canossa in 1077.
4. In 1080 Gregory again excommunicated Henry; in return, Henry invaded Rome.
5. In 1122, the lay investiture controversy was finally settled in a conference at Worms.
   a. The emperor surrendered the right to choose bishops.
   b. However, lay rulers retained a veto over ecclesiastical choices.
6. In the long run, the investiture crisis perpetuated the political division of Germany and encouraged the rise of a very strong noble class.
C. The papacy in the High Middle Ages
1. Pope Urban II laid the foundation for the papal curia, which henceforth administered the church and was its court of law.
   a. The papal curia developed into the court of final appeal for all of Christian Europe.
   b. Most of the cases involved property disputes, ecclesiastical elections, and marriage and annulment.
2. By the early thirteenth century, papal reform had succeeded, but in the following decades the papal bureaucracy became greedy and indifferent.
IV. The Crusades of the eleventh and twelfth centuries
A. The Crusades reflect papal influence in society and the church's new understanding of the noble warrior class.
1. The Crusades, or holy wars to recover the Holy Lands from the Muslims grew out of the Christian-Muslim conflict in Spain.
2. Many knights participated in the Crusades, which manifested both the religious and chivalric ideals of medieval society.
3. The Crusades began with Pope Urban II's plea in 1095 for a crusade to take Jerusalem from the Turks.

4. The Crusades offered a variety of opportunities for many people.
    a. Religious convictions imspired many.
    b. The lure of foreign travel and excitement was also strong.
    c. The Crusades also gave kings an opportunity to get rid of troublesome knights.
C. The results of the Crusades
    1. The First Crusade (1096) was marked by disputes among the great lords and much starvation and disease.
        a. The Crusaders captured Jerusalem in 1099.
        b. Crusader kingdoms were founded in Jerusalem, Edessa, Tripoli, and Antioch.
    2. There were eight papally approved expeditions to the East between 1096 and 1270, but none of the later ones accomplished much.
        a. The Third Crusade was precipitated by the recapture of Jerusalem in 1187.
        b. The Fourth Crusade made the split between the Western and Eastern churches permanent when the Crusaders sacked Byzantium.
    3. Crusades were also fought against the heretical Albegensians and against Emperor Frederick II.
    4. Some women, such as Eleanor of Aquitaine, went on Crusades, while many found that the Crusades brought new economic opportunities.
    5. The Crusades brought few cultural changes, since strong economic and intellectual ties with the East had already been made.
    6. The long struggle between Christians and Muslims left a legacy of deep bitterness.
    7. However, the Christian West benefited from commercial contact with the Middle East.

Review Questions

Check your understanding of this chapter by answering the following questions.

1. Describe the political revival that took place in the ninth and tenth centuries. Who were the chief participants in this revival and what did they accomplish?
2. What role did the church play in the recovery of Europe from a period of war and invasion?
3. Why did the population of Europe begin to increase in the eleventh century?
4. What were the goals of the Cluniac reformers? Why were they interested in isolation from lay society?
5. Describe the condition of the clergy and church leadership prior to Leo IX's reform movement. What were the major abuses?
6. Was it inevitable that Pope Gregory would come into conflict with the monarchs of Europe? Explain.
7. What was the investiture controversy? Who held ultimate power in medieval society?
8. Describe the conflict between Pope Gregory VII and Henry IV. What was the outcome?
9. In the long run who were the winners in the investiture controversy? How did this controversy affect the political development of Germany?
10. What was the role and function of the papal curia?
11. What were the various reasons for the Crusades? Were they primarily theological, economic, or imperialistic?

14. In the tenth and eleventh centuries, Nicolaites were
    a. reformed monks.
    b. married priests.
    c. priests who bought and sold church offices.
    d. none of the above

15. The Crusades originated as reaction to
    a. Christian-Muslim conflict in Spain.
    b. the decline of Christian influence in Turkey.
    c. the decline of Christian influence in Italy.
    d. new economic opportunities in southern Italy.

16. The goal of the Gregorian reform movement was
    a. the end of Philip I's adulterous marriage.
    b. the abolition of simony.
    c. the moral reform of the clergy and the centralization of the Catholic church under papal authority.
    d. the excommunication of William of Normandy.

17. Emperor Henry IV opposed Pope Gregory VII because
    a. the pope was too inflexible.
    b. Gregory VII was a peasant.
    c. the pope wanted Henry's strict obedience.
    d. Henry relied on the services of churchmen whom the pope wanted to make responsible solely to papal authority.

18. The pontificate of Innocent III represents the high point of medieval papal authority because
    a. Innocent launched the Crusades.
    b. he composed important legal treatises.
    c. he exerted power all over Europe.
    d. he secured the end of clerical marriage.

19. The papal curia was important as
    a. a symbol of papal power and authority.
    b. the first strong monarchial bureaucracy.
    c. a final court of appeals for Christians all over Europe.
    d. all of the above

20. The crusade that resulted in Christian fighting Christian was the
    a. Fourth Crusade.
    b. Second Crusade.
    c. Eastern Crusade.
    d. First Crusade.

21. The tenth- and eleventh-century advance in energy use centered on
    a. coal mining.
    b. the building of dams.
    c. the development of the steam engine.
    d. the water wheel and the windmill.

22. By the last quarter of the eleventh century monastic observance and spiritual fervor declined because of
    a. the economic depression of the monasteries.
    b. war.
    c. the increased wealth of the monasteries.
    d. competition from the Cistercian orders.

23. The investiture struggle between church and state had its largest impact on
    a. Germany.
    b. France.
    c. England.
    d. Italy.

24. Compared to the dukes of Normandy and Aquitaine, the first Capetian kings of France were
    a. rich and powerful.
    b. able to use royal law and coinage to unify France.
    c. weak.
    d. militarily superior but not hereditary.

25. Which of the following statements best describes the effect of the Crusades on the women of Europe?
    a. They made it impossible for any women to experience foreign travel.
    b. They further limited the possibilities of female independence.
    c. They lowered the birthrate.
    d. They provided greater economic opportunities for women.

Major Political Ideas

The Gregorian reform movement ushered in the idea of "freedom of the church," which meant, in part, ending the practice of lay investiture. Discuss and define the terms *freedom of the church* and *lay investiture*. Include in your discussion an account of the conflict between Henry IV and Pope Gregory VII.

Issues for Essays and Discussion

The High Middle Ages were a period of growth and achievement. What were the chief political and religious changes of the age? Make specific reference to increased political stability in western Europe, the monastic revival, and the Gregorian revolution.

Interpretation of Visual Sources

Study the illustration entitled "Henry IV and Gregory VII" on page 269 of the textbook. What is going on in this scene? Who are the participants and what appears to be the resolution of the problem? Who was the eventual victor?

Geography

Study Map 9.1 in the textbook and then answer the following questions: Why did the First Crusade begin in France? Approximately how many miles did the Crusaders travel before they reached Jerusalem? What is the significance of the cities of Edessa, Antioch, Tripoli, Damascus, and Acre? Why did the Third Crusade take three different routes? Where did the Fourth Crusade end? Why?

Understanding History Through the Arts

1. How did the Crusades affect the art and architecture of the High Middle Ages? To begin a study of the art and architecture of the Crusades, see the chapter titled "Crusader Art and Architecture" in J. R. Strayer, ed., *The Dictionary of the Middle Ages*, vol. 4 (1984).

2. What were the ideas and stories that inspired the imagination and dreams of medieval people? Who were their heroes? The myths of any period are important because they make up the backbone of the culture. Seven myths and hero stories of the Middle Ages are retold in N. L. Goodrich, *The Medieval Myths** (1961).

3. What contributions did the Cistercian monks make to architecture? For discussion of this subject, begin with R. Stalley, *The Cistercian Monasteries of Ireland* (1988).

Problems for Further Investigation

1. What was life like for people who lived during the early Middle Ages? This is one subject dealt with in the fascinating book *Medieval People** (1963) by E. Power.

2. How did Cluny come to exert such a strong religious influence? G. Barraclough's *Medieval Papacy** (1968) is an interesting study for anyone interested in the power of the papacy and the Cluniac movement.

3. What was the relationship between politics and religion in medieval society? Politics and royal justice? Begin your investigation with the standard work on medieval political ideals, J. Morrall, *Political Thought in Medieval Times* (1962).

4. What makes the Crusades such an intriguing period of history? The success, glory, idealism, and political aspects of the religious Crusades have fascinated historians for generations. Students interested in further research in this area should begin with *The Crusades** (1939) by J. A. Brundage.

---

*Available in paperback.

Chapter 10
Life in Christian Europe in the High Middle Ages

Chapter Questions

After reading and studying this chapter you should be able to answer the following questions:

How did the peasants, nobles, and monks of the Middle Ages live and what were their interests? How much social mobility existed in the Middle Ages?

Chapter Summary

This chapter describes and analyzes life in medieval society. It focuses on the three most representative groups within medieval society: the peasants, who worked; the nobles, who fought; and the monks, who prayed. Despite the rise of towns and the beginning of a merchant class, most of the people were peasants or serfs, who lived and labored on the land. These men and women toiled on the land of the manors to scratch out a meager existence for themselves and to support their noble lords in noble fashion. The agricultural productivity of the average manor was low because there was a lack of fertilizer and it was necessary to leave as much as half of the land fallow each year. Between the ninth and thirteenth centuries, however, it appears that agricultural productivity doubled—a remarkable achievement. Nonetheless, the diet of the peasantry was very limited and seldom adequate. A major problem of the Middle Ages was that the birthrate tended always to outpace the food supply.

The manor was the basic unit of medieval rural life, and Christianity was the center of the day-to-day world on the manor. The church provided an explanation for the meaning of life, and it also supplied the community with much of its entertainment and political leadership. Women held a pivotal position in the family and village economy.

The aristocratic nobility was a class with special power and legal status. It had its own lifestyle and goals. The size of noble families, aristocratic patterns of child rearing, marriage, and sex, and women's role were determined by the fact that males were the holders of property.

The monasteries of Europe had a great civilizing influence, and provided important opportunities for aristocratic men and women. They contributed to both literacy and agricultural improvement in the Middle Ages. Monastic life varied from order to order and from district to district, but daily life in all monasteries centered around the liturgy.

Study Outline

Use this outline to preview the chapter before you read a particular section in your textbook and then as a self-check to test your reading comprehension after you have read the chapter section.

I. Those who work
  A. The condition of the peasantry varied according to geographic location, and there were many levels of peasantry.
  B. Slavery, serfdom, and upward mobility
    1. Slavery was not common in Europe.
      a. The church played a key role in opposing the enslavement of Christians.
      b. The distinction between slave and serf was not always clear, but a serf could not be bought and sold like a slave could.
    2. Serfs had to perform labor services on the lord's land.
      a. Serfs often had to pay fees to the lord.
      b. Serfs were tied to the land, and serfdom was a hereditary condition.
      c. Serfs could obtain freedom in several ways: from their lord, by purchase by a third party, or by being in a town guild for a year and a day.
    3. Settlement on new land meant opportunities for social mobility and freedom.
  C. The manor as the basic unit of medieval rural life
    1. The manor—the estate of the lord—was the basic unit of medieval rural organization and the center of rural life.
      a. Manors varied in size.
      b. A manor usually contained a village.
    2. All the arable land of the manor was divided into strips.
      a. The demesne was cultivated for the lord.
      b. The other part was held by the peasantry.
    3. Each manor usually had pastures and forests.
  D. Agricultural methods
    1. Usually half the land was left fallow for one year (the open-field system).
      a. Every peasant had strips in both halves.
      b. All farmers on the manor shared in the level of productivity.
    2. Animal manure was the major form of fertilizer.
    3. The increase in iron production after 1100 meant better tools.
    4. The development of the padded horse collar led to the use of horses in agriculture and thus a great increase in productivity.
    5. Yields were low, but they improved from the ninth to the thirteenth centuries.
  E. Life on the manor
    1. Medieval village life was provincial and dull but secure.
    2. Most peasant households consisted of a nuclear family.
    3. Women worked the fields, managed the household, and dominated in the production of beer and ale.
    4. Diet included vegetables, some fruit, grains, beer, cheese, some fish, and wild meat— with possibly a great increase in meat consumption by the mid-thirteenth century—but the mainstay was bread.
    5. Children helped with the family chores.

F. Popular religion
1. The Christian religion infused and regulated daily life.
2. Religious ritual and practice synthesized many elements—Jewish, pagan, Roman, and Christian.
3. The church was the center of village social, political, and economic life.
4. Popular religion consisted largely of symbolic rituals and ceremonies.
5. In the eleventh century a great emphasis on the devotion to Mary evolved.
6. Peasants believed that God intervened directly in human affairs, and that sin was caused by the Devil.
7. Few peasants lived beyond the age of forty; pilgrimages offered adventure and hope in a world of gloom.
   a. The church granted indulgences (remissions of penalties for sin) to those who visited the shrines of great saints.
   b. Indulgences and pilgrimages came to be equated with salvation.

II. Those who fight
A. The nobility strongly influenced all aspects of medieval culture.
1. The social structure of the nobility varied from region to region.
2. The nobility was an elite, self-conscious social class.
3. Nobles held political power and had a special legal status.
4. Nobles were professional fighters.
   a. Their function was to protect the weak, the poor, and the churches.
   b. Nobles were supposed to display the chivalric virtues of courage, courtesy, loyalty, generosity, and graciousness.
5. The medieval nobility developed independently of knighthood—all nobles were knights, but not all knights were noble.
   a. In France and England, the term *knight* connoted moral values, consciousness of family, and participation in a superior hereditary caste.
   b. In Germany, a large caste of nonnoble knights, or ministerials, existed.
B. Infancy and childhood in aristocratic families
1. Ignorant medical care contributed to the high infant mortality rate.
2. Infanticide probably decreased during this period, but abandonment of infants, which was socially acceptable, increased.
3. Children were often sold or given to monasteries as oblates.
4. Other family-planning strategies, such as primogeniture, late marriages, and birth control were used to preserve family estates.
5. Most young aristocratic children had a great deal of playtime and freedom.
6. At about age seven, aristocratic boys served in a lord's household and received formal training in arms.
   a. Formal training concluded at age twenty-one with the ceremony of knighthood.
   b. Once knighted, a young man was supposed to be loyal and brave.
C. Youth in aristocratic families
1. Unless a young man's father was dead, he was still considered a youth and could not marry.
2. Knighted men whose fathers were alive had to find activities, such as travel, tournaments, and carousing, to occupy themselves.

      3. Aristocratic women married early; their families provided large marriage portions, or dowries.

      4. Generational disputes were common in aristocratic families in the twelfth and thirteenth centuries.

      5. Sexual tensions arose from aristocratic marriage practices, which brought together young wives, older husbands, and young, unmarried men.

  D. Power and responsibility in the aristocracy

      1. A male member of the nobility became an adult when he came into possession of his property.

      2. Aristocrats saw lavish living as a sign of status and power, but it often meant debt.

      3. As a vassal, a noble was required to fight for the lord or for the king when called on to do so.

      4. He was also obliged to attend his lord's court on important occasions.

      5. He had to look after his own estates, which usually required frequent travel.

      6. Holding the manorial court was one of his major duties.

      7. Women played an important role in running the estate.

III. Those who pray

  A. Prayer was a vital social service performed by monks; they also performed other important cultural and economic services.

  B. Recruitment

      1. Many who became monks did so because of their parents' decision to give them to the church as oblates.

      2. Monasteries provided careers for aristocratic children.

      3. In the later Middle Ages the monasteries recruited from the middle class.

  C. The nuns

      1. Convents were established for women of the noble class.

        a. The abbess or prioress was customarily a woman of high social standing.

        b. Some abbesses achieved national prominence.

      2. The duties of a nun varied from religious duties to administration to sewing and perhaps manuscript copying.

        a. Hildegard of Bingen represents the scholarly life of many nuns.

        b. Isabella of Lancaster represents the type of prioress who was active in court life and travel.

  D. Prayer and other work

      1. Daily life in the monasteries centered around the liturgy.

        a. The need to praise God justified the spending of a great deal of money on objects to enhance the liturgy.

        b. The liturgy this inspired a great deal of art.

      2. The lords gave the monasteries land.

      3. Aristocratic monks, or choir monks, did not till the land, but relied on lay brothers supervised by a cellarer for this.

      4. The almoner took care of the poor, the precentor the library, the sacristan the liturgy materials, and the novice master the training of recruits.

      5. Law and medicine were studied and practiced—sometimes in the royal court.

      6. Raising and breeding of horses was undertaken, as was the conversion of wasteland to agriculture.

7. The Cistercians were important in agricultural developments in the Low Countries, Germany, France, and England.
8. Some monasteries got involved in iron and lead mining.
9. Most monasteries were involved in providing social services such as schools, hospitals, and hostels for travelers.
E. Economic difficulties
    1. By the late Middle Ages many monasteries, such as Cluny, did not have enough income to support their lavish lifestyle.
    2. Many fell into debt.

Review Questions

Check your understanding of this chapter by answering the following questions.

1. How could a serf obtain freedom?
2. Describe a medieval manor. How did it work and what agricultural methods governed its existence? Was it "efficient"?
3. What was the role of women in medieval society? What evidence exists to suggest that women might have held considerable power within the family unit?
4. How important was religion in medieval manor life?
5. What do you believe to have been the world-view of the average medieval peasant? How would peasant men and women have thought about themselves and their environment?
6. What was the function of the nobility? What were its characteristics as a class?
7. How did medieval people treat their children? Why was child abandonment so widespread and what were the responses of society to it?
8. Why did aristocratic men marry late and aristocratic women marry early?
9. Why was aristocratic society marked by sexual tension and generational conflict?
10. What were the responsibilities and lifestyles of aristocratic men and women?
11. What was the social background of most medieval monks? How did this tend to change in the later Middle Ages?
12. What were the major functions of the medieval monasteries? Were they solely spiritual institutions?
13. Why was the monastic movement important to the aristocratic families of Europe?
14. Describe the economic dilemma that many monasteries faced in the late Middle Ages.

Study-Review Exercises

Define the following key concepts and terms.

slave

serf

villein

manor (demesne)

open-field system

child abandonment

oblate

nobility

almoner

choir monks

lay brothers

Identify and explain the significance of the following people and terms.
ministerials

abbey of Cluny

Cistercian Order

Orderic Vitalis

The Leech Book of Bald

chevaliers

knighthood

"Salve Regina"

Describe each of the following aspects of medieval life.
monastic recruitment

medieval agricultural system

aristocratic marriage patterns

medieval peasants' diet

Test your understanding of the chapter by providing the correct answers.
1. The evidence about infanticide makes it *certain/uncertain* that it increased in the Middle Ages.

2. The use of horses rather than oxen in farming meant *greater/less* productivity.

3. In medieval society, women *did/did not* play an important economic role in the manor and the family.

4. The word _____ derives from a Latin term meaning "dwelling," "residence," or "homestead."

5. In medieval society women were *frequently/never* raised to the nobility.

6. By the late Middle Ages it was the *groom/bride* who provided the marriage dowry.

7. Most noblemen married relatively *early/late* in life.

8. Formal military training for the medieval aristocratic boy was concluded with the

   ceremony of _____ .

9. Slavery *was/was* not common in medieval European society.

10. Some scholars believe that the use of the _____ in agriculture was one of the decisive ways in which Europe advanced over the rest of the world.

Multiple-Choice Questions

1. Which of the following statements about the medieval village church is *false*?
   a. It was often a business center.
   b. It was often a center for medieval drama.
   c. It was the chief educational center.
   d. It was often open only to aristocratic participation.

2. In the twelfth century many of the older monastic houses found themselves in economic difficulties because
   a. they could no longer recruit monks.
   b. peasants refused to pay their levies.
   c. building and living expenses increased faster than revenue.
   d. knights no longer placed their estates under their authority when they went on Crusades.

3. Which of the following statements about medieval nobility is *false*?
   a. All nobles were knights.
   b. Their function was primarily military and political.
   c. Father-son ties tended to be strong and loving.
   d. A castle was an aristocratic status symbol.

4. Generally, the monasteries recruited their members from
   a. the middle class.
   b. the aristocracy.
   c. the peasantry.
   d. village church schools.

5. For noblemen, adulthood came with
   a. knighthood.
   b. the age of eighteen.
   c. the acquisition of property.
   d. the demonstration of military prowess.

6. The difference between a free person and a serf was that the
   a. free person was tied to the land and the serf was not.
   b. serf had no obligations to the lord, while the free person had many.
   c. serf paid rent to his lord, while the free person paid nothing at all.
   d. serf was bound to the land by the obligations he owed his lord, while the free person usually just paid rent.

7. Medieval farmers
   a. generally farmed the land in strips scattered throughout the manor.
   b. did not use any kind of fertilizer.
   c. never used iron for tools.
   d. were unable to show any improvement in agricultural output in nearly a thousand years.

8. Medieval peasants
    a. traveled widely and visited many foreign countries.
    b. had a sense of community and pride of place.
    c. hardly ever drank alcoholic beverages.
    d. refused to let women work in the fields.

9. Peasants usually did not consume
    a. vegetables, particularly cabbage.
    b. large quantities of meat.
    c. bread.
    d. beer.

10. Medieval treatment of infants and children was characterized by
    a. a low rate of mortality.
    b. an increase in infanticide.
    c. legal prohibitions on sale of children.
    d. widespread child abandonment.

11. In medieval society, noblewomen
    a. usually married late in life.
    b. had the right to select their husbands.
    c. were customarily required to present a dowry to the groom and his family.
    d. generally married men younger than themselves.

12. Monastic life in general was
    a. a combination of attention to liturgy and manual work.
    b. devoted exclusively to prayer.
    c. so different from place to place that it is impossible to generalize about it.
    d. centered exclusively on manufacturing and farming.

13. Which of the following statements about medieval serfs and freedom is true?
    a. There were very few immigration possibilities within Europe for serfs.
    b. Serfs had little chance of purchasing freedom with cash.
    c. Serfs could obtain freedom by fleeing from the manor and living in town for a year and a day.
    d. Serfs had no possibility of freedom as long as they remained on the manor.

14. Chevaliers were
    a. wealthy monks.
    b. members of a religious order that stressed agricultural reform.
    c. horsemen, or knights.
    d. court painters and architects.

15. A medieval manor was
    a. an estate of at least ten villages.
    b. a plantation.
    c. the estate of a lord and his dependent tenants.
    d. an estate of at least three villages.

16. To provide food for all the people on the manor, the land had to yield at least
    a. six times the amount of seeds planted.
    b. ten times the amount of seeds planted.
    c. three times the amount of seeds planted.
    d. five times the amount of seeds planted.

17. A person became a noble by
    a. thrift, hard work, and sobriety.
    b. clever business acumen.
    c. birth or remarkable service to king or lord.
    d. buying a patent of nobility.

18. Most of the education of medieval aristocrats was in
    a. the Bible.
    b. the Latin classics.
    c. canon law.
    d. the arts of war and chivalry.

19. The opportunities and responsibilities of aristocratic women in the Middle Ages were
    a. significant, particularly in terms of the administration of the manorial estate.
    b. limited to bearing and raising children.
    c. considerable, but only at times of crusade when the husband was away.
    d. centered on noneconomic activities, such as music and reading.

20. Until the fourteenth century, most monks were drawn from the
    a. business classes.
    b. peasantry.
    c. petty bourgeoisie.
    d. nobility.

21. Management of the monastic estate was the basic responsibility of the
    a. abbot.
    b. novices.
    c. cellarer.
    d. almoner.

22. The monastic order that excelled in the development of new agricultural techniques and methods was the
    a. Dominicans.
    b. Benedictines.
    c. Franciscans.
    d. Cistercians.

23. In general, the monasteries regarded their major social responsibility to be
    a. academic work.
    b. providing for the poor.
    c. educating the children of the nobility.
    d. prayer.

24. The opinion of most scholars is that medieval peasant households were
    a. usually composed of unmarried couples.
    b. extended families with many grandparents and married children present.
    c. mostly small nuclear families.
    d. on average composed of teen parents and five to seven children.

25. English serfs were called
    a. *ministerials.*
    b. *miles.*
    c. *villeins.*
    d. *chevalier.*

Major Political Ideas

1. Compare and contrast the concepts of serfdom and freedom. How was freedom acquired in medieval society?

2. What political role did the nobility play in medieval society? What was the relationship between the nobility and the monarchy in terms of power and the dispensing of justice? Who was more important in medieval society, the nobles or the monarch?

Issues for Essays and Discussion

Describe the opportunities for social and economic mobility for both men and women in the three general groups within the High Middle Ages—those who fought, those who prayed, and those who worked. Who among these people had the greatest opportunities? In what way did these opportunities tend to expand or contract during this period, and who made the greatest contribution to society?

Interpretation of Visual Sources

Study the reproduction of the painting showing a French castle under siege on page 299 of the textbook. Describe the types of weapons depicted. What military advantages do those inside the castle seem to enjoy? How might their defenses be weakened? What advantages do the aggressors appear to have? What factors might result in their loss of the siege? Compare the attire of the knights shown here with those in the picture on textbook page 272. How does their armor differ? What might account for the differences in the way both groups of knights are dressed?

Geography

Study Figure 10.1, "A Medieval Manor," in your textbook (page 283), and then answer the following questions: (1) How many fields are there, and what does it mean that one lies "fallow"? (2) What percent of the arable land on this manor is demesne? (3) Why are the village houses surrounded by fences? (4) What was the function of the meadow, the common, and the woodland? (5) Would the horse that is shown in the field have been used for agricultural labor?

Understanding History Through the Arts

1. How do the illuminated manuscripts created in the Carolingian, Byzantine, and Norman empires compare with one another? Begin your study with H. Buchthal et al., *The Place of Book Illumination in Byzantine Art* (1975), J. J. G. Alexander, *Norman Illumination at Mont St. Michael* (1970), and G. Braziller, *Carolingian Painting* (1976). For the relationship between Russian and Byzantine art, see A. Voyce, *The Art and Architecture of Medieval Russia* (1967), and for the remarkable artistic developments in Ireland, see P. Harbison et al., *Irish Art and Architecture, From Pre-History to the Present* (1978).

2. How does poetry help us understand medieval life? *Carmina Burana* by C. Orff is a series of songs based on poems written in the thirteenth century by wandering students and disillusioned monks in Germany who celebrated their carousing and lovemaking in verse. Orff put these intensely physical, scenic, and entertaining poems to vibrant music in 1937, and it is available in many recordings.

3. How aware were medieval women poets of the issue of womanhood? A recent study of feminine poetry, *Sister of Wisdom: St. Hildegard's Theology of the Feminine* (1987), by B. Newman, shows how one woman of the twelfth century used symbolic theology to explore the issue of gender.

Problems for Further Investigation

1. Did the peasants really starve? What are some of the modern world's mistaken beliefs about sex, marriage, and family in medieval times? These and other questions are considered in a ground-breaking social history, *The World We Have Lost** (1965) by P. Laslett.

2. Did aristocratic women have any power in the churches or households of this military society? Were children mistreated in the medieval family? Historians are just beginning to investigate how childhood and the status of women in society have changed over the course of history. Some good starting points for research on childhood are L. de Mause, ed. , *The History of Childhood** (1974); *The History of Childhood Quarterly;* and a collection of essays, *Women as Mothers in Pre-Industrial England,* V. Fildes, ed. (1990). For medieval women see E. Power, *Medieval Women,** M. M. Postan, ed. (1976), and S. Shahar, *The Fourth Estate: A History of Women in the Middle Ages* (1984). Much of the work on medieval women is on women in the world of religion. The best of these works is G. Nichols and L. Shank, *Medieval Religious Women,* vol. 1: *Distant Echoes* (1984). A good place to begin a study on women as mystics and the masculine-feminism issues in religion is C. Bynum, *Jesus as a Mother: Studies in the Spirituality of the High Middle Ages* (1982).

---

*Available in paperback.

Chapter 11
The Creativity and Vitality of the High Middle Ages

Chapter Questions

After reading and studying this chapter you should be able to answer the following questions:

How did medieval rulers in England, France, and Germany solve their problems of government and lay the foundations of the modern state? How did medieval towns originate and how do they reflect radical change in medieval society? Why did towns become the center of religious heresy? How did universities develop and what needs of medieval society did they serve? What does the Gothic cathedral reveal about the ideals, attitudes, and interests of medieval people?

Chapter Summary

The High Middle Ages—roughly, the twelfth and thirteenth centuries—was an era of remarkable achievement in law, the arts, philosophy, and education. The modern idea of the sovereign nation-state took root in this period. By means of war, taxation, and control over justice, the kings of England and France were able to strengthen royal authority and establish a system of communication with all of their people.

The Normans were important in bringing a centralized feudal system to England by using the sheriff, the writ, and other devices to replace baronial rule with royal power. Out of this process emerged the concept of common law and, with the Magna Carta, the idea of supremacy of the law. The process, however, was not altogether smooth, as the conflict between Henry II and Becket illustrates. The evolution of the territorial state in France was not quite as rapid as in England. France was less of a geographical unit than England, and the creation of strong royal authority involved more armed conflict between king and barons. And in Germany, royal power failed to develop at all, despite a good start by Emperor Frederick Barbarossa. Part of the reason was the historic connection between Germany and Italy. The church-state struggle was another major reason why royal authority in Germany was destined to remain weak.

The rise of the universities accompanied the emergence of the strong secular states because the new states needed educated administrators to staff their bureaucracies. The new universities became centers for the study of law and medicine.

Improvement in agriculture, coupled with a reopening of the Mediterranean to Christian traders, fostered the growth of towns and commerce. Flanders and Italy led the way in this urban revival. The growth of towns was one of the most important developments in Western history. Towns meant a new culture and social order, increased economic opportunities, and the beginnings of modern capitalism.

Religious heresy grew as the traditional Christian religion was unable to meet the needs of urban dwellers. The result of the heretical crisis was the evolution of several new religious orders of Friars, which counteracted the heretical movement by putting emphasis on a nonmaterialistic clergy that could preach to the needs of the people and at the same time manage the process of reconversion.

Few periods in history can claim as many artistic achievements as the High Middle Ages. The Gothic cathedrals, shimmering in stone and glass, stand not only as spiritual and artistic testimony to the age but also as a reflection of the economic power and civic pride of the great cities. By 1300, the energy of the High Middle Ages had been spent.

Study Outline

Use this outline to preview the chapter before you read a particular section in your textbook and then as a self-check to test your reading comprehension after you have read the chapter section.

I. The medieval origins of the modern state
    A. Unification and communication in England
        1. England was united under one king under the pressure of the Viking invasions of the ninth and tenth centuries.
            a. England was divided into shires, each under the jurisdiction of an unpaid sheriff appointed by the king.
            b. All the English thegns (local chieftains) recognized the central authority of the king.
        2. William the Conqueror replaced the Anglo-Saxon sheriffs with Normans.
        3. Sheriffs, the writ, the Norman inquest, and *Domesday Book* were used to centralize royal power.
        4. The Angevin dynasty began with William's grandson, Henry II.
    B. Unification and communication in France
        1. In the early twelfth century, France consisted of virtually independent provinces; the king's goal was to increase the royal domain and extend his authority.
        2. Philip II began the process of unifying France.
        3. By the end of the thirteenth century, most of the provinces of modern France had been added to the royal domain through diplomacy, marriage, war, and inheritance, and the king was stronger than his nobles.
        4. Philip Augustus devised a system of royal agents called baillis and seneschals to help enforce royal law.
        5. Unlike England, where administration was based on unpaid local officials, royal administration in France rested on a professional bureaucracy.

C. Unification and communication in Germany
1. The eleventh-century investiture controversy left Germany split into many provinces, duchies, and cities.
2. The German emperors were weak and lacked a strong royal domain to serve as a source of revenue and a power base.
3. Frederick Barbarossa tried to unify Germany by creating royal officials, called ministerials, to enforce his will.
   a. He tried to make feudalism work as a way of government.
   b. He tried to restore the Holy Roman Empire by joining Germany and Italy but was defeated as Legnano in 1176.
D. Finance
1. Henry I of England established a bureau of finance called the Exchequer to keep track of income.
2. French kings relied on royal taxes, mostly from the church, the tallage, and the conversion of feudal dues to cash payments.
3. Medieval people believed that royal taxation should be imposed only in times of emergency.
4. Sicily is a good example of an efficient financial bureaucracy.
   a. Roger de Hauteville introduced feudalism to the island.
   b. Frederick II Hohenstaufen centralized royal power in Sicily by taxing regularly, building an advanced bureaucracy, taking control of local government, founding a university, and regulating the economy but destroyed the centralizing efforts of Frderick Barbarossa in Germany by granting huge concessions to the local rulers.
E. Law and justice in medieval Europe
1. A system of royal justice, founded by Louis IX, unified France.
   a. He established the Parlement of Paris as a kind of supreme court.
   b. He sent royal judges to all parts of the country.
   c. He was the first French monarch to publish laws for the entire kingdom.
2. Beginning with Henry II the English kings developed and extended the common law, which was accepted by the whole country.
   a. Henry II established a jury system and improved procedure in criminal justice.
   b. The trial by jury replaced the trial by ordeal.
3. Becket and Henry II quarreled over legal jurisdiction.
   a. Becket claimed that crimes by clerics should be tried in church courts ("benefit of clergy").
   b. He was assassinated by the king's friends in 1170.
   c. Henry gave up his attempt to bring clerics under the authority of the royal court.
4. King John's conflict with church and barons led to the Magna Carta (1215), which claims that everyone, including the king, must obey the law.
5. The English common law system was strikingly different from the system of continental (Roman) law.
   a. The common law relied on precedents and thus was able to evolve.
   b. The Roman law tradition used the fixed legal maxims of the Justinian *Code*.

6. Various factors, including economic competition and fear of foreigners, led to pressure for social conformity.
   a. By the late twelfth century, anti-Semitism was on the rise.
   b. By 1300, homosexuality, which had been accepted for centuries, had been declared illegal.

II. Economic revival
   A. The rise of towns
      1. Some historians believe that towns began as fortifications (boroughs).
      2. The historian Henri Pirenne claimed that towns resulted from trade and commerce.
      3. Others believe that towns sprang up around religious centers.
      4. All towns had a few common characteristics: a town wall, a central market, a court, and a monetary system.
      5. The bourgeoisie, or townspeople, became a new class in medieval society.
   B. Town liberties
      1. Townspeople worked hard to acquire social, political, and legal liberties, or special privileges.
         a. The most important privilege a medieval townsperson could gain was personal freedom.
         b. The liberty of personal freedom that came with residence in a town contributed greatly to the emancipation of the serfs in the High Middle Ages.
      2. Merchant and craft guilds evolved to provide greater economic security; they bargained with kings and lords for political independence.
      3. Women played an important role in the household, the guilds, and the town economy.
   C. Town life
      1. Medieval towns served as places of trade and protection.
         a. The place where a product was made and sold was also usually the merchant's residence.
         b. Towns grew without planning or regulation.
         c. Air and water pollution were serious problems.
      2. As the bourgeoisie grew wealthier, more and more churches were built.
   D. The revival of long-distance trade in the eleventh century
      1. Groups of merchants would pool capital to finance trading expeditions.
      2. Italian and Flemish cities dominated the trade market.
         a. Venice led the West in trade and controlled the Oriental market.
         b. Flanders controlled the cloth trade.
      3. England was the major supplier of wool for Flanders.
         a. Wool was the cornerstone of the English medieval economy.
         b. Eventually cloth manufacture was taken up in English towns.
   E. The commercial revolution of the eleventh through thirteenth centuries
      1. The growth of medieval commerce meant the rise of capitalist ideas and practices.
      2. The Hanseatic League developed new trade routes and established new "factories" (foreign trading centers) and business techniques like the business register.
      3. The commercial revolution meant a higher standard of living and new opportunities.

4. Kings allied with the middle classes to defeat feudal lords and build modern states, while many serfs used the commercial revolution to improve their social position.
5. The slow transformation of European society from rural isolation to a more urban sophistication was the commercial revolution's greatest effect.

III. Medieval universities
   A. Origins
      1. Prior to the twelfth century, only monasteries and cathedral schools existed, and there weren't very many of them.
      2. During the twelfth century, cathedral schools in France and municipal schools in Italy developed into universities.
         a. The first universities were at Bologna and Salerno in Italy.
         b. Bologna became a law school, while medicine was studied in Salerno.
         c. The cathedral school at Notre Dame in Paris became an international center of learning.
   B. Instruction and curriculum
      1. The Scholastic method of teaching was used.
         a. In this method of reasoning and writing, questions were raised and authorities cited on both sides of the question.
         b. Its goal was to arrive at definite answers and provide a rational explanation for what was believed on faith.
         c. Aristotle's texts were reinterpreted in a Christian context.
         d. By asking questions about nature and the universe, Scholastics laid the foundations for later scientific work.
         e. Scholastic philosophers dealt with many theological issues.
         f. They published *summa*, or reference books, on many topics, the most famous—Aquinas's *Summa Theologica*—became the fundamental text of Roman Catholic doctrine.
      2. The standard method of teaching was the lecture accompanied by a gloss, or interpretation.
      3. Oral examinations came when students applied for their degree.

IV. Gothic art
   A. After 1000, church building increased greatly; most churches were in the Romanesque style, with thick walls, small windows, and rounded arches.
   B. From Romanesque gloom to "uninterrupted light"
      1. The Gothic style was created by Suger, the abbot of St. Denis.
         a. The Gothic style has several distinct features: the pointed arch, the ribbed vault, flying buttresses, and interior brightness.
         b. The Gothic style spread rapidly throughout Europe.
   C. The creative outburst of cathedral building
      1. Bishops, nobility, and the commercial classes supported cathedral building.
      2. Cathedrals became symbols of bourgeois civic pride, and towns competed to build the largest and most splendid church.
      3. Cathedrals served many purposes, secular as well as religious.
      4. The architecture of the cathedrals was a means of religious instruction.

     5. Tapestry making and drama were first used to convey religious themes to ordinary people, then emerged as distinct art forms.
        a. Early tapestries depicted religious themes, but the later ones, produced for the knightly class, bore secular designs.
        b. Mystery plays, which combined farce and serious religious scenes, were very popular.

V. Heresy and the friars
   A. Heresy flourished most in the most economically advanced and urbanized areas.
     1. Neither traditional Christian theology nor the isolated monastic orders addressed the problems of mercantile society.
     2. Townspeople desired a pious clergy who would meet their needs.
   B. Heresy, originally meaning "individual choosing," was seen as a threat to social cohesion and religious unity.
     1. The Gregorian injunction against clerical marriage made many priests vulnerable to the Donatist heresy, which held that sacraments given by an immoral priest were useless.
     2. Various heretics, such as Arnold of Brescia, Peter Waldo, the Albigensians, and others denounced wealth, the sacraments, and material things.
        a. The Albigensian heresy grew strong in southern France and was the subject of a political-religious crusade.
        b. Heretical beliefs became fused with feudal rebellion against the French crown.
   C. As a response to heretical cults, two new religious orders were founded.
     1. Saint Dominic's mission to win back the Albigensians led to the founding of a new religious order of "Preaching Friars" (the Dominicans).
     2. Saint Francis of Assisi founded an order (the Franciscans) based on preaching and absolute poverty of the clergy.
     3. These new orders of friars were urban, based on the idea of poverty, and their members were drawn from the burgher class.
   D. The friars met the spiritual and intellectual needs of the thirteenth century.
     1. The friars stressed education and intellectual pursuit.
     2. Their emphasis on an educated and nonmaterialistic clergy won them the respect of the bourgeoisie.
     3. The friars successfully directed the Inquisition, and heresy was virtually extinguished.
   E. A challenge to religious authority
     1. Pope Boniface VIII refused to let King Edward I of England and Philip the Fair of France tax the clergy to finance their war.
     2. In the *Unam Sanctam* (1302), Boniface declared that all Christians are subject to the pope, whereupon French mercenaries arrested him.

Review Questions

Check your understanding of this chapter by answering the following questions.

1. Define the modern state. What are its characteristics and goals?
2. Describe the unification and centralization of royal power in England. Who were the participants and what methods did they use?
3. What problems did the French kings face in unifying France under royal authority? What techniques did they use?
4. Why was unification in Germany so much more difficult than in England or France? What were the factors that weakened and divided Germany?
5. Evaluate the work of Frederick Barbarossa. In what did he succeed, and why, in the end, did he fail?
6. Why was Frederick II Hohenstaufen called "The Transformer of the World"? What was so modern about him? What effect did he have on Germany?
7. Describe the evolution of common law and royal justice in England. Who were the important participants and what were their methods and accomplishments?
8. What were the principal reasons for the rise of urban society in the eleventh century?
9. Evaluate the various theories advanced to explain the rise of towns in late medieval society. Which do you believe to be the most plausible?
10. How did the new townspeople manage to gain political status and liberty for their towns?
11. Why did Venice and the Flemish towns become leaders in long-distance trade?
12. What impact did the rise of towns and the commercial revolution have on the way people lived?
13. What were the purpose and origins of the medieval universities?
14. Who were the medieval Scholastics? What were their basic beliefs about knowledge and education and what were their methods of acquiring knowledge?
15. What were the chief features of the Gothic style?
16. Why were cathedrals symbols of civic pride?
17. How did architecture become the servant of theology in the High Middle Ages? Give examples.
18. What were the reasons for the rise of heretical cults? Why and how were they extinguished?

Study-Review Exercises

Define the following key concepts and terms.

thegn

Gothic

scholasticism

universitas

common law

Roman law

Hanseatic League

burgher

Define each of the following terms and explain how it contributed to the evolution of the modern state.
writ

sheriff

baillis and seneschals

Exchequer

jury

tallage

Identify and explain the significance of the following people and terms.
cult of Saint Denis

merchant guild

heresy

Frederick II Hohenstaufen

Philip II of France

Saint Thomas Aquinas

Suger, abbot of St. Denis

Henry II of England

Peter Abelard

Summa Theologica

Louis IX of France

Saint Dominic

Saint Francis of Assisi

Explain what the following events were and why they are important in understanding the High Middle Ages.
Domesday survey

crusade against the Albigensians

Inquisition

Frederick Barbarossa's Italian wars

William of Normandy's conquest of England

conflict between Pope Boniface VIII and King Philip the Fair of France

Test your understanding of the chapter by providing the correct answers.

1. This letter declared that everyone must submit to the papacy. _____

2. The English royal bureau of finance. _____

3. The emperor of Germany who tried to unify Germany. _____

4. William the Conqueror's survey of English wealth. _____

4. The European country best known for its common law. _____

6. The area that underwent development by Frederick II Hohenstaufen.

    _____

7. This document implied that in English society the law is above the king.

    _____

8. The method of teaching at medieval universities. _____

9. The architectural style that reflects Roman and early Christian models.

    _____

10. Medieval reference books. _____

11. A league of German cities with its center at Lübeck. _____

12. Author of *Sic et Non*. _____

13. The bishop who was murdered as the result of a church-state struggle. _____

14. A kind of French supreme court. _____

Multiple-Choice Questions

1. The Jewish members of most medieval towns had the reputation of being
    a. rich landowners who retired to the town.
    b. the town's military class.
    c. semibarbaric.
    d. rich and learned.

2. By origin and definition, a burgher, or bourgeois, was
    a. a person involved in trade or commerce.
    b. a person who lived within town walls.
    c. a resident of Hamburg, Germany.
    d. a person who lived on hamburgers.

3. The modern scholar who identified the growth of medieval towns with the development of trade was
    a. Josiah Cox Russell.
    b. Eileen Power.
    c. Henri Pirenne.
    d. Marc Bloch.

4. Towns were most successful in gaining rights in the area of
    a. political freedom from the monarchy.
    b. emancipation from the influence of religion and the church.
    c. judicial independence.
    d. military influence in the larger state.

5. Artisans and craftspeople in medieval towns formed
    a. courts to try corrupt businessmen.
    b. craft guilds.
    c. merchant guilds.
    d. the *scutage*.

6. The French government, as conceived by Philip Augustus, was characterized by
    a. centralization at the local level and diversity at the top.
    b. diversity at the local level and centralization at the top.
    c. complete local government.
    d. a system identical to England's.

7. Frederick Barbarossa's success in restoring order to the Holy Roman Empire was spoiled by his involvement in
    a. France.
    b. Germany.
    c. England.
    d. Italy.

8. The principle implied in the Magna Carta was
    a. democracy.
    b. that all people, even the king, are subject to the law.
    c. that the king is above the law.
    d. that the people rule the monarch.

9. Which of the following is *not* a characteristic of a Gothic cathedral?
    a. Pointed arches
    b. Ribbed vaults
    c. Thick walls
    d. Flying buttresses

10. The surge of cathedral building in the twelfth and thirteenth centuries was closely associated with
    a. the increase of university-trained architects.
    b. financial hard times, which caused people to turn to religion.
    c. the low cost of building materials.
    d. the growth of towns and the increase of commercial wealth.

11. The university in the Europe of the High Middle Ages
    a. was borrowed from the Muslims.
    b. was a unique contribution of western Europe.
    c. was copied from the Greek model.
    d. was copied from the Roman model.

12. The duties of sheriffs in Norman England included all of the following *except*
    a. maintaining law and order.
    b. collecting taxes when instructed by the king.
    c. raising infantry at the king's request.
    d. supervising the remaining Anglo-Saxon sheriffs.

13. Heresy flourished
    a. in the most economically advanced and urbanized areas.
    b. in backward rural areas.
    c. only in southern France.
    d. in urban areas suffering from plague and economic depression.

14. The two European states that first developed efficient state bureaucracies were
    a. England and Sicily.
    b. England and France.
    c. England and Italy.
    d. Sicily and France.

15. Which of the following financial problems eventually forced England's King John to sign the Magna Carta?
    a. The debts incurred from Richard the Lionhearted's crusading zeal
    b. The ransom paid for Richard the Lionhearted
    c. The war debt caused by John in his attempt to regain Normandy from France
    d. John's attack on Scotland

16. The first European universities were located in
    a. England.
    b. France.
    c. Italy.
    d. Germany.

17. Prior to the systematization of law in the thirteenth century, homosexuality was
    a. socially accepted.
    b. outlawed.
    c. uncommon.
    d. unknown.

18. The origin of Western universities were
    a. manor schools.
    b. monasteries.
    c. cathedral schools.
    d. medieval public schools.

19. The standard method of teaching in medieval universities was
    a. summa.
    b. a gloss.
    c. reading assignment in books.
    d. lecture.

20. Common law differed from the system of Roman law in that it
    a. applied only to the peasant class.
    b. was more permanent and static.
    c. relied on precedents.
    d. relied heavily on torture.

21. By the end of the twelfth century, the general European attitude toward the Jews in society
    a. became increasingly intolerant
    b. moved in the direction of greater acceptance
    c. led to political emancipation of the Jews
    d. had not changed over that of the previous generations

22. The major function of the medieval city was that of
    a. an ecclesiastical center.
    b. a political center.
    c. a royal stronghold.
    d. a vast marketplace.

23. The *Summa Theologica* was written by
    a. John of Salisbury.
    b. Peter Abelard.
    c. Thomas Aquinas.
    d. William of Sens.

24. The Waldensians were
    a. a heretical group that attacked the sacraments and church hierarchy.
    b. the political and financial supporters of the German princes.
    c. the merchant bankers of Hamburg.
    d. the religious order that built the abbey church at Saint Denis.

25. The followers of Domingo de Guzman became known as the
    a. Albigensians.
    b. bourgeois.
    c. masters of the Cathederal School at Paris.
    d. "Preaching Friars."

Major Political Ideas

1. Define and describe the concept of the sovereign nation-state. How does it contrast to the early medieval idea of government?

2. What is meant by common law? How and why did it evolve?

3. The history of towns is also the history of merchants' efforts to acquire liberties. What does *liberties* mean and what role did the merchant and craft guilds and their members play in its evolution?

Issues for Essays and Discussion

The High Middle Ages witnessed remarkable achievements in the areas of political organization, law and justice, the evolution of the town, and art. What were the major developments in these areas? How did they differ in England, France, Germany, and elsewhere? What were the reasons for these developments and were there any negative effects?

Interpretation of Visual Sources

Study the section of the Bayeaux Tapestry reproduced on page 313 of your text. What is the subject of this tapestry? What information about medieval life does it provide? What is the political significance of the event depicted?

Geography

1. On Outline Map 11.2 provided, and using Map 11.2 in the textbook as a reference, mark the following: the royal domain, or crown lands, of France as they existed in 1180, the names of the territories added by Philip Augustus, the territories added from 1223 to 1270, and the territories added from 1270 to 1314.

2. Study Map 11.4 in the textbook. In the space below (1) list the four largest cities in Europe in ca the late thirteenth century, (2) what part of Europe was the most urbanized? (3) use Map 11.5 to explain the evolution of the urban concentration indicated on Map 11.4.

   _____

   _____

   _____

3. Using Map 11.5 and the text discussion as your sources, describe the various trade routes used by the Italians, the Flemish, and the Hanseatic League.

   _____

   _____

   _____

Outline Map 11.2

Understanding History Through the Arts

1. How was medieval architectural style affected by the needs of those men and women who commissioned it? Begin with M. W. Thompson, *The Decline of the Castle* (1988). Those interested in medieval cathedral building will want to see J. Harvey, *The Medieval Architect* (1972). See also Chapters 3 and 4 of N. Pevsner, *An Outline of European Architecture** (7th ed., 1963). For France, the center of Gothic achievement, see J. Evans, *Art in Medieval France, 987–1498* (1969).

2. What does the Bayeaux Tapestry reveal about medieval life? This problem of historical interpretation is dealt with in D. Bernstein, *The Mystery of the Bayeaux Tapestry* (1987).

Problems for Further Investigation

1. What are the origins of the modern state? New interpretations and ideas for research on the rise of the modern state are found in a collection of essays edited by H. Lubasz, *The Development of the Modern State** (1964).

2. Why was Thomas Becket murdered? Many possible research and term-paper topics are suggested in T. M. Jones, ed. , *The Becket Controversy* (1970). The conflict between King Henry II and Archbishop Becket has produced some interesting literature, such as Jean Anouilh, *Becket; or the Honor of God*, L. Hill, trans. (1960), and T. S. Eliot, *Murder in the Cathedral* (1935).

3. What was life like for aristocratic women during this period? One of the most fascinating women of the Middle Ages was Eleanor of Aquitaine, wife to the king of France and the king of England and mother to two kings of England. She is the subject of a spellbinding biography, *Eleanor of Aquitaine and the Four Kings** (1950) by A. Kelly.

4. What caused the rise of individualism in European life? What impact did the cult of individualism have on European society? The best book on this subject is M. Colin, *The Discovery of the Individual, 1050–1200** (1973). See also R. Hanning, *The Individual in Twelfth-Century Romance* (1977).

5. Did the emergence of urban life result in a clash between Christianity and urban values? Did urbanization force Christianity to re-evaluate its traditional antimaterialistic position? A good place to begin your investigation is with an excellent synthesis of the new urban life and Christianity: L. Little, *Religion, Poverty, and the Profit Economy in Medieval Europe* (1978).

---

*Available in paperback.

Primary Sources
Three Documents from the Thirteenth Century

The thirteenth century was a century of progress and change. Each of the following documents represents a particular aspect of that change.

Magna Carta, 1215*

Although its initial purpose was to protect the interests of the barons under King John of England (1199–1216), the Magna Carta eventually came to protect the interests of other social classes as well. As a result, the document was regarded as a guarantee of certain rights. Sections 6, 7, 8, included below, were interpreted to allow women some powers. What were these? Sections 13, 20, and 35 afforded merchants of the towns a greater degree of freedom. What were these? Sections 39 and 40 contain the germ of the modern legal idea of due process of law for all people. On the other hand, Articles 10 and 11 reflect anti-Semitic attitudes deep in medieval society. In what ways do they indicate discrimination?

6. Heirs shall be married with disparagement; yet so that, before the marriage is contracted, it shall be announced to the blood-relatives of the said heir.

7. A widow shall have her marriage portion and inheritance immediately after the death of her husband and without difficulty; nor shall she give anything for her dowry or for her marriage portion or for her inheritance—which inheritance she and her husband were holding on the day of that husband's death. And after his death she shall remain in the house of her husband for forty days, within which her dowry shall be assigned to her.

8. No widow shall be forced to marry so long as she wishes to live without a husband; yet so that she shall give security against marrying without our consent if she holds of us, or without the consent of her lord if she holds of another.

---

*Source: Carl Stephenson and Frederick G. Morcham, *Sources of English Constitutional History* (New York: Harper & Brothers, 1937).

10. If any one has taken anything, whether much or little, by way of loan from Jews, and if he dies before that debt is paid, the debt shall not carry usury so long as the heir is under age, from whomsoever he may hold. And if that debt falls into our hands, we will take only the principal contained in the note.

11. And if any one dies owing a debt to Jews, his wife shall have her dowry and shall pay nothing on that debt. And if the said deceased is survived by children who are under age, necessities shall be provided for them in proportion to the tenement that belonged to the deceased; and the debt shall be paid from the remained, saving the service of the lords. In the same way let action be taken with regard to debts owed to others besides Jews.

13. And the city of London shall have all its ancient liberties and free customs, both by land and by water. Besides we will and grant that all the other cities, boroughs, towns, and ports shall have all their liberties and free customs.

20. A freeman shall be amerced [punished] for a small offence only according to the degree of the offence; and for a grave offence he shall be amerced according to the gravity of the offence, saving his contentment. And a merchant shall be amerced in the same way, saving his merchandise; and a villein in the same way, saving his wainage [agricultural implements]—should they fall into our mercy. And none of the aforesaid amercements shall be imposed except by the oaths of good men from the neighbourhood.

35. There shall be one measure of wine throughout our entire kingdom, and one measure of ale; also one measure of grain, namely the quarter of London; and one width of dyed cloth, russet [cloth], and hauberk [cloth], namely, two yards between the borders. With weights, moreover, it shall be as with measures.

39. No freeman shall be captured or imprisoned or disseised [unlawfully removed] or outlawed or exiled or in any way destroyed, nor will we go against him or send against him, except by the lawful judgement of his peers or by the law of the land.

40. To no one will we sell, to no one will we deny or delay right or justice.

The Rule of Saint Francis, 1223*

The medicants, or orders of begging friars, were founded as a response to the spiritual needs of a growing urban society. Chief among these orders was the order of friars founded by Saint Francis of Assisi. Can you tell what the goals and practices of the Franciscans were? How did they differ from the older monastic orders like the Benedictines and Cistercians? What in these rules indicates that the Franciscans are involved in an urban as opposed to a monastic society?

Source: Oliver J. Thatcher and Edgar H. McNeal, eds. and trans., *A Source Book for Medieval History* (New York: Scribner's, 1905), 499–507.

This is the rule and life of the Minor Brothers, namely, to observe the holy gospel of our Lord Jesus Christ by living in obedience, in poverty, and in chastity. Brother Francis promises obedience and reverence to Pope Honorius and to his successors who shall be canonically elected, and to the Roman Church. The other brothers are bound to obey brother Francis, and his successors . . .

I counsel, warn, and exhort my brothers in the Lord Jesus Christ that when they go out into the world they shall not be quarrelsome or contentious, nor judge others. But they shall be gentle, peaceable, and kind, mild and humble, and virtuous in speech, as is becoming to all. They shall not ride on horseback unless compelled in manifest necessity or infirmity to do so. When they enter a house they shall say, "Peace be to this house." According to the holy gospel, they may eat of whatever food is set before them.

I strictly forbid all the brothers to accept money or property either in person or through another. Nevertheless, for the needs of the sick, and for clothing the other brothers, the ministers and guardians may, as they see that necessity requires, provide through spiritual friends, according to the locality, season, and the degree of cold which may be expected in the region where they live. But, as has been said, they shall never receive money or property.

Those brothers to whom the Lord has given the ability to work shall work faithfully and devotedly, so that idleness, which is the enemy of the soul, may be excluded and not extinguish the spirit of prayer and devotion to which all temporal things should be subservient. As the price of their labors they may receive things that are necessary for themselves and the brothers, but not money or property. And they shall humbly receive what is given them, as is becoming to the servants of God and to those who practise the most holy poverty.

The brothers shall have nothing of their own, neither house, nor land, nor anything, but as pilgrims and strangers in this world, serving the Lord in poverty and humility, let them confidently go asking alms. Nor let them be ashamed of this, for the Lord made himself poor for us in this world. This is that highest pitch of poverty which has made you, my dearest brothers, heirs and kings of the kingdom of heaven, which has made you poor in goods, and exalted you in virtues . . . .

I strictly forbid all the brothers to have any association or conversation with women that may cause suspicion. And let them not enter nunneries, expect those which the pope has given them special permission to enter. Let them not be intimate friends of men or women, lest on this account scandal arise among the brothers or about brothers.

Ordinance of the Silk Spinsters in Paris, 1254–1271*

This ordinance of the silk merchants' guild in the mid-thirteenth century tells us a great deal about women in industry in the High Middle Ages. How did women control their trade? Consider how the ordinance seeks to regulate the size of particular establishments and the number of workers in them, sets the number of years of training, prevents "raiding" of businesses, sets standards for the quality of the silk cloth, and seeks to build loyalty to the silk manufacturer's guild.

Source: Merry E. Wiesner, trans., unpublished ordinance in Memmingen Stadtarchiv, Zünfte, 471-1.

Any woman who wishes to be a silk spinster on large spindles in the city of Paris—i.e., reeling, spinning, doubling and retwisting—may freely do so, provided she observe the following customs and usages of the craft:

No spinster on large spindles may have more than three apprentices, unless they be her own or her husband's children born in true wedlock; nor may she contract with them for an apprenticeship of less than seven years or for a fee of less than 20 Parisian sols to be paid to her, their mistress. The apprenticeship shall be for eight years if there is no fee, but she may accept more years and money if she can get them. . . .

No woman of the said craft may hire an apprentice or workgirl who has not completed her years of service with the mistress to whom she was apprenticed. If a spinster has assumed an apprentice, she may not take on another before the first has completed her seven years unless the apprentice die or forswear the craft forever. If an apprentice spinster buy her freedom before serving the said seven years, she may not herself take on an apprentice until she has practiced the craft for seven years. If any spinster sell her apprentice, she shall owe six deniers to the guardians appointed in the King's name to guard the [standards of the] craft. The buyer shall also owe six deniers. . . .

If a working woman comes from outside Paris and wishes to practice the said craft in the city, she must swear before two guardians of the craft that she will practice it well and loyally and conform to its customs and usages.

If anyone gives a woman of the said craft silk to be spun and the women pawn it and the owner complain, the fine shall be 5 sols.

No workwoman shall farm out another's silk to be worked upon outside her own house.

The said craft has as guardians two men of integrity sworn in the King's name but appointed and changed at the will of the provost of Paris. Taking an oath in the provost's presence, they shall swear to guard the craft truly, loyally, and to their utmost, and to inform him or his agents of all malpractices discovered therein.

Any spinster who shall infringe any of the above rules shall pay the King a fine of 5 sols for each offense . . . [from which the craft guardians deduct their own expense].

Chapter 12
The Crisis of the Later Middle Ages

Chapter Questions

After reading and studying this chapter you should be able to answer the following questions:

What economic difficulties did Europe experience in the later Middle Ages? What were the causes and the effects of the repeated attacks of plague and disease? Was war a catalyst for change? What political and social developments do new national literatures express? What provoked the division in the church in the fourteenth century? What impact did the schism have on the common people? What were the dominant features of life for ordinary people during this era?

Chapter Summary

The fourteenth century was a time of disease, war, crime, and violence. The art and literature of the period are full of the portrayal of death, just as the historical accounts are full of tales of conflict and violence. There were several major causes for this century of human suffering. Natural disaster—including changes in climate and horrible new diseases—attacked Europe. A long series of wars between France and England not only brought death and economic ruin but increased personal violence and crime as well. In addition, a serious shortage of labor, created by the bubonic plague, resulted in intense social conflict among landlords. Economic crisis during the century also resulted in a bitter struggle between urban workers and their guild masters.

Amid such violence the church lost power and prestige, partly because of the religious disillusionment that accompanied the plague. In short, the institutional church failed to fill the spiritual vacuum left by the series of disasters. A more immediate reason for the decline of the church's influence and prestige was the Babylonian Captivity and the Great Schism. The call for reform, often in the form of the conciliar movement, by people such as Marsiglio of Padua and John Wyclif, was a signal of things to come in the sixteenth century.

But the century of disaster was also a century of change, some of it for the good of ordinary people. It is in this light that the chapter examines some important changes in marriage practices, family relations, and the life of the people. The decline in population meant that those who survived had better food and higher wages. Peasants in western Europe used the labor-shortage problem to demand higher wages and freedom from serfdom. These demands often resulted in conflict with their lords. The disillusionment with the organized church also led to greater lay independence and, ultimately, ideas of social and political equality. The wars actually fostered the development of constitutionalism in England. All in all, it was a period of important changes.

Study Outline

Use this outline to preview the chapter before you read a particular section in your textbook and then as a self-check to test your reading comprehension after you have read the chapter section.

I. Death and disease in the fourteenth century
    A. Prelude to disaster
        1. Poor harvests led to famines in the years 1315–1317 and 1321.
        2. Diseases killed many people and animals.
        3. Economies slowed down and population growth came to a halt.
        4. Weak governments were unable to deal with these problems.
    B. The Black Death
        1. Genoese ships brought the bubonic plague—the Black Death—to Europe in 1347.
           a. The bacillus lived in fleas that infested black rats.
           b. The bubonic form of the disease was transmitted by rats; the pneumonic form was transmitted by people.
           c. Unsanitary and overcrowded cities were ideal breeding grounds for the black rats.
        2. Most people had no rational explanation for the disease, and out of ignorance and fear many blamed it on Jews, causing thousands of Jews to be murdered.
        3. The disease, which killed millions, recurred often and as late as 1700.
    C. The social and psychological consequences of the Black Death
        1. The plague hit the poor harder than the rich, but all classes suffered; the clergy was particularly affected.
        2. Labor shortages meant that wages went up and social mobility increased, as did per capita wealth.
        3. The psychological consequences of the plague were enormous: pessimism, gross sensuality, religious fervor, flagellantism, and obsession with death.
II. The Hundred Years' War (ca 1337–1453)
    A. The causes of the war
        1. Edward III of England, the grandson of the French king Philip the Fair, claimed the French crown by seizing the duchy of Aquitaine in 1337.
        2. French barons backed Edward's claim as a way to thwart the centralizing goals of their king.
        3. Flemish wool merchants supported the English claim to the crown.
        4. Both the French and the English saw military adventure as an excuse to avoid domestic problems.

B. The popular response to the war
 1. Royal propaganda for war and plunder was strong on both sides.
 2. The war meant opportunity for economic or social mobility for poor knights, criminals, and great nobles.
C. The Indian summer of medieval chivalry
 1. Chivalry, a code of conduct for the knightly class, enjoyed its final days of glory during the war.
 2. Chivalry and feudal society glorified war.
D. The course of the war to 1419
 1. The battles took place in France and the Low Countries.
 2. At the Battle of Crécy (1346), the English disregarded the chivalric code and used new military tactics: the longbow and the cannon.
 3. The English won major battles at Poitiers (1356) and Agincourt (1415) and had advanced to Paris by 1419.
E. Joan of Arc and France's victory
 1. Joan of Arc participated in the lifting of the British siege of Orleans in 1429.
 2. She was turned over to the English and burned as a heretic in 1431.
F. Costs and consequences
 1. The war meant economic and population decline for both France and England.
 2. Taxes on wool to finance the war caused a slump in the English wool trade.
 3. In England, returning soldiers caused social problems.
 4. The war encouraged the growth of parliamentary government, particularly in England.
  a. The "Commons" (knights and burgesses) acquired the right to approve all taxes and developed its own organization.
  b. In France, neither the king nor the provincial assemblies wanted a national assembly.
 5. The war generated feelings of nationalism in England and France.
III. Vernacular literature
A. The emergence of national consciousness is seen in the rise of literature written in national languages—the vernacular.
B. Three literary masterpieces manifest this new national pride.
 1. Dante's *Divine Comedy*, a symbolic pilgrimage through Hell, Purgatory, and Paradise to God, embodies the psychological tensions of the age and contains bitter criticism of some church authorities.
 2. Chaucer, in the *Canterbury Tales*, depicts the materialistic, worldly interests of a variety of English people in the fourteenth century.
 3. Villon used the language of the lower classes to portray the reality, beauty, and hardships of life here on earth.
IV. The decline of the church's prestige
A. The Babylonian Captivity (1309–1377)
 1. The pope had lived at Avignon since the reign of King Philip the Fair of France and thus was subject to French control.
  a. The Babylonian Captivity badly damaged papal prestige.
  b. It left Rome poverty-stricken.
 2. Pope Gregory XI brought the papacy back to Rome in 1377, but then Urban VI alienated the church hierarchy in his zeal to reform the church.

3. A new pope, Clement VII, was elected, and the two popes both claimed to be legitimate.

B. The Great Schism (1378–1417)

    1. England and Germany recognized Pope Urban VI, while France and others recognized the antipope, Clement VII.

    2. The schism brought the church into disrepute and wakened the religious faith of many.

C. The conciliar movement was based on the idea of reform through a council of church leaders.

    1. Marsiglio of Padua had claimed in 1324, in *Defensor Pacis*, that authority within the church should rest with a church council and not the pope and that the church was subordinate to the state.

    2. John Wyclif attacked papal authority and called for even more radical reform of the church.

        a. He believed that Christians should read the Bible for themselves, prompting the first English translation of the Bible.

        b. His followers, called Lollards, disseminated his ideas widely.

    3. Wyclif's ideas were spread to Bohemia by John Hus.

    4. An attempt in 1409 to depose both popes and select another led to a threefold schism.

    5. Finally, the council at Constance (1414–1418) ended the schism with the election of Pope Martin V.

V. The life of the people in the fourteenth and fifteenth centuries

A. Marriage and the family

    1. Marriage usually came at 16 to 18 years for women and later for men.

    2. Legalized prostitution existed in urban areas and was the source of wealth for some women.

    3. Economic factors, rather than romantic love, usually governed the decision to marry.

    4. Divorce did not exist.

    5. Many people did not observe church regulations and married without a church ceremony.

B. Life in the parish

    1. The land and the parish were the centers of life.

    2. Opportunities to join guilds declined in the fourteenth century, and strikes and riots became frequent.

    3. Cruel sports, such as bullbaiting, and bearbaiting, as well as drunkenness, reflect the violence and frustrations of the age.

    4. Lay people increasingly participated in church management.

C. Fur-collar crime

    1. In England, nobles returning from war had little to do and were in need of income; thus they resorted to crime.

    2. Kidnaping, extortion, and terrorism by the upper classes were widespread.

    3. Because governments were not able to stop abuses, outlaws such as Robin Hood sought to protect the people.

D. Peasant revolts
   1. Peasants revolted against the nobility in France in 1358 (the *Jacquerie*), 1363, 1380, and 1420, and in England in 1381.
      a. One cause of the Peasant's Revolt of 1381 was the lords' attempt to freeze wages.
      b. In general, peasants were better off; the revolts were due to rising expectations.
      c. The 1381 revolt in England was due to economic grievances, antiaristocratic sentiment, and protest against taxes.
   2. Workers in Italy (the *ciompi*), Germany, and Spain also revolted.

Review Questions

Check your understanding of this chapter by answering the following questions.

1. What were the causes of the population decline that began in the early fourteenth century?
2. What was the source of the bubonic plague and why did it spread so rapidly in Europe?
3. What impact did the plague have on wages and the demand for labor? What happened to land values?
4. Describe the psychological effects of the plague. How did people explain this disaster?
5. What were the immediate and other causes of the Hundred Years' War?
6. Why did the people support their kings in war?
7. Did feudalism tend to encourage or prevent war? Explain.
8. What were the results of the Hundred Years' War? Who were the winners and losers within both countries?
9. How did the Babylonian Captivity greatly weaken the power and prestige of the church?
10. Why were there three popes in 1409? Who were they and how did this situation occur?
11. What was the conciliar movement and who were its advocates? Was this a revolutionary idea?
12. Why was Wyclif a threat to the institutional church?
13. What was fur-collar crime and why did it become a central feature of European life in the fourteenth and fifteenth centuries?
14. Did peasants' lives improve or deteriorate in the fourteenth and fifteenth centuries? In what ways?
15. What were the reasons for the French Jacquerie of 1358 and the English Peasants' Revolt of 1381?
16. Why did a great amount of conflict and frustration among guild members develop in the fourteenth century?

Study-Review Exercises

Define the following key concepts and terms.
Pasteurella pestis

fur-collar crime

English Statute of Labourers

conciliar movement

vernacular literature

craft guild

Identify and explain the significance of the following people and terms.
Queen Isabella of England

Hundred Years' War

Robin Hood

Marsiglio of Padua

Battle of Crécy (1346)

Martin V

Joan of Arc

Babylonian Captivity

Margaret Paston

Lollards

House of Commons

Edward III

John Hus

John Wyclif

Jacquerie

Explain the importance of each of the following concepts in late medieval life and describe what changes it was subject to in this period.

marriage

feudal chivalry

individual Christian faith

leisure time

nationalism

Test your understanding of the chapter by providing the correct answers.

1. In reaction to the calls for reform in the fourteenth century, the church *did/did not* enter into a period of reform and rejuvenation.

2. Prior to the plague in 1348, Europe experienced a period of unusually *good/bad* harvests.

3. The Hundred Years' War was between the kings of _____ and

   _____ .

4. The followers of the English theologian Wyclif. _____

5. Up to the nineteenth century, *economic/romantic* factors usually determined whom and when a person married.

6. For the most part, job mobility within the late medieval guilds tended to *increase/decrease*.

Place the following events in correct chronological order.

First instance of the bubonic plague in Europe
Babylonian Captivity
Start of the Hundred Years' war
Council of Constance
Battle of Crécy
Jacquerie
Dante's *Divine Comedy*
Great Schism

1.

2.

3.

4.

5.

6.

7.

8.

Multiple-Choice Questions

1. The conciliar movement was
   a. an effort to give the pope the power to use councils to wipe out heresy.
   b. the effort by the French lords to establish a parliament.
   c. a new monastic order vowing poverty.
   d. an attempt to place ultimate church authority in a general council.

2. The plague was probably brought into Europe by
   a. Chinese soldiers.
   b. Spanish warriors returning from South America.
   c. English soldiers pushing into France.
   d. Genoese ships from the Crimea.

3. In general, farm laborers who survived the bubonic plague faced
   a. higher wages.
   b. food shortages.
   c. the need to migrate.
   d. excommunication from the church.

4. Generally, the major new source of criminals after the Hundred Years' War was
   a. the urban mobs.
   b. the rural peasants.
   c. the nobility.
   d. the bourgeoisie.

5. Which of the following statements about the fourteenth century is *false?*
   a. The population declined.
   b. The standard of living fell drastically.
   c. The power of the church declined.
   d. War between England and France was frequent.

6. Most people in the fourteenth century believed that the Black Death was caused by
   a. bad air.
   b. poor sanitation and housing.
   c. a bacillus living in fleas.
   d. black rats.

7. Generally, the plague disaster of the fourteenth century resulted in all but which of the following for European society?
   a. Higher wages for most workers
   b. A severe decline in the number of German clergymen
   c. A decline in flagellantism
   d. An obsession with death

8. Which of the following did *not* participant in the Hundred Years' War?
   a. Edward III of England
   b. King Philip the Fair
   c. Joan of Arc
   d. The Dauphin Charles of France

9. One reason for peasant-landlord conflict in the fourteenth century was
   a. peasants' opposition to declining wages and inflation.
   b. landlords' attempts to legislate wages.
   c. land scarcity.
   d. peasants' refusal to be drafted for war service.

10. The author of *Defensor Pacis* and proponent of the idea that authority in the Christian church rested in a general council rather than in the papacy was
    a. Cardinal Robert of Geneva.
    b. Pope Urban V.
    c. John Wyclif.
    d. Marsiglio of Padua.

11. Which of the following statements about the Hundred Years' War is true?
    a. It discouraged representative government.
    b. It depressed the English wool trade.
    c. It increased the amount of arable land in England.
    d. It created a surplus of manpower.

12. The followers of the English theologian-reformer Wyclif were called
    a. Protestants.
    b. outlaws.
    c. Lollards.
    d. flagellants.

13. *Fur-collar crime* is a term used to describe
    a. the robbery and extortion inflicted on the poor by the rich.
    b. the criminal activity carried out by bandits such as Robin Hood.
    c. crimes committed by churchmen.
    d. the illegal activities of noblewomen.

14. After 1347, the Black Death generally moved
    a. from north to south.
    b. from west to east.
    c. from south to north.
    d. from east to west.

15. Initially the Hundred Years' War was fought over
    a. Aquitaine.
    b. King Edward III's claim to the French crown.
    c. the control of the Flemish wool trade.
    d. religion.

16. English military innovation(s) during the Hundred Years' War included
    a. the crossbow.
    b. the cannon and the longbow.
    c. cavalry.
    d. the pike.

17. Which of the following statements about marriage during the Middle Ages is true?
    a. Most marriages were based on romantic love.
    b. Most marriages were arranged.
    c. Divorce was common.
    d. Marriage without the church's sanction was unheard of.

18. Which of the following was a writer of vernacular literature?
    a. Dante
    b. Jacques de Vitry
    c. Clement VII
    d. Marsiglio of Padua

19. Which of the following statements about Joan of Arc is *false*?
    a. She dressed like a man.
    b. The English king was her greatest supporter.
    c. She was accused of being a heretic and was burned.
    d. She was from a peasant family.

20. For the French, the turning point of the Hundred Years' War was
    a. the relief of Paris.
    b. the defeat of the English fleet in the English Channel.
    c. the relief of Orléans.
    d. the Battle of Poitiers.

21. Prostitution in late medieval society
    a. did not exist.
    b. existed only among the lower classes.
    c. was not respected but was legalized.
    d. existed in the countryside but not the city.

22. In the fourteenth century craft guilds began to change in that
    a. master and journeyman distinctions began to disappear.
    b. the guilds lost control over the production process.
    c. apprenticeship was abandoned.
    d. membership became more restrictive and master-journeyman relations deteriorated.

23. Chaucer's *Canterbury Tales* is important because
    a. it depicts the impact of the plague on Italian life.
    b. it reflects the cultural tensions of the times.
    c. it illustrates the highly religious interests of most people.
    d. it show how people were obsessed with the next world.

24. The effect of the Hundred Years' War on England was that it
    a. brought great wealth in the form of cash reserves to England.
    b. caused a great increase in wool exports.
    c. allowed many English knights to become very rich.
    d. resulted in a great net loss in cash.

25. The English Peasants' Revolt most probably
    a. was the largest single uprising of the entire Middle Ages.
    b. was an event of little significance at the time.
    c. affected only a very small number of people.
    d. was engineered by the landowners.

Major Political Ideas

1. Define nationalism. How did the Hundred Years' War encourage nationalism? What is the purpose and function of a national assembly? Why did a national representative assembly emerge in England but not in France?

2. What were the ideas set forth by Marsiglio of Padua in his *Defensor Pacis*? What were the political implications of these ideas?

Issues for Essays and Discussion

Some historians have argued that war is the engine of change. Does this theory have any validity for the fourteenth century? Discuss this in terms of the political, economic, and social experience of the fourteenth century.

Interpretation of Visual Sources

Study the reproduction of the painting *The Plague-Stricken* on page 358 of the textbook. How did people respond to this mysterious disease? Look carefully at the figures in this painting. Who seems to be in control of the situation? Does the group of figures in the upper left-hand corner provide any information as to what was thought to be the origins of the disease?

Geography

Use maps 12.2 and 12.3 in the textbook to complete the following:

1. Locate the extent of the English possessions in France. What were the origins of English claims to French land?
2. Why was it unlikely that England could have held these territories permanently?
3. Locate the main centers of popular revolt in France and England.
4. Why were so many of the English revolts in the highly populated and advanced areas of the country?

Understanding History Through the Arts

1. What was the music of this period like? An excellent introduction is a recording, *Instruments of the Middle Ages and Renaissance,* with an accompanying illustrated book by David Munro (Angel recording number SB2-3810 [1976]). For the French chansons and the English madrigals, listen to the recording titled *The King's Singers Sing of Courtly Pleasures,* which includes text and translations (Angel recording number s-37025 [1974]).

2. How did the Black Death affect art? While some members of society responded to the plague with religious fervor, others merely looked to enjoy life as best they could. The fourteenth-century Italian writer Boccaccio wrote the *Decameron,* a series of bawdy tales told by a group of Florentine men and women who fled to the countryside to escape the plague.

Problems for Further Investigation

1. How can a single disease affect the course of history? Students interested in the plague should begin with G. C. Coulton, *The Black Death* (1929); P. Zeigler, *The Black Death: A Study of the Plague in Fourteenth Century Europe* (1969); and W. McNeill, *Plagues and Peoples* (1976).

2. What was the cause of the Hundred Years' War? What effect did it have on English and French society? E. Perroy, *The Hundred Years' War** (1951), is a good start for anyone interested in that subject.

3. Why did the peasant revolts start? Those interested in popular protest during this age should consult M. Mullett, *Popular Culture and Popular Protest in Medieval and Early Modern Europe* (1987). The fourteenth century is analyzed in the interesting book, *A Distant Mirror: The Calamitous Fourteenth Century* (1978) by B. W. Tuchman.

---

*Available in paperback.

4. What was the cause of the conflict between Philip the Fair of France and the pope? Was the French king out to destroy the power of the papacy? These and other questions are debated by a number of historians in C. T. Wood, ed., *Philip the Fair and Boniface VIII** (1967).

5. How did the plague affect religion? One of the results of the Black Death was a revival of Christian mysticism—a search for meaning in life through a personal relationship with God. One of the most popular books of this movement was *The Imitation of Christ** by Thomas à Kempis.

6. What was medieval chivalry and how did it reflect changes in medieval society? Begin your study with R. Barber, *The Knight and Chivalry** (1990). You may want to supplement this with M. W. Thompson, *The Decline of the Castle* (1988).

---

*Available in paperback.

Chapter 13
European Society in the Age of the Renaissance

Chapter Questions

After reading and studying this chapter you should be able to answer the following questions:

What does the term *Renaissance* mean? How did the Renaissance influence politics, government, and social organization? What were the intellectual and artistic hallmarks of the Renaissance? Did the Renaissance cause shifts in religious attitudes? What developments occurred in the evolution of the nation-state?

Chapter Summary

The Renaissance was an era of intellectual and artistic brilliance unsurpassed in European history. It is clear that some thinking people in this era, largely a mercantile elite, saw themselves living in an age more akin to that of the bright and creative ancient world than that of the recent dark and gloomy Middle Ages. Although many of the supposedly "new" Renaissance ideas are actually found in the Middle Ages, scholars generally agree that the Renaissance was characterized by a number of distinctive ideas about life and humanity—individualism, secularism, humanism, materialism, and hedonism.

The Renaissance began in Florence, Italy, in the late thirteenth century. It subsequently spread to the rest of Italy—particularly Rome—and then to northern Europe, where it developed somewhat differently. The best-known expressions of the bold new Renaissance spirit can be seen in the painting, sculpture, and architecture of the period. New attitudes were also found in education, politics, and philosophy; in Northern Europe new ideas of social reform developed. Although the Renaissance brought some benefits to the masses of people, such as the printing press, it was basically an elitist movement. A negative development of the age was a deterioration in the power and position of women in society.

In politics, the Renaissance produced an approach to power and the state that historians often call "new monarchies. " The best known and most popular theoretician of this school was the Florentine Niccolò Machiavelli. Its most able practitioners are the fifteenth- and sixteenth-century monarchs of France, England, and Spain. In Italy, the city-state system led to wealthy and independent cities that were marvelously creative but also vulnerable to invasion and control from the outside by powerful Spanish and French kings.

Study Outline

Use this outline to preview the chapter before you read a particular section in your textbook and then as a self-check to test your reading comprehension after you have read the chapter section.

I. The evolution of the Italian Renaissance
   A. Beginnings
      1. The Renaissance was a period of commercial, financial, political, and cultural achievement in two phases, from 1050 to 1300 and from 1300 to about 1600.
      2. The northern Italian cities led the commercial revival, especially Venice, Genoa, and Milan.
      3. The first artistic and literary flowerings of the Renaissance appeared in Florence.
         a. Florentine mercantile families dominated European banking.
         b. The wool industry was the major factor in the city's financial expansion and population increase.
   B. Communes and republics
      1. Northern Italian cities were communes—associations of free men seeking independence from the local lords.
         a. The nobles, attracted by the opportunities in the cities, often settled there and married members of the mercantile class, forming an urban nobility.
         b. The *popolo*, or middle class, was excluded from power.
         c. Popolo-led republican governments failed, which led to the rule of despots (*signori*) or oligarchies.
         d. In the fifteenth century, the princely courts of the rulers were centers of wealth and art.
   C. The balance of power among the Italian city-states
      1. Italy had no political unity; it was divided into city-states such as Milan, Venice, and Florence, the Papal States, and a kingdom of Naples in the south.
      2. The political and economic competition among the city-states prevented centralization of power.
      3. Shifting alliances among the city-states led to the creation of permanent ambassadors.
      4. After 1494 a divided Italy became a European battleground.
II. Intellectual hallmarks of the Renaissance
   A. Many, like the poet and humanist Petrarch, saw the fourteenth century as a new golden age and a revival of ancient Roman culture.
   B. Individualism
      1. Literature specifically concerned with the nature of individuality emerged.
      2. Renaissance people believed in individual will and genius.
   C. The revival of antiquity
      1. Italians copied the ancient Roman lifestyle.
      2. The study of the classics led to humanism, an emphasis on human beings.
         a. Humanists sought to understand human nature through a study of pagan and classical authors *and* Christian thought.
         b. The humanist writer Pico della Mirandola believed that there were no limits to what human beings could accomplish.
      3. Ancient Latin style was considered superior to medieval Latin.

D. Secular spirit
   1. *Secularism* means a concern with materialism rather than religion.
   2. Unlike medieval people, Renaissance people were concerned with money and pleasure.
      a. In *On Pleasure*, Lorenzo Valla defended the pleasure of the senses as the highest good.
      b. In the *Decameron*, Boccaccio portrayed an acquisitive and worldly society.
   3. The church did little to combat secularism; in fact, many popes were Renaissance patrons and participants.
E. Art and the artist
   1. The *quattrocento* (1400s) and the *cinquecento* (1500s) saw dazzling artistic achievements, led by Florence and Rome.
   2. Art and power
      a. In the early Renaissance, powerful urban groups commissioned works of art, which remained overwhelmingly religious.
      b. In the later fifteenth century, individuals and oligarchs began to sponsor works of art as a means of self-glorification.
      c. As the century advanced, art became more and more secular, and classical subjects became popular.
   3. The style of art changed in the fifteenth century.
      a. The individual portrait emerged as a distinct genre.
      b. Painting and sculpture became more naturalistic and realistic, and the human body was glorified, as in the work of the sculptors Donatello and Michelangelo.
      c. A new "international style" emphasized color, decorative detail, and curvilinear rhythms.
      d. In painting, the use of perspective was pioneered by Brunelleschi and della Francesca.
   4. The status of the artist
      a. The status of the artist improved during the Renaissance; most work was done by commission from a prince.
      b. The creative genius of the artist was recognized and rewarded.
      c. The Renaissance was largely an elitist movement; Renaissance culture did not directly affect the middle classes.
III. Social change during the Renaissance
   A. Education and political thought
      1. Vergerio wrote a treatise on education that stressed the teaching of history, ethics, and rhetoric (public speaking).
      2. Castiglione's *The Courtier*, which was widely read, describes the model Renaissance gentleman as a man of many talents, including intellectual and artistic skills.
      3. Machiavelli's *The Prince* describes how to acquire, maintain, and increase political power.
         a. Machiavelli believed that the politician should manipulate people and use any means to gain power.
         b. Machiavelli did not advocate amoral behavior but believed that political action cannot be governed by moral considerations.

B. The printed word
1. The invention in 1455 of movable type by Gutenberg, Fust, and Schöffer made possible the printing of a wide variety of texts.
2. Printing transformed the lives of Europeans by making propaganda possible, encouraging a wider common identity, and improving literacy.

C. Women in Renaissance society
1. Compared to women in the previous age, the status of upper-class women declined during the Renaissance.
2. Although the Renaissance brought improved educational opportunities for women, they were expected to use their education solely to run a household.
3. Women's status declined with regard to sex and love.
   a. Renaissance humanists laid the foundations for the bourgeois double standard.
   b. The rape of women by upper-class men was frequent and not considered serious.
4. Because of poverty, infanticide and abandonment of children were frequent and eventually led to the establishment of foundling hospitals.

D. Blacks in Renaissance society
1. Beginning in the fifteenth century, black slaves were brought into Europe in large numbers.
2. Blacks as slaves and freemen filled a variety of positions, from laborers to dancers and actors and musicians.
3. The European attitude toward blacks was ambivalent—blackness symbolized both evil and humility.
4. In the Renaissance, blacks were displayed as signs of wealth.

IV. The Renaissance in the north began in the last quarter of the fifteenth century
A. It was more Christian than the Renaissance in Italy, and it stressed social reform based on Christian ideals.
B. Christian humanists sought to create a more perfect world by combining the best elements of classical and Christian cultures.
1. Humanists like Lefèvre believed in the use of the Bible by common people.
2. Thomas More, the author of *Utopia*, believed that society, not people, needed improving.
3. The Dutch monk Erasmus best represents Christian humanism in his emphasis on education as the key to a moral and intellectual improvement and inner Christianity.
C. The stories of the French humanist Rabelais were distinctly secular but still had a serious purpose.
1. Like More, Rabelais believed that institutions molded individuals and education was the key to moral life.
2. He combined a Renaissance zest for life with a classical insistence on the cultivation of body and mind.
D. Northern art and architecture were more religious than in Italy and less influenced by classical themes and motifs.
1. Van Eyck painted realistic, incredibly detailed works.
2. Bosch used religion and folk legends as themes.

V. Politics and the state in the Renaissance (ca 1450–1521)
   A. The "new" monarchs
      1. The fifteenth century saw the rise of many powerful and ruthless rulers interested in the centralization of power and the elimination of disorder and violence.
      2. Many of them, such as Louis XI of France, Henry VII of England, and Ferdinand and Isabella of Spain, seemed to be acting according to Machiavelli's principles.
      3. These monarchs invested kingship with a strong sense of royal authority and national purpose.
      4. The ideas of the new monarchs were not entirely original—some of them had their roots in the Middle Ages.
   B. France after the Hundred Years' War
      1. Charles VII ushered in an age of recovery and ended civil war.
         a. He expelled the English, reorganized the royal council, strengthened royal finances, reformed the justice system, and remodeled the army.
         b. He made the church subject to the state.
      2. Louis XI expanded the French state and laid the foundations of later French absolutism.
   C. England
      1. Feudal lords controlled the royal council and Parliament in the fifteenth century.
      2. Between 1455 and 1471, the houses of York and Lancaster fought a civil war called the Wars of the Roses that hurt trade, agriculture, and domestic industry.
      3. Edward IV and his followers began to restore royal power.
      4. The English Parliament had become a power center for the aristocracy but was manipulated by Henry VII into becoming a tool of the king.
      5. Henry VII used the royal council and the court of Star Chamber to check aristocratic power.
      6. Henry and his successors won the support of the upper middle class by linking government policy with their interests.
   D. Spain
      1. The *reconquista* was the centuries-long attempt to unite Spain and expel Arabs and Jews.
      2. The marriage of Ferdinand and Isabella was the last major step in the unification and Christianization of Spain.
         a. Under their reign, however, Spain remained a loose confederation of separate states.
         b. They used the *hermandades*, or local police forces, to administer royal justice.
      3. They restructured the royal council to curb aristocratic power.
      4. The church was also used to strengthen royal authority.
      5. Ferdinand and Isabella completed the *reconquista* in 1492, but many Jews remained.
         a. Jews were often financiers and professionals; many (called *conversos*) had converted but were still disliked and distrusted.
         b. Ferdinand and Isabella revived the Inquisition and used its cruel methods to unify Spain and expel the Jews.

Review Questions

Check your understanding of this chapter by answering the following questions.

1. What new social class developed in twelfth-century Italy? How did this social class affect the movement toward republican government?
2. What five powers dominated the Italian peninsula in the fifteenth century? How did the Italian city-states contribute to modern diplomacy?
3. How does the concept of individualism help explain the Renaissance?
4. How do Valla and Boccaccio illustrate and represent what Renaissance people were like?
5. What is humanism? What do humanists emphasize?
6. According to Vergerio, what is the purpose of education? Was he a humanist?
7. How does Castiglione's *The Courtier* define the "perfect Renaissance man"? How does this book serve as an example of humanism?
8. How did the invention of movable type revolutionize European life?
9. How did the Renaissance in northern Europe differ from that of Italy?
10. Discuss Christian humanism by describing the works and ideas of Thomas More and Desiderius Erasmus.
11. Why did Italy became a battleground for the European superpowers after 1494?
12. What were the obstacles to royal authority faced by the kings of France in the fifteenth century? How did Charles VII and his successors strengthen the French monarchy?
13. What devices did Henry VII of England use to check the power of the aristocracy and strengthen the monarchy?
14. Why is the reign of Ferdinand and Isabella one of the most important in Spanish history? What were their achievements in the areas of national power and national expansion?
15. Why were blacks valued in Renaissance society? What roles did they play in the economic and social life of the times?
16. In what ways did life for upper-class women change during the Renaissance?
17. How was Renaissance art different from medieval art? How did the status of the artist change?

Study-Review Exercises

Define the following key concepts and terms.

Renaissance

oligarchy

signori

communes

popolo

reconquista

humanism

secularism

individualism

materialism

hermandades

Machiavellian

Identify and explain the significance of the following people and terms.
English Royal Council and Court of Star Chamber

conquest of Granada

Habsburg-Valois wars

Brunelleschi's Founding Hospital in Florence

Pico della Mirandola

Desiderius Erasmus

Jan van Eyck

Thomas More

Donatello

Baldassare Castiglione

Niccolò Machiavelli

Johan Gutenberg

Lefèvre d'Etaples

Saint John Chrysostom

Lorenzo Valla

Savonarola

Jerome Bosch

François Rabelais

Explain why each of the following is considered a "new monarch."
Louis XI of France

Henry VII of England

Ferdinand and Isabella of Spain

Charles VII of France

Cesare Borgia

Test your understanding of the chapter by providing the correct answers.

1. The author of a best-selling political critique called *The Prince*. _____

2. Renaissance humanists tended to be *more/less* concerned about religion than about people.

3. In the fifteenth century, infanticide *increased/decreased*.

4. An important English humanist and the author of *Utopia*. _____

5. Generally, the legal status of upper-class women *improved/declined* during the Renaissance.

6. It *is/is not* clear that the economic growth and the material wealth of the Italian cities were direct causes of the Renaissance.

Multiple-Choice Questions

1. Which of the following statements about the earliest printed books is *false*?
   a. They dealt mainly with economic and business subjects.
   b. They encouraged literacy.
   c. Movable type was first developed in Mainz, Germany.
   d. They had an effect on the process of learning.

2. The Renaissance began in
   a. the Low Countries.
   b. Rome.
   c. France.
   d. Florence

3. The patrons of the Renaissance were mostly
   a. churchmen.
   b. the popes.
   c. the common people.
   d. merchants and bankers.

4. The frail and ugly king who began French economic and political recovery in the early fifteenth century was
   a. Henry Tudor.
   b. Charles VII.
   c. Philip the Fair.
   d. Louis XI.

5. It appears that in Renaissance society blacks were
   a. valued as soldiers.
   b. valued as servants and entertainers.
   c. considered undesirable and not allowed in society.
   d. not much in demand.

6. A major difference between northern and Italian humanism is that northern humanism stressed
   a. economic gain and materialism.
   b. social reform based on Christian ideals.
   c. pagan virtues.
   d. scholastic dogma over reason.

7. Local groups in Spain that were given royal authority to administer justice were the
   a. *conversos*.
   b. liberals.
   c. *hermandades*.
   d. royal tribunal.

8. The court of Star Chamber in England was
   a. a common-law court.
   b. under the control of the barons in the House of Lords.
   c. done away with by the powerful Tudors.
   d. used to check aristocratic power.

9. The superiority of the French monarch over the church was the object of the
   a. Pragmatic Sanction of Bourges.
   b. Habsburg-Valois wars.
   c. Declaration of Calais.
   d. Hundred Years' War.

10. Most of the northern Renaissance thinkers agreed that
    a. democracy, not monarchy, was the only workable political system.
    b. humanity is basically sinful.
    c. Christianity is unacceptable.
    d. society is perfectible.

11. The late-fifteenth-century ruler of England who ended the civil war and strengthened the crown was
    a. John I.
    b. William III.
    c. Henry II.
    d. Henry VII.

12. Which of the following statements about Florence at the time of the Renaissance is *false*?
    a. Its major industry was wool production.
    b. It lost probably half its population to the Black Death.
    c. It was a major banking center.
    d. It was an important Mediterranean port city.

13. The dome of St. Peter's in Rome is considered to be the greatest work of
    a. Brunelleschi.
    b. Donatello.
    c. Michelangelo.
    d. Ghiberti.

14. The term *Renaissance* means
    a. a rise in the average standard of living among the masses.
    b. a resurgence of art and culture in the fourteenth through sixteenth centuries.
    c. an increase in the population after the ravaging effects of the "Four Horsemen of the Apocalypse."
    d. the recovery of the church from economic and moral decline.

15. The financial and military strength of the towns of northern Italy was directly related to
    a. their wealth, which enabled them to hire mercenary soldiers to protect their commercial interests.
    b. their contractual and marital alliances with the rural nobility.
    c. protections provided them by the Holy Roman Emperor.
    d. their alliance with the papacy.

16. The northern Renaissance differed from the Italian Renaissance in that the former was characterized by all of the following *except*
    a. interest in biblical scholarship.
    b. an emphasis on secular and pagan themes in art.
    c. the combination of the best aspects of antiquity and Christianity.
    d. an emphasis on the use of reason.

17. Erasmus advocated
    a. paganism.
    b. Christian education for moral and intellectual improvement.
    c. a monastic life of contemplation and divorce from the material world.
    d. obedience to church doctrine and ritual.

18. The Renaissance artist of talent and ability often lived a life
    a. of economic desperation.
    b. of economic security through patronage.
    c. of luxury, but without social status.
    d. like that of the masses.

19. The most influential book on Renaissance court life and behavior was
    a. Castiglione's *The Courtier*.
    b. Machiavelli's *The Prince*.
    c. Augustine's *City of God*.
    d. Boccaccio's *Decameron*.

20. The best description of Machiavelli's *The Prince* is that it is
    a. a description of how government should be organized and implemented.
    b. a satire on sixteenth-century politics.
    c. a call for Italian nationalism.
    d. an accurate description of politics as practiced in Renaissance Italy.

21. The Wars of the Roses were
    a. civil wars between the English ducal houses of York and Lancaster.
    b. between England and France.
    c. civil wars between the English king, Henry VI, and the aristocracy.
    d. minor disputes among English gentry.

22. Just before the advent of Ferdinand and Isabella, the Iberian Peninsula could best be described as
    a. a homogeneous region sharing a common language and cultural tradition.
    b. a heterogeneous region consisting of several ethnic groups with a diversity of linguistic and cultural characteristics.
    c. tolerant of religious and ethnic traditions different from Christianity.
    d. a region dominated equally by Arabs and Jews.

23. Thomas More's ideas, as best expressed in his book *Utopia,* centered on the belief that
    a. evil exists because men and women are basically corrupt.
    b. political leaders must learn how to manipulate their subjects.
    c. social order is only an unattainable ideal.
    d. corruption and war are due to acquisitiveness and private property.

24. Renaissance men's view of educated women was that they should
    a. be encouraged and given an equal place in society.
    b. have a voice in the affairs of the city.
    c. not be encouraged in any manner.
    d. be allowed to add a social touch to the household, but otherwise remain subservient to men.

25. The culture of the Renaissance
    a. was largely limited to a small mercantile elite.
    b. was widely spread and practiced by a broad middle class.
    c. was confined to the church.
    d. affected all classes, including the peasants.

Major Political Ideas

1. What were the political ideas behind the concept of the "new monarch"?

2. In what ways does Machiavelli represent a change in political thought? What were his suggestions for and philosophy of the acquisition and meaning of political power?

Issues for Essays and Discussion

The Renaissance was a period during which many people began to think and act in different ways. Sometimes this is referred to as a "self-conscious awareness," a stress on "humanism," and a "secular spirit. " What do these terms mean? Answer by making specific reference to developments in literature, political thought, and art.

Interpretation of Visual Sources

1. Study the reproduction of the painting entitled *Death and the Miser* by Jerome Bosch on page 409 of your textbook. Describe how this painting reflects the religious orientation of the Renaissance in the north of Europe. What is happening in this scene? Account for as many symbolic references as you can. What do you believe to be Bosch's message?

2. Study the reproduction of the painting *Journey of the Magi* on page 397 of your textbook. How does this painting reflect corporate patronage of the arts? Is it a religious or a secular painting?

Geography

On Outline Map 13.1 provided, and using Map 13.1 in the textbook as a reference, mark the following: the names of the Italian city-states and their principal cities, underlining the five major powers of Venice, Milan, Florence, the Papal States, and the kingdom of Naples.

Outline Map 13.1

Understanding History Through the Arts

1. What does the music of the Renaissance tell us about the period? The music of the Renaissance is introduced in two recordings, *From the Renaissance* (STL-150) and *From the Renaissance-Concert* (STL-160), in the Time-Life series *The Story of Great Music* (1967), which also includes a book with a good introduction to the period and its musical styles, art, and history. Good written introductions to Renaissance music are H. Brown, *Music in the Renaissance** (1976), and G. Reese, *Music in the Renaissance* (1954).

2. What impact did Renaissance thinking have on the arts? Fine illustrations and a discussion of new directions in the arts are woven into a number of interesting essays on the age in D. Hay, *The Renaissance* (1967).

3. What were the interests and motives of Renaissance artists? A good introduction to Renaissance art and the life of the artist and writer is J. H. Plumb, *The Renaissance* (1961), which includes biographies of Michelangelo, Petrarch, da Vinci, and others and includes hundreds of color plates and a comprehensive history of Renaissance art.

4. How did the art of Rome and Florence differ? What characteristics did they share? Begin your study with R. Goldthwaite, *The Building of Renaissance Florence** (1983); M. Andres et al., *The Art of Florence*, 2 vols. (1989); and J. Andreae, *The Art of Rome* (1989). For the northern Renaissance see O. Benesch, *The Art of the Renaissance in Northern Europe* (1965). Two of the finest Renaissance artists are the subjects of M. Kemp and J. Roberts, *Leonardo Da Vinci, Artist, Scientist, Inventor* (1989), and M. Levey, *Giambattista Tiepolo* (1987).

Problems for Further Investigation

1. Was the Renaissance an age of progress and advancement? Urban and rural life, court life, war, and witchcraft are among the many aspects of Renaissance life covered in E. R. Chamberlin, *Everyday Life in Renaissance Times** (1967).

2. What did popular Renaissance writers believe to be important about the age in which they lived? One of the best ways to understand the Renaissance is to read the works of its participants. Three works dealt with in this chapter are Niccolò Machiavelli, *The Prince** (a number of paperback translations are available); Baldassare Castiglione, *The Courtier,** Charles Singleton, trans. (1959); and Thomas More, *Utopia.**

3. How did the Renaissance alter the status of women? Begin your study by reading J. Kelly-Gadol, "Did Women Have a Renaissance?" in R. Bridenthal and C. Koontz, eds., *Becoming Visible: Women in European History* (1977), and M. Rose et al., *Women in the Middle Ages and the Renaissance: Literary and Historical Perspectives* (1986).

---

*Available in paperback.

4. The Swiss historian Jacob Burckhardt called the Renaissance the "mother" of our modern world. Was the Renaissance as important as Burckhardt and others have claimed? Did it dramatically change the way people acted and the direction history was to take? These and other questions are considered in several historical debates on the Renaissance: D. Hay, ed., *The Renaissance Debate** (1965); B. Tierney et al., *Renaissance Man—Medieval or Modern?** (1967); and K. H. Dannenfeldt, ed., *The Renaissance—Medieval or Modern?** (1959).

---

*Available in paperback.

Studying Effectively—Exercise 3

Learning How to Identify Main Points That Are Effects, Results, Consequences

In the introduction to this *Study Guide* and in the "Studying Effectively" exercises 1 and 2, we noted that learning to underline properly plays an important part in college work. Underlining (or highlighting with a felt-tipped pen) provides a permanent record of what you study and learn. It helps you review, synthesize, and do your best on exams.

We suggested three simple guidelines for effective underlining or highlighting:*

1. Be selective; do not underline or highlight too much.
2. Underline or highlight the main points.
3. Consider numbering the main points.

These guidelines will help you in courses in many different subjects.

Cause and Effect in History

The study of history also requires learning to recognize special kinds of main points. These points are *explanatory* in nature. *They answer why and how questions,* thereby helping you to interpret and make sense of the historical record.

Two particularly important types of why and how questions focus on *cause* and *effect* in history. You are already familiar with questions of this nature, questions that provide much of history's fascination and excitement. "Why did the Roman Empire decline and fall?" That is, what *causes* explain the decline and fall of the Roman Empire? "What were the *effects* of the Black Death?" You should pay particular attention to questions of cause and effect. They give history meaning. They help you increase your ability to think and reason in historical terms.

Two other insights will help you greatly in identifying main points involving cause and effect. First, historians use a number of different words and verbal constructions to express these concepts. Thus "causes" often become "reasons" or "factors," or things that "account for," "contribute to," or "play a role in" a given development. "Effects" often become "results" or

---

*The guidelines for underlining are from *RSVP: The Houghton Mifflin Reading, Study, & Vocabulary Program,* third edition, by James F. Shepherd (Houghton Mifflin, 1988). We urge students to consult this very valuable book for additional help in improving their reading and study skills.

"consequences," or are "the product of an impact." In most cases students can consider such expressions as substitutes for cause and effect, although they should be aware this historians are not of one mind on these matters.

Second, cause and effect are constantly interrelated in the historical process. Yesterday's results become today's causes, which will in turn help bring tomorrow's results. To take examples you have studied, the *causes* of the fall of the Roman Empire (such as increasing economic difficulties) brought *results* (such as the self-sufficient agrarian economy) that contributed to—helped *cause*—the rise of Benedictine monasticism. In short, *a historical development can usually be viewed as a cause or an effect, depending on what question is being answered.*

Exercise A

Read the following passage once as a whole. Read it a second time to underline or highlight it in terms of main points identified as effects or results. Consider numbering the effects in the margin. Then do Exercise B at the end of the passage.

The effects of the invention of movable-type printing were not felt overnight. Nevertheless, within a half-century of the publication of Gutenberg's Bible of 1456, movable type brought about radical changes. Printing transformed both the private and the public lives of Europeans. Governments that "had employed the cumbersome methods of manuscripts to communicate with their subjects switched quickly to print to announce declarations of war, publish battle accounts, promulgate treaties or argue disputed points in pamphlet form. Theirs was an effort 'to win the psychological war.' " Printing made propaganda possible, emphasizing differences between various groups, such as Crown and nobility, church and state. These differences laid the basis for the formation of distinct political parties. Printed materials reached an invisible public, allowing silent individuals to join causes and groups of individuals widely separated by geography to form a common identity; this new group consciousness could compete with older, localized loyalties.

Printing also stimulated the literacy of lay people and eventually came to have a deep effect on their private lives. Although most of the earliest books and pamphlets dealt with religious subjects, students, housewives, businessmen, and upper- and middle-class people sought books on all subjects. Printers responded with moralizing, medical, practical, and travel manuals. Pornography as well as piety assumed new forms. Broadsides and flysheets allowed great public festivals, religious ceremonies, and political events to be experienced vicariously by the stay-at-home. Since books and printed materials were read aloud to the illiterate, print bridged the gap between written and oral cultures.

Exercise B

Study the last paragraph again. Can you see how it is a good example of the historical interaction of cause and effect? Do you see how a given development is an effect or a cause *depending on what historical question is being asked?* Be prepared for such "reversals" in the text, in lecture and class discussion, and on exams.

Hint: In the last paragraph, what is an *effect* of the invention of the printing press? (Ideas could be spread more rapidly.) What "stimulated"—helped *cause*—the spread of literacy? (The invention of the printing press. The authors develop this point further in Chapter 14.)

Chapter 14
Reform and Renewal in the Christian Church

Chapter Questions

After reading and studying this chapter you should be able to answer the following questions:

What late medieval religious developments paved the way for the adoption and spread of Protestant thought? What role did social and political factors play in the several reformations? What were the consequences of religious division? Why did Luther's ideas trigger political, social, and economic reactions and how did the Catholic church respond?

Chapter Summary

A great religious upheaval called the Protestant Reformation ended the centuries-long religious unity of Europe and resulted in a number of important political changes. In the sixteenth century, cries for reform were nothing new, but this time they resulted in revolution. There were a number of signs of disorder within the church, pointing to the need for moral and administrative reform. For example, it was the granting of indulgences that propelled Martin Luther into the movement for doctrinal change in the church. Luther had come to the conclusion that salvation could not come by good works or indulgences, but only through faith. This was to be one of the fundamental tenets of Protestantism and one of the ideas that pushed Luther and the German nobility to revolt against not only Rome but Rome's secular ally, the Holy Roman Emperor.

It is important to recognize that Luther's challenge to the authority of the church and to Catholic unity in Europe invited and supported an attack on the emperor by the German nobility. The pope and the emperor, as separate powers and allies, represented religious and political unity and conformity in Germany. Thus, the victory of Luther and the nobility was a victory for decentralized authority. It meant the collapse of Germany as a unified power in Europe. This is one reason Catholic France usually supported the German Protestants in their quarrel with Rome.

Outside of Germany the Protestant reformer Calvin had a greater impact on Europe than Luther. Calvin's harsh and dogmatic religion spread from Geneva into northern Europe, England, and Scotland. It was England, in fact, that eventually became the political center of Protestantism. Initiated by Henry VIII, the English Protestant Reformation was at first motivated by the personal and political interests of the king himself. The type of Protestantism eventually adopted by the Church of England was much more moderate—and closer to Catholicism—than that of Scotland.

With the Council of Trent of 1545–1563, the Catholic church, finding the Habsburgs unable to destroy the heretical Protestantism, launched a massive and partly successful Counter-Reformation to convince dissidents to return to the church.

All in all, Protestantism developed and spread for economic and political reasons as well as religious ones. In the end, Protestantism meant greater spiritual freedom for some individuals, but spiritual disunity and disorganization for Europe as a whole. In England, Scotland, the Scandinavian countries, and elsewhere, it contributed to the power of the nation and thus meant a further political division of Europe, while in Germany it slowed down the movement toward nationhood.

Study Outline

Use this outline to preview the chapter before you read a particular section in your textbook and then as a self-check to test your reading comprehension after you have read the chapter section.

I. The condition of the church (ca 1400–1517)
   A. The declining prestige of the church
      1. The Babylonian Captivity and the Great Schism damaged the church's prestige.
      2. Secular humanists satirized and denounced moral corruption within the church.
   B. Signs of disorder in the early sixteenth century
      1. The parish clergy, largely poor peasants, brought spiritual help to the people.
      2. Critics of the church wanted moral and administrative reform in three areas.
         a. Clerical immorality (neglect of celibacy, drunkenness, gambling) created a scandal among the faithful.
         b. The lack of education of the clergy and law standards of ordination were condemned by Christian humanists.
         c. The absenteeism, pluralism (holding of several benefices, or offices), and wealth of the greater clergy bore little resemblance to Christian gospel.
      2. The prelates and popes of the period, often members of the nobility, lived in splendor and moral corruption.
   C. Signs of vitality in the late fifteenth and early sixteenth centuries
      1. Sixteenth-century Europe remained deeply religious, and calls for reform testify to the spiritual vitality of the church.
      2. New organizations were formed to educate and minister to the poor.
         a. The Brethren of the Common Life in Holland lived simply and sought to make religion a personal, inner experience based on following the scriptures.
         b. *The Imitation of Christ* by Thomas à Kempis urged Christians to seek perfection in a simple way of life.
         c. The Oratories of Dive Love in Italy were groups of priests who worked to revive the church through prayer and preaching.
      3. Pope Julius II summoned an ecumenical council on reform in the church called the Lateran Council (1512–1527).

II. Martin Luther and the birth of Protestantism
   A. Luther's early years
      1. Luther was a German monk and professor of religion whose search for salvation led him to the letters of St. Paul.
      2. He concluded that faith was central to Christianity and the only means of salvation.
   B. Luther's Ninety-five Theses (October 1517)
      1. Luther's opposition to the sale of indulgences (remissions of penalties for sin) prompted his fight with Rome.
      2. His Ninety-five Theses, or propositions on indulgences, raised many theological issues and initiated a long period of debate in Europe.
         a. Luther rejected the idea that salvation could be achieved by good works, such as indulgences.
         b. He also criticized papal wealth.
      3. Luther later denied the authority of the pope and was excommunicated and declared an outlaw by Charles V at Worms in 1521.
   C. Basic theological tenets of Protestantism
      1. Protestant thought was set forth in the Confession of Augsburg, in which Luther provided new answers to four basic theological issues.
         a. He believed that salvation derived through faith alone, not faith and good works.
         b. He stated that religious authority rests with the Bible, not the pope.
         c. He believed that the church consists of the entire community of Christian believers.
         d. And he believed that all work is sacred and everyone should serve God in his or her individual vocation.
      2. Protestantism, therefore, was a reformulation of Christian beliefs and practices
III. The social impact of Luther's beliefs
   A. By 1521 Luther's religious ideas had a vast following among all social classes.
      1. Luther's ideas were popular because of widespread resentment of clerical privileges and wealth.
      2. Luther's ideas attracted many preachers, and they became Protestant leaders.
      3. Peasants cited Luther's theology as part of their demands for economic reforms.
         a. Luther did not support the peasants' revolts; he believed in obedience to civil authority.
         b. Widespread peasant revolts in 1525 were brutally crushed, but some land was returned to common use.
      4. Luther's greatest weapon was his mastery of the language, and his words were spread by the advent of printing.
         a. Zwingli and Calvin were greatly influenced by his writings.
         b. The publication of Luther's German translation of the New Testament in 1523 democratized religion.
         c. Catechisms and hymns enabled people, especially the young, to remember central points of doctrine.
   B. Luther's impact on women
      1. Luther gave dignity to domestic work, stressed the idea of marriage and the Christian home, ended confession, and encouraged education for girls.

      2. Luther held enlightened views on sex and marriage, although he claimed that women should be no more than efficient wives.

IV. Germany and the Protestant Reformation
   A. The Holy Roman Empire in the fourteenth and fifteenth centuries
      1. The Golden Bull of 1356 gave each of the seven electors virtual sovereignty.
      2. Localism and chronic disorder allowed the nobility to strengthen their territories and reduced the authority of the emperor.
   B. The rise of the Habsburg dynasty
      1. The Habsburgs gave unity to much of Europe, especially with the marriage of Maximilian I of Austria and Mary of Burgundy in 1477.
      2. Charles V, their grandson, inherited much of Europe and was committed to the idea of its religious and political unity.
   C. The political impact of Luther's beliefs
      1. The Protestant Reformation stirred nationalistic feelings in Germany against the wealthy Italian papacy.
      2. Luther's appeal to patriotism earned him the support of the princes, who used religion as a means of gaining more political independence and preventing the flow of German money to Rome.
      3. The Protestant movement proved to be a political disaster for Germany.
         a. The dynastic Habsburg-Valois wars advanced the cause of Protestantism and promoted the political fragmentation of Germany.
         b. By the Peace of Augsburg of 1555, Charles recognized Lutheranism as a legal religion and each prince was permitted to determine the religion of his territory.

V. The Growth of the Protestant Reformation
   A. Calvinism
      1. Calvin believed that God selects certain people to do his work and that he was selected to reform the church.
      2. Under Calvin, Geneva became a theocracy, in which the state was subordinate to the church.
      3. Calvin's central ideas, expressed in *The Institutes of Christian Religion*, were his belief in the omnipotence of God, the insignificance of humanity, and predestination.
      4. Austere living and intolerance of dissenters characterized Calvin's Geneva.
         a. The Genevan Consistory monitored the private morals of citizens.
         b. Michael Servetus was burned at the stake for denying the Christian dogma of the Trinity and rejecting child baptism.
      5. The city of Geneva was the model for international Protestantism, and Calvinism, with its emphasis on the work ethic, became the most dynamic and influential form of Protestantism.
   B. The Anabaptists
      1. This Protestant sect believed in adult baptism, revelation, religious tolerance, pacifism, and the separation of church and state.
      2. Their beliefs and practices were too radical for the times, and they were bitterly persecuted.

C. The English Reformation
1. The Lollards, although driven underground in the fifteenth century, survived and stressed the idea of a direct relationship between the individual and God.
2. The English humanist William Tyndale began printing an English translation of the New Testament in 1525.
3. The wealth and corruption of the clergy, as exemplified by Thomas Wolsey, stirred much resentment.
4. Henry VIII desired a divorce from his queen, Catherine, daughter of Ferdinand and Isabella of Spain, so he could marry Anne Boleyn.
5. Pope Clement VII (who did not wish to admit papal error) refused to annul Henry's marriage to Catherine.
6. Archbishop Cranmer, however, engineered the divorce.
7. The result was the nationalization of the English church and a break with Rome as Henry used Parliament to legalize the Reformation.
   a. Henry needed money so he dissolved the monasteries and confiscated their lands, but this did not lead to more equal land distribution.
   b. Some traditional Catholic practices, such as confession and the doctrine of transubstantiation, were maintained.
   c. Nationalization of the church led to changes in governmental administration, resulting in greater efficiency and economy.
8. Under Edward VI, Henry's heir, England shifted closer to Protestantism.
9. Mary Tudor attempted to bring Catholicism back to England.
10. Under Elizabeth I a religious settlement requiring outward conformity to the Church of England was made.

D. The establishment of the Church of Scotland
1. Scotland was an extreme case of clerical abuse and corruption.
2. John Knox brought Calvinism to Scotland from Geneva.
3. The Presbyterian church became the national church of Scotland.

E. Protestantism in Ireland
1. The English ruling class in Ireland adopted the new faith.
2. Most of the Irish people defiantly remained Catholic.

F. Lutheranism in Scandinavia
1. In Sweden, Norway, and Denmark the monarchy led the religious reformation.
2. The result was Lutheran state churches.

VI. The Catholic and the Counter-Reformations
A. There were two types of reform within the Catholic church in the sixteenth and seventeenth centuries.
1. The Catholic Reformation sought to stimulate a new religious fervor.
2. The Counter-Reformation started in the 1540s as a reaction to Protestantism and progressed simultaneously with the Catholic Reformation.

B. The slowness of institutional reform
1. Too often the popes were preoccupied with politics or sensual pleasures.
2. Popes resisted calls for the formation of a general council because it would limit their authority.

C. The Council of Trent
1. Pope Paul III called the Council of Trent (1545–1563).
   a. An attempt to reconcile with the Protestants failed.

      b.   International politics hindered the theological debates.
    2.   Nonetheless, the principle of papal authority was maintained, considerable reform was undertaken, and the spiritual renewal of the church was begun.
      a.   Tridentine decrees forbade the sale of indulgences and outlawed pluralism and simony.
      b.   Attempts were made to curb clerical immorality and to encourage education.
      c.   Great emphasis was placed on preaching.
  D. New religious orders
    1.   The Ursuline order of nuns gained enormous prestige for the education of women.
      a.   The Ursulines sought to re-Christianize society by training future wives and mothers.
      b.   The Ursulines spread to France and North America.
    2.   The Society of Jesus played a strong international role in resisting Protestantism.
      a.   Obedience was the foundation of the Jesuit tradition.
      b.   With their schools, political influence, and missionary work, they brought many people into the Catholic fold.
  E. The Sacred Congregation of the Holy Office
    1.   This group, established by Pope Paul III in 1542, carried out the Roman Inquisition as a way to combat heresy.
    2.   It had the power to arrest, imprison, and execute, but its influence was confined to papal territories.

Review Questions

Check your understanding of this chapter by answering the following questions.

1.   What was the condition of the church in 1517? Were the village clergy useless and corrupt?
2.   What were some of the signs of disorder within the early sixteenth-century church? What impact did church wealth have on the condition of the church?
3.   What were some of the signs of religious vitality in fifteenth- and early sixteenth-century society?
4.   What circumstances prompted Luther to post his Ninety-five Theses?
5.   Describe the practice of indulgence selling. What authority did Luther question and on what argument did he base his position?
6.   What were Luther's answers, as delineated in the Confession of Augsburg, to the four basic theological issues?
7.   What effect did Luther's concept of state authority over church authority have on German society and German history?
8.   Why was the condemnation of Luther in 1521 at Worms not enforced by the German nobility? What was the result?
9.   Why was Calvin's Geneva called "the city that was a church"? What is a theocracy?
10. In what ways were the Anabaptists radical for their time? Why did many of their beliefs cause them to be bitterly persecuted?
11. What were the causes and results of the English Reformation?
12. What was the Elizabethan Settlement?

13. What were the repercussions of the marriage of Maximilian and Mary? What impact did this marriage have on France?
14. Charles V has been considered a medieval emperor. In what respects is this true? What were the origins of his empire?
15. What were the goals and methods of the Ursuline order and the Society of Jesus?
16. Why was reform within the Catholic church often unwelcome and slow in coming?
17. What were the achievements of the Council of Trent?
18. What was the Inquisition? How extensive was its power?

Study-Review Exercises

Identify and explain the significance of the following people and terms.

Brethren of the Common Life

John Knox

Pope Paul III

Archbishop Cranmer

John Tetzel

Martin Luther

Angela Merici

Henry VIII

Charles V

Mary Tudor

Pope Alexander VI

Council of Trent

Counter-Reformation

Elizabethan Settlement

Act of Restraint of Appeals

pluralism

benefices

Peace of Augsburg

Ninety-five Theses

preacherships

Explain the subject matter and historical significance of the following works.
The Imitation of Christ

Appeal to the Christian Nobility of the German Nation

The Institutes of the Christian Religion

Define the basic beliefs of the following Christian religions and churches.
Roman Catholicism

Lutheranism

Calvinism

Anabaptism

Church of England

Presbyterian Church of Scotland

Test your understanding of the chapter by providing the correct answers.

1. The Council of Trent *did/did not* reaffirm the seven sacraments, the validity of tradition, and transubstantiation.

2. The English Supremacy Act of 1534 declared the _____ to be the Supreme Head of the Church of England.

3. For the most part, the English Reformation under Henry VIII dealt with *political/theological* issues.

4. He wrote: "How comes it that we Germans must put up with such robbery and such

   extortion of our property at the hands of the pope?" _____

5. This pope's name became a synonym for moral corruption. _____

6. Mary Tudor, the English queen and daughter of Henry VIII, *was/was not* interested in the restoration of Catholicism in England.

7. In general, Protestantism tended to *strengthen/weaken* Germany as a political unit.

8. During the reign of Elizabeth, the English church moved in a moderately *Protestant/Catholic* direction.

Multiple-Choice Questions

1. Under the Presbyterian form of church government, the church is governed by
   a. bishops.
   b. the king of Scotland.
   c. ministers.
   d. the people.

2. Which one of the following did *not* come from the Anabaptist tradition?
   a. Congregationalists
   b. Puritans
   c. Quakers
   d. Jesuits

3. According to Luther, salvation comes through
   a. good works.
   b. faith.
   c. indulgences.
   d. a saintly life.

4. The cornerstone of Calvin's theology was his belief in
   a. predestination.
   b. indulgences.
   c. the basic goodness of man.
   d. religious tolerance and freedom.

5. John Knox and the Reformation movement in Scotland were most influenced by which of the following?
   a. Catholicism
   b. Calvinism
   c. Lutheranism
   d. The Church of England

6. Which of the following is *not* identified with corrupt practices in the early sixteenth-century church?
   a. Pluralism
   b. The Brethren of the Common Life
   c. Pope Alexander VI
   d. Absenteeism

7. Which of the following clearly did *not* support Luther?
   a. The German peasants
   b. The German nobility
   c. Charles V
   d. Ulrich Zwingli

8. Overall, Henry VIII's religious reformation in England occurred
   a. strictly for economic reasons.
   b. for religious reasons.
   c. mostly for political reasons.
   d. mostly for diplomatic reasons.

9. The Reformation in Germany resulted in
   a. a politically weaker Germany.
   b. a politically stronger Germany.
   c. no political changes of importance.
   d. a victory for imperial centralization.

10. The great Christian humanists of the fifteenth and sixteenth centuries believed that reform could be achieved through
    a. the use of violent revolution.
    b. education and social change.
    c. mass support of the church hierarchy.
    d. the election of a new pope.

11. Luther tacked his Ninety-five Theses to the door in Wittenberg as a response to
    a. the sale of indulgences and papal wealth.
    b. a revelation he experienced instructing him to start a new church.
    c. the illiteracy of the clergy.
    d. the oppressive rule of Frederick of Saxony.

12. The peasants who revolted in 1525 wanted all of the following *except*
    a. the abolition of serfdom.
    b. the reform of the clergy.
    c. the suppression of Luther's movement.
    d. an end to taxes and tithes.

13. Luther's success was a result of all of the following *except*
    a. his appointment by the pope to a church position.
    b. the development of the printing press.
    c. his appeal to the nobility and the middle classes.
    d. a strong command of language.

14. The Holy Roman Emperor who tried to suppress the Lutheran revolt was
    a. Christian III.
    b. Charles V.
    c. Adrian VI.
    d. Henry VII.

15. By 1555 the Protestant Reformation had spread to all but
    a. England.
    b. Scandinavia.
    c. Spain.
    d. Scotland.

16. The chief center of the Protestant reformers in the sixteenth century was
    a. Paris.
    b. Geneva.
    c. Zurich.
    d. Cologne.

17. The Anabaptists appealed to
    a. the nobility.
    b. the poor, uneducated, and unemployed.
    c. the intellectuals.
    d. the merchant classes.

18. Henry VIII dissolved the monasteries largely because
    a. he wanted to distribute the land more equitably.
    b. they were symbolic of papal authority.
    c. he needed the wealth they would bring.
    d. they were a burden on the state.

19. The Scandinavian countries were most influenced by the religious beliefs of
    a. Martin Luther.
    b. John Knox.
    c. Olaus Petri.
    d. the Jesuits.

20. A vow of the Jesuit order making it uniquely different from others was
    a. poverty.
    b. chastity.
    c. obedience to the pope.
    d. pacifism.

21. Luther's German translation of the New Testament
    a. proved that the state was supreme over the church.
    b. convinced women that they had no constructive role in life.
    c. democratized religion.
    d. turned the common people away from the church.

22. The marriage of Maxmilian of Habsburg and Mary of Burgandy in 1477 was a decisive event in early modern history in that
    a. Austria became an international power.
    b. France emerged as the leading continental power.
    c. England became tied to Spain.
    d. German principalities became tied to Austria.

23. The man who wrote *The Institutes of the Christian Religion* and did the most to internationalize Protestantism was
    a. John Knox
    b. Martin Luther
    c. Ulrich Zwingli
    d. John Calvin

24. Henry VIII of England's divorce from his wife Catherine was complicated by the fact that Catherine's nephew was
    a. the pope.
    b. the emperor, Charles V.
    c. the king of France.
    d. the leader of the English Parliament.

25. The *Index of Prohibited Books* was published by
    a. the Calvinist government of Geneva.
    b. the princes who supported Luther.
    c. the Sacred Congregation of the Holy Office of the pope.
    d. the Anabaptists.

Major Political Ideas

1. In what ways was Protestantism a political idea? Did it help or hinder the development of the nation-state? Compare and contrast the religious settlements made in the German states, England, Scotland, and Ireland. Why was Protestantism on the one hand a source of national strength and on the other a source of national weakness?

2. What was the political message behind Luther's 1520 book *Appeal to the Christian Nobility of the German Nation*?

Issues for Essays and Discussion

Was the Reformation a blessing or a disaster for the people of Europe? Support your argument by making specific reference to Germany, England, and Scotland. What impact did the Reformation have on the power of the monarchs, the well-being of the common man and woman, and the overall balance of European power?

Interpretation of Visual Sources

Study the sixteenth-century woodcut titled *The Folly of Indulgences* on page 429 of your textbook. Describe the participants and the event. What is the message? What image of the church does this woodcut present to the popular mind? How important do you believe such prints were in forming public opinion?

Geography

On Outline Map 14.2 provided, and using maps 14.1 and 14.2 in the textbook as a reference, mark the following: the boundary of the Holy Roman Empire, the territory under the control of Charles V, the approximate areas of Lutheran influence, the approximate areas of Calvinist influence.

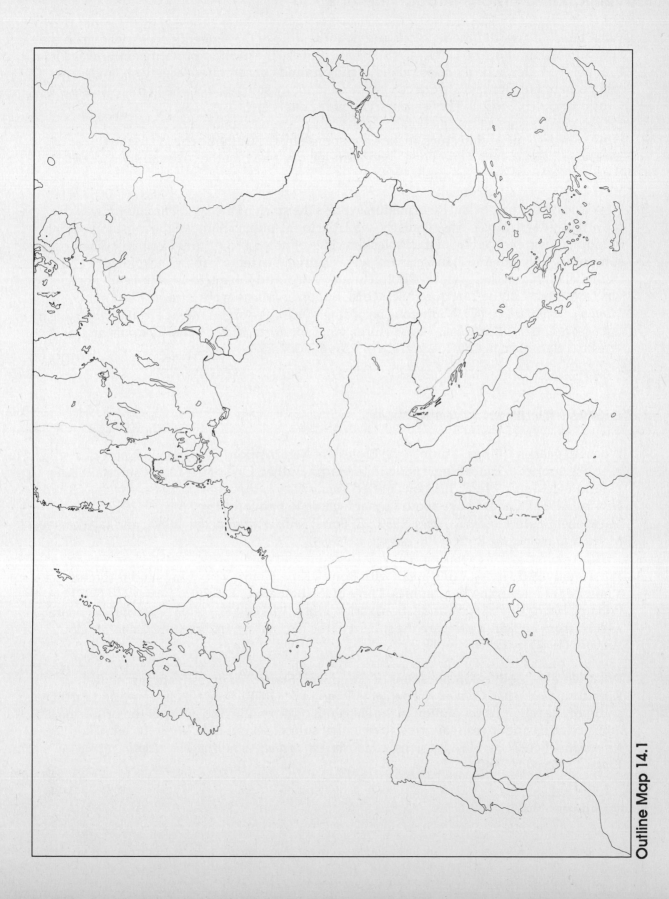

Understanding History Through the Arts

1. What effect, if any, did the religious and political strife of the sixteenth century have on the arts? In northern Europe in the later sixteenth century the most important painter was Pieter Bruegel the Elder, who avoided religious subjects and concentrated largely on landscapes and peasant life. Bruegel's work can be found in many sources, but one of the best is F. Grossmann, ed., *Bruegel, The Paintings: Complete Edition* (1956).

2. How was baroque architecture, in part, a response by the Catholic church to the threat of heresy and loss of believers? For a good introductory essay on the baroque style, see H. W. Janson, *History of Art*, Chapter 6 (1963).

3. How does the music of the Reformation express the spirit of the age? The church was the only place where music was regularly available to the public. Some of the most important baroque music evolved from the Protestant cities of north and central Germany. The leading composers of organ music in Germany were Dietrich Buxtehude in Lübeck, Johann Pachebell in Nuremberg, George Bohm in Luneburg, and Johann Sebastian Bach. For a written account of the baroque style, see M. Bukofzer, *Music in the Baroque Era: From Monteverdi to Bach* (1947). Numerous recording of baroque organ music are available; one of the best is *Dietrich Buxtehude, Organ Works*, vol. 1, performed by Michel Chapuis on Das Alte Werke, Telefunken. 6.42001.AF., and vol. 2. as 6.35307.EK.

Problems for Further Investigation

1. What led Martin Luther to launch the Protestant Reformation? Few men in history have been the subject of more biographies than Martin Luther. One of the most important is a psychological study by E. Erikson entitled *Young Man Luther: A Study in Psychoanalysis and History** (1962). Other books about Luther include R. Bainton, *Here I Stand** (1950); E. Schwiebert, *Luther and His Times* (1952); G. Forel, *Faith Active in Love* (1954); and J. Atkinson, *Martin Luther and the Birth of Protestantism** (1968).

2. What motivated Henry VIII's break with Rome? King Henry VIII of England is the subject of a number of interesting biographies. Three of the best are L. B. Smith, *Henry VIII* (1971); A. F. Pollard, *Henry VIII** (1905); and J. Scarisbrick, *Henry VIII* (1968). Henry's marital problems, as seen from his wife's side, are the subject of the fascinating and exciting *Catherine Of Aragon** (1941) by G. Mattingly.

3. What were the political implications of Calvinism? Start your investigation with R. Kingdom, *Calvin and Calvinism: Sources of Democracy** (1970). Students interested in further study of the religious revolution of the sixteenth century will find some of the problems of interpretation and investigation relative to that subject set out in L. W. Spitz, ed., *The Reformation** (1972), and K. Sessions, ed., *Reformation and Authority: The Meaning of the Peasant's Revolt** (1968).

---

*Available in paperback.

4. What is the relationship between the Protestant religion and economic growth? This historical problem is defined in R. Green, ed., *Protestantism, Capitalism, and Social Science* (1973).

5. How successful was the Counter-Reformation? Students interested in the Counter-Reformation should begin with E. M. Bums, *The Counter Reformation** (1964).

---

*Available in paperback.

Primary Sources
Two Sixteenth-Century Thinkers

Niccolò Machiavelli and Martin Luther were both mirrors of the sixteenth century, and both contributed to a new view of the relationship between man, God, and the state. However, Machiavelli is viewed as a man of the Renaissance, while Luther is largely associated with the Reformation. The following selections illustrate some of the similarities and some of the differences in their thought.

Niccolò Machiavelli, *The Prince**

Machiavelli was a political analyist, not a theoretician. He based his observations on politics and government and on practical reality, not an ideal state. What does he say here about effective political leadership? How could this be misconstrued to support authoritarian rule?

Here the question arises: is it better to be loved than feared, or vice versa? I don't doubt that every prince would like to have both; but since it is hard to accommodate these qualities, if you have to make a choice, to be feared is much safer than to be loved. For it is a good general rule about men, that they are ungrateful, fickle, liars, and deceivers, fearful of danger and greedy for gain. While you serve their welfare, they are all yours, offering their blood, their belongings, their lives, and their children's lives, as we noted above—so long as the danger is remote. But when the danger is close at hand, they turn against you. Then, any prince who has relied on their words and has made no other preparations will come to grief; because friendships that are bought at a price, and not with greatness and nobility of soul, may be paid for but they are not acquired, and they cannot be used in time of need. People are less concerned with offending a man who makes himself loved than one who makes himself feared: the reason is that love is a link of obligation which men, because they are rotten, will break any time they think doing so serves their advantage; but fear involves dread of punishment, from which they can never escape.

Still, a prince should make himself feared in such a way that, even if he gets no love, he gets no hate either; because it is perfectly possible to be feared and not hated, and this will be the

---

Source: Reprinted from *The Prince* by Niccolò Machiavelli, Translated and Edited by Robert M. Adams. A Norton Critical Edition. With the permission of W. W. Norton & Company, Inc. Copyright © 1977 by W. W. Norton & Company, Inc.

result if only the prince will keep his hands off the property of his subjects or citizens, and off their women. When he does have to shed blood, he should be sure to have a strong justification and manifest cause; but above all, he should not confiscate people's property, because men are quicker to forget the death of a father than the loss of a patrimony. Besides, pretexts for confiscation are always plentiful; it never fails that a prince who starts living by plunder can find reasons to rob someone else. Excuses for proceeding against someone's life are much rarer and more quickly exhausted.

But a prince at the head of his armies and commanding a multitude of soldiers should not care a bit if he is considered cruel; without such a reputation, he could never hold his army together and ready for action. Among the marvelous deeds of Hannibal, this was prime: that, having an immense army, which included men of many different races and nations, and which he led to battle in distant countries, he never allowed them to fight among themselves or to rise against him, whether his fortune was good or bad. The reason for this could only be his inhuman cruelty, which, along with his countless other talents, [virtù], made him an object of awe and terror to his soldiers; and without the cruelty, his other qualities [le altre sua virtù] would never have sufficed. The historians who pass snap judgements on these matters admire his accomplishments and at the same time condemn the cruelty which was their main cause.

When I say, "His other qualities would never have sufficed," we can see that this is true from the example of Scipio, an outstanding man not only among those of his own time, but in all recorded history; yet his armies revolted in Spain, for no other reason than his excessive leniency in allowing his soldiers more freedom than military discipline permits. Fabius Maximus rebuked him in the senate for his failing, calling him the corrupter of the Roman armies. When a lieutenant of Scipio's plundered the Locrians, he took no action in behalf of the people; and did nothing to discipline that insolent lieutenant; again, this was the result of his easygoing nature. Indeed, when someone in the senate wanted to excuse him on this occasion, he said there are many men who knew better how to avoid error themselves than how to correct error in others. Such a soft temper would in time have tarnished the fame and glory of Scipio, had he brought it to the office of emperor; but as he lived under the control of the senate, this harmful quality of his not only remained hidden but was considered creditable.

Returning to the question of being feared or loved, I conclude that since men love at their own inclination but can be made to fear at the inclination of the prince, a shrewd prince will lay his foundations so what is under his own control, not on what is controlled by others. He should simply take pains not to be hated, as I said.

Sermon Preached by Martin Luther in Erfurt, Germany, 1521*

On his way to the Diet of Worms in 1521, Martin Luther preached this sermon to the citizens of Erfurt. What teachings of the Roman church did he criticize? What ideas of his own did he emphasize? And how did Luther think salvation was to be achieved? If you did not know who had written this sermon, how would you describe its author's mind and education?

Now it is clear and manifest that every person likes to think that he will be saved and attain to eternal salvation. This is what I propose to discuss now.

You also know that all philosophers, doctors and writers have studiously endeavored to teach and write what attitude man should take to piety. They have gone to great trouble, but, as is evident, to little avail. Now genuine and true piety consists of two kinds of work: those done for others, which are the right kind, and those done for ourselves, which are unimportant. In order to find a foundation, one man builds churches; another goes on a pilgrimage to St. James' or St. Peter's; a third fasts or prays, wears a cowl, goes barefoot, or does something else of the kind. Such works are nothing whatever and must be completely destroyed. Mark these words: none of our works have any power whatsoever. For God has chosen a man, the Lord Christ Jesus, to crush death, destroy sin, and shatter hell, since there was no one before he came who did not inevitably belong to the devil. The devil therefore thought he would get a hold upon the Lord when he hung between the two thieves and was suffering the most contemptible and disgraceful of deaths, which was cursed both by God and by men [cf. Deut. 21:23; Gal. 3:13]. But the Godhead was so strong that death, sin, and even hell were destroyed.

Therefore you should note well the words which Paul writes to the Romans [Rom. 5:12–21]. Our sins have their sources in Adam, and because Adam ate the apple, we have inherited sin from him. But Christ has shattered death for our sake, in order that we might be saved by his works, which are alien to us, and not by our works.

But the papal dominion treats us altogether differently. It makes rules about fasting, praying, and butter-eating, so that whoever keeps the commandments of the pope will be saved and whoever does not keep them belongs to the devil. It thus seduces the people with the delusion that goodness and salvation lies in their own works. But I say that none of the saints, no matter how holy they were, attained salvation by their works. Even the holy mother of God did not become good, was not saved, by her virginity or her motherhood, but rather by the will of faith and the works of God, and not by her purity, or her own works. Therefore, mark me well: this is the reason why salvation does not lie in our own works, no matter what they are; it cannot and will not be effected without faith.

Now, someone may say: Look, my friend, you are saying a lot about faith, and claiming that our salvation depends solely upon it; now, I ask you, how does one come to faith? I will tell you. Our Lord Christ said, "Peace be with you. Behold my hands, etc." [John 20:26–27]. [In other words, he is saying:] Look, man, I am the only one who has taken away your sins and redeemed you, etc.; now be at peace. Just as you inherited sin from Adam—not that you committed it, for I did not eat the apple, any more than you did, and yet this is how we came to be in sin—so we have not suffered [as Christ did], and therefore we were made free from death and sin by God's work, not by our works. Therefore God says: Behold, man, I am your redemption [cf. Isa. 43:3]; just as Paul said to the Corinthians: Christ is our justification and redemption, etc. [I Cor. 1:30]. Christ is our justification and redemption, as Paul says in this passage. And here our [Roman] masters say: Yes, Redemptor, Redeemer; this is true, but it is not enough.

Therefore, I say again: Alien works, these made us good! Our Lord Christ says: I am your justification. I have destroyed the sins you have upon you. Therefore only believe in me; believe that I am he who has done this; then you will be justified. For it is written, Justicia est fides, righteousness is identical with faith and comes through faith. Therefore, if we want to have faith, we should believe the gospel, Paul, etc., and not the papal breves, or the decretals, but rather guard ourselves against them as against fire. For everything that comes from the pope cries out: Give, give; and if you refuse, you are of the devil. It would be a small matter if they were only exploiting the people. But, unfortunately, it is the greatest evil in the world to lead the people to believe that outward works can save or make a man good.

In conclusion, then, every single person should reflect and remember that we cannot help ourselves, but only God, and also that our works are utterly worthless. So shall we have the peace of God. And every person should so perform his work that it benefits not only himself alone, but also another, his neighbor. If he is rich, his wealth should benefit the poor. If he is poor, his service should benefit the rich. When persons are servants or maidservants, their work should benefit their master. Thus no one's work should benefit him alone; for when you note that you are serving only your own advantage, then your service is false. I am not troubled; I know very well what man-made laws are. Let the pope issue as many laws as he likes, I will keep them all so far as I please.

Therefore, dear friends, remember that God has risen up for our sakes. Therefore let us also arise to be helpful to the weak in faith, and so direct our work that God may be pleased with it. So shall we receive the peace he has given to us today. May God grant us this every day. Amen.

Chapter 15
The Age of European Expansion and Religious Wars

Chapter Questions

After reading and studying this chapter you should be able to answer the following questions:

Why and how did Europeans gain control over distant continents? What effect did overseas expansion have on Europe and on conquered societies? What were the causes of religious wars in France, the Netherlands, and Germany? How did the religious wars affect the status of women? How and why did African slave labor become the dominant form of labor organization in the New World? What religious and intellectual developments led to the growth of skepticism? What literary masterpieces did this period produce?

Chapter Summary

In this chapter we see how the trends in the High Middle Ages toward centralized nations ruled by powerful kings and toward European territorial expansion were revitalized. The growth of royal power and the consolidation of the state in Spain, France, and England accompanied and supported world exploration and a long period of European war.

The Portuguese were the first to push out into the Atlantic, but it was Spain, following close behind, that built a New World empire that provided the economic basis for a period of Spanish supremacy in European affairs. In the short run, Spanish gold and silver from the New World made the Spanish Netherlands the financial and manufacturing center of Europe, and Spain became Europe's greatest military power. In the long run, however, overseas expansion ruined the Spanish economy, created massive European inflation, and brought the end of Spain's empire in Europe.

The attempts by Catholic monarchs to re-establish European religious unity and by both Catholic and Protestant monarchs to establish strong centralized states led to many wars among the European states. Spain's attempt to keep religious and political unity within her empire led to a long war in the Netherlands—a war that pulled England over to the side of the Protestant Dutch. There was bitter civil war in France, which finally came to an end with the reign of

Henry of Navarre and the Edict of Nantes in 1598. The Thirty Years' War in Germany from 1618 to 1648 left that area a political and economic shambles.

The sixteenth century also saw a vast increase in witch-hunting and the emergence of modern racism, sexism, and skepticism. Generally, the power and status of women in this period did not change. Protestantism meant a more positive attitude toward marriage, but the revival of the idea that women were the source of evil and the end of the religious orders for women caused them to become increasingly powerless in society. North American slavery and racism had their origins in the labor problems in America and in Christian and Muslim racial attitudes. Skepticism was an intellectual reaction to the fanaticism of both Protestants and Catholics and a sign of things to come, while the Renaissance tradition was carried on by Shakespeare's work in early sixteenth-century England.

Study Outline

Use this outline to preview the chapter before you read a particular section in your textbook and then as a self-check to test your reading comprehension after you have read the chapter section.

I. Discovery, reconnaissance, and expansion (1450–1650)
   A. Overseas exploration and conquest
      1. The outward expansion of Europe began with the Viking voyages, then the Crusades, but the presence of the Ottoman Turks in the East frightened the Europeans and forced their attention westward.
      2. Political centralization in Spain, France, and England prepared the way for expansion.
      3. The Portuguese, under the leadership of Prince Henry the Navigator, pushed south from North Africa.
         a. By 1500 Portugal controlled the flow of gold to Europe.
         b. Diaz, da Gama, and Cabral established trading routes to India.
         c. The Portuguese gained control of the Indian trade by overpowering Muslim forts in India.
      4. Spain began to play a leading role in exploration and exploitation.
         a. Columbus sailed under the Spanish flag and opened the Caribbean for trade and conversion of the Indians.
         b. Spanish exploitation in the Caribbean led to the destruction of the Indian population.
         c. In 1519 Magellan sailed southwest across the Atlantic for Charles V of Spain; his expedition circumnavigated the earth.
         d. Cortez conquered the Aztec Empire and founded Mexico City as the capital of New Spain.
         e. Pizarro crushed the Inca empire in Peru and opened the Potosí mines, which became the richest silver mines in the New World.
      5. The Low Countries, particularly the cities of Antwerp and Amsterdam, had been since medieval times the center of European trade.
         a. The Dutch East India Company became the major organ of Dutch imperialism.
         b. The Dutch West India Company gained control of much of the African and American trade.

6. France and England made sporadic efforts at exploration and settlement.
B. The explorers' motives
   1. The desire to Christianize the Muslims and pagan peoples played a central role in European expansion.
   2. Limited economic and political opportunity for upper-class men in Spain led to emigration.
   3. Government encouragement was also important.
   4. Renaissance curiosity caused people to seek out new worlds.
   5. Spices were another important incentive.
   6. The economic motive—the quest for material profit—was the basic reason for European exploration and expansion.
C. Technological stimuli to exploration
   1. The development of the cannon aided European expansion.
   2. New sailing and navigational developments, such as the caravel ship, the magnetic compass, and the astrolabe, also aided the expansion.
D. The economic effects of Spain's discoveries in the New World
   1. Enormous amounts of American gold and silver poured into Spain in the sixteenth century.
   2. It is probable that population growth and not the flood of American bullion caused inflation in Spain.
   3. European inflation hurt the poor the most.
E. Colonial administration
   1. The Spanish monarch divided his new world into four viceroyalties, each with a viceroy and *audiencia*, or board of judges that served as an advisory council and judicial body.
   2. The intendants were royal officials responsible directly to the monarch.
   3. The Spanish acted on the mercantilist principle that the colonies existed for the financial benefit of the mother country.
      a. The Crown claimed the *quinto*, one-fifth of all precious metals mined in South America.
      b. The development of native industries were discouraged.
   4. Portuguese administration in Brazil was similar to Spain's, although one unique feature was the thorough mixture of the races.
II. Politics, religion, and war
A. The Spanish-French wars ended in 1559 with a Spanish victory, leading to a variety of wars centering on religious and national issues.
   1. These wars used bigger armies and gunpowder, and led to the need for administrative reorganization.
   2. Governments had to use various propaganda devices, including the printing press, to arouse public opinion.
   3. The Peace of Westphalia (1648) ended religious wars but also ended the idea of a unified Christian society.
B. The origins of difficulties in France (1515–1559)
   1. By 1500, France was recovering from plague and disorder, and the nobility began to lose power.

2. The French kings, such as Francis I and Henry II, continued the policies of centralization and were great patrons of Renaissance art but spent more money than they raised.
3. The wars between France and Emperor Charles V—the Habsburg-Valois wars—were also costly.
4. To raise money, Francis sold public offices and signed the Concordat of Bologna (1516), in which he recognized the supremacy of the papacy in return for the right to appoint French bishops.
   a. This settlement established Catholicism as the state religion in France.
   b. It also perpetuated corruption within the French church.
   c. The corruption made Calvinism attractive to Christians eager for reform: some clergy and members of the middle and artisan classes.
C. Religious riots and civil war in France (1559–1589)
   1. The French nobility, many of them Calvinist, attempted to regain power over a series of weak monarchs.
   2. Frequent religious riots symbolized the struggle for power in the upper classes and serious religious concerns among the lower classes.
   3. The Saint Bartholomew's Day massacre of Calvinists in 1572 led to the War of the Three Henrys, a damaging conflict for secular power.
   4. King Henry IV's Edict of Nantes (1598) saved France from further civil war by allowing Protestants to worship.
D. The Netherlands under Charles V
   1. The Low Countries were part of the Habsburg empire and enjoyed commercial success and relative autonomy.
   2. In 1556 Charles V abdicated and divided his empire between his brother, Ferdinand, and his son, King Philip of Spain.
E. The revolt of the Netherlands (1556–1587)
   1. Calvinism took deep root among the merchants and financiers.
   2. Regent Margaret attempted to destroy Protestantism by establishing the Inquisition in the Netherlands.
   3. She also raised taxes, causing those who opposed the repression of Calvinism to unite with those who opposed the taxes.
   4. Popular support for Protestantism led to the destruction of many Catholic churches.
   5. The duke of Alva and his Spanish troops were sent by Philip II to crush the disturbances in the Low Countries.
   6. Alva's brutal actions only inflamed the religious war, which raged from 1568 to 1578.
   7. The Low Countries were finally split into the Spanish Netherlands in the south, under the control of the Spanish Habsburgs, and the independent United Provinces of the Netherlands in the north.
      a. The north was Protestant and ruled by the commercial aristocracy.
      b. The south was Catholic and ruled by the landed nobility.
   8. Elizabeth I of England supported the northern, or Protestant, cause as a safeguard against Spain attacking England.
      a. The wars in the Low Countries had badly hurt the Enlish economy.
      b. She had her rival Mary, Queen of Scots, beheaded.

F.   Philip II and the Spanish Armada
   1.   Philip II planned war on England for several reasons.
     a.   He wanted to keep England in the Catholic fold.
     b.   He believed he would never conquer the Dutch unless he defeated England first.
   2.   The destruction of the Spanish Armada of 1588 did not mean the end of the war, but it did prevent Philip from forcibly unifying western Europe.
   3.   In 1609, Philip III agreed to a truce, recognizing the independence of the United Provinces.

G.   The Thirty Years' War (1618–1648)
   1.   Protestant Bohemian revolt over religious freedom led to war in Germany.
   2.   The Bohemian phase (1618–1625) was characterized by civil war in Bohemia between the Catholic League and the Protestant Union.
     a.   The Bohemians fought for religious liberty and independence from Habsburg rule.
     b.   Ferdinand II wiped out Protestantism in Bohemia.
   3.   The Danish phase of the war (1625–1629) led to further Catholic victory.
   4.   The Swedish phase of the war (1630–1635) ended the Habsburg plan to unite Germany.
   5.   The French phase (1635–1648) ended with a destroyed Germany and an independent Netherlands.
     a.   The "Peace of Westphalia" recognized the independent authority of the German princes.
     b.   The treaties allowed France to intervene at will in German affairs.
     c.   They also denied the pope the right to participate in German religious affairs.

H.   Germany after the Thirty Years' War
   1.   The war was economically disastrous for Germany.
   2.   The war led to agricultural depression in Germany, which in turn encouraged a return to serfdom for many peasants.

III.   Changing attitudes
  A.   The status of women
   1.   Literature on women and marriage called for a subservient wife, whose household was her first priority, and a protective, firm-ruling, and loyal husband.
     a.   Catholic marriages could not be dissolved, while Protestants held that divorce and remarriage were possible.
     b.   Women did not lose their identity or meaningful work, but their subordinate status did not change.
   2.   Prostitution was common, and brothels were licensed.
   3.   Protestant reformers believed that convents were antifeminist and that women would find freedom in marriage.
   4.   With the closing of convents, marriage became virtually the only occupation for upper-class Protestant women.

  B.   The great European witch hunt
   1.   Growth in religion and the advent of religious struggle led to a rise in the belief in the evil power of witches.
   2.   The thousands of people executed as witches represent society's drift toward social and intellectual conformity.

3. Witch-hunting reflects widespread misogyny and a misunderstanding of women.
C. European slavery and the origins of American racism
    1. Black slavery originated with the end of white slavery (1453) and the widespread need for labor, particularly in the new sugar-producing settlements.
    2. Africans were brought to America to replace the Indians beginning in 1518.
    3. Settlers brought to the Americas the racial attitudes they had absorbed in Europe from Christianity and Islam, which by and large depicted blacks as primitive and inferior.
IV. Literature and art
    A. The origins of modern skepticism in the essays of Montaigne
        1. Skeptics doubt whether definitive knowledge is ever attainable.
        2. Montaigne is the best representative of early modern skepticism and a forerunner of modern attitudes.
            a. In the *Essays* he advocated open-mindedness, tolerance, and rejection of dogmatism.
            b. He rejected the claim that one culture may be superior over another, and he inaugurated an era of doubt.
    B. Elizabethan and Jacobean literature
        1. Shakespeare reflects the Renaissance appreciation of classical culture, individualism, and humanism.
        2. The *Authorized Bible* of King James I (*King James Bible*) is a masterpiece of English vernacular writing.
    C. Baroque art and music
        1. In the late sixteenth century, the papacy and the Jesuits encouraged the growth of an emotional, exuberant art intended to appeal to the senses and kindle the faith of ordinary churchgoers.
        2. The baroque style took definite shape in Italy after 1600 and developed with exceptional vigor in Catholic countries.
            a. Rubens developed a sensuous, colorful style of painting characterized by animated figures and monumental size.
            b. In music the baroque style reached its culmination with Bach.

Review Questions

Check your understanding of this chapter by answering the following questions.

1. Describe the Portuguese explorations. Who were the participants and what were their motives?
2. What role did Antwerp and Amsterdam play in international commerce?
3. Why was there such severe inflation in the sixteenth century?
4. What role did technology play in European expansion?
5. What were the major reasons for European expansion in the fifteenth and sixteenth centuries?
6. What were the causes and consequences of the French civil war of 1559 to 1589? Was the war chiefly a religious or a political event?

7. What were the origins and the outcome of the war between the Netherlands and Spain in the late sixteenth and early seventeenth centuries?
8. What were the circumstances surrounding Elizabeth's decision to aid the United Provinces in their war against Spain? What was the Spanish reaction?
9. Why did Catholic France side with the Protestants in the Thirty Years' War?
10. What were the political, religious, and economic consequences of the Thirty Years' War in Europe?
11. What was the social status of women between 1560 and 1648?
12. What do the witch hunts tell us about social attitudes toward women?
13. What were the origins of North American racism?
14. What is skepticism? Why did faith and religious certainty begin to come to an end in the first part of the seventeenth century?
15. What were the major literary masterpieces of this age? In what ways can Shakespeare be regarded as a true Renaissance man?
16. What was the baroque style?

Study-Review Questions

Define the following key concepts and terms.

mercantilism

inflation

sexism

racism

skepticism

misogyny

baroque

Identify and explain the significance of the following people and terms.

politiques

Elizabeth I of England

Huguenots

Philip II of Spain

Prince Henry the Navigator

Michel de Montaigne

Christopher Columbus

Bartholomew Diaz

Hernando Cortez

Habsburg-Valois wars

quinto

audiencia

corregidores

Thirty Years' War

defeat of the Spanish Armada

Concordat of Bologna

Peace of Westphalia

Saint Bartholomew's Day massacre

War of the Three Henrys

Edict of Nantes

Test your understanding of the chapter by providing the correct answers.

1. The war that brought destruction and political fragmentation to Germany.

   _____

2. The Spanish explorer who conquered the Aztecs. _____

3. The law of 1598 that granted religious freedom to French Protestants.

   _____

4. Spain's golden century. _____

5. The king of Sweden who intervened in the Thirty Years' War. _____

6. After 1551, the seven northern provinces of the Netherlands were called

   _____.

7. The city that became the financial capital of Europe by 1600. _____

8. The monarch of Britain at the time of the Spanish Armada. _____

9. The idea that nothing is completely knowable. _____

10. The emperor who divided the Habsburg empire into two parts. _____

11. The 1516 compromise between church and state in France. _____

12. The first European country to establish sea routes to the east. _____

Multiple-Choice Questions

1. Which of the following was a motive for Portuguese exploration in the late fifteenth and sixteenth centuries?
   a. The search for gold
   b. The conversion of peoples to the Islamic religion
   c. The discovery of sea routes to North America
   d. The conquest of Constantinople

2. Beginning in 1581, the northern Netherlands revolted against their political overlord, which was
   a. France.
   b. Spain.
   c. Elizabeth I of England.
   d. Florence.

3. North American racist attitudes toward African blacks originated in
   a. South America.
   b. Spain.
   c. France.
   d. England.

4. In the Thirty Years' War, France supported
   a. the German Catholics.
   b. the Holy Roman Emperor.
   c. Spain.
   d. the German Protestants.

5. Which of the following statements about the Spanish Armada of 1588 is *false?*
   a. It was the beginning of a long war with England.
   b. It failed in its objective.
   c. It prevented Phillip II from reimposing unity on western Europe by force.
   d. It made possible Spanish conquest of the Netherlands.

6. The nation that considered itself the international defender of Catholicism was
   a. France.
   b. Spain.
   c. Italy.
   d. England.

7. Columbus, like many of his fellow explorers, was principally motivated by
   a. a desire to discover India.
   b. a desire to Christianize the Americans.
   c. the desire of Spain to control the New World.
   d. the Spanish need to control the Mediterranean.

8. The earliest known explorers of North America were
   a. the Spanish.
   b. the Vikings.
   c. the Italians.
   d. the English.

9. Which of the following statements describes a feature of Spanish colonial policy?
   a. The New World was divided into four vice-royalties.
   b. Native industries were established.
   c. Each territory had local officials, or *corregidores*, who held judicial and military powers.
   d. The Spanish crown had only indirect and limited control over colonies.

10. To gain control of the spice trade of the Indian Ocean, the Portuguese had to defeat
    a. Spain.
    b. England.
    c. the Muslims.
    d. France.

11. The main contribution of Cortez and Pizarro to Spain was
    a. the tapping of the rich silver resources of Mexico and Peru.
    b. the Christianizing of the New World peoples.
    c. the further exploration of the Pacific Ocean.
    d. the discovery of South Africa.

12. The flow of huge amounts of gold and silver from the New World caused
    a. serious inflation in Spain and the rest of Europe.
    b. the Spanish economy to become dependent on New World gold and silver.
    c. the suffering of the poor because of the dramatic rise in food prices.
    d. Spain's economic strength and dominance in Europe.

13. By which treaty did the king of France, Francis I, recognize the supremacy of the papacy?
    a. The Treaty of Westphalia
    b. The treaty of Cateau-Cambrésis
    c. The Concordat of Bologna
    d. The Edict of Nantes

14. France was saved from religious anarchy when religious principles were set aside for political necessity by King
    a. Henry III.
    b. Francis I.
    c. Henry IV of Navarre.
    d. Charles IX.

15. Calvinism was appealing to the middle classes for each of the following reasons *except*
    a. its heavy moral emphasis.
    b. its stress on leisure and ostentatious living.
    c. its intellectual emphasis.
    d. its approval of any job well done, hard work, and success.

16. The vast palace of the Spanish monarchs, built under the direction of Philip II, was called
    a. Versailles.
    b. the Escorial.
    c. Tournai.
    d. Hampton Court.

17. The Treaty of Westphalia, which ended the Thirty Years' War
    a. further strengthened the Holy Roman Empire.
    b. completely undermined the Holy Roman Empire as a viable state.
    c. maintained that only Catholicism and Lutheranism were legitimate religions.
    d. refused to recognize the independence of the United Provinces of the Netherlands.

18. Who among the following best represents early modern skepticism?
    a. Las Casas
    b. James I
    c. Calvin
    d. Montaigne

19. The Spanish missionary Las Casas convinced Charles V to import Africans to Brazil because of all the following *except*
    a. the enslavement of Africans seemed more acceptable to the church.
    b. he believed they could endure better than the Indians.
    c. the native Indians were not durable enough under such harsh conditions.
    d. the native Indians revolted and refused to work as slave labor.

20. The Portuguese explorer who first reached India was
    a. Bartholomew Diaz.
    b. Prince Henry the Navigator.
    c. Vasco da Gama.
    d. Hernando Cortez.

21. The style of art popular in late-eighteenth-century Europe was called
    a. Elizabethan.
    b. Jacobean.
    c. skepticism.
    d. baroque.

22. The appearance of gunpowder in Europe
    a. made the common soldier inferior to the gentleman soldier.
    b. changed the popular belief that warfare bettered the individual.
    c. eliminated the need for governments to use propaganda to convince their people to support war.
    d. had little effect on the nature of war

23. The ten southern provinces of the Netherlands, known as the Spanish Netherlands, became the future
    a. Netherlands.
    b. Bohemia.
    c. Belgium.
    d. Schleswig.

24. The Thirty Years' war was fought primarily
    a. on German soil.
    b. in France.
    c. in eastern Europe.
    d. in Spain.

25. The Ottoman capture of Constantinople in 1453 was significant in the history of slavery and racism in that it
    a. introduced the concept of slavery to the Christian European world.
    b. ended the transport of black slaves to Europe.
    c. caused Europeans to turn to sub-Saharan Africa for their slaves.
    d. ushered in a flow of slaves from the Indies.

Major Political Ideas

1. This chapter emphasizes how the medieval concept of a unified Christian society under one political ruler and one church began to break down. What was the cause of this breakdown?

2. *Misogyny* and *racism* are "political" terms in that they help to explain the distribution of power within society. Discuss each of these terms in the context of the sixteenth and seventeenth centuries.

3. It is suggested in this chapter (see pages 473–474) that Calvinism contributed to Dutch ideas of national independence. Explain the connection. Do you agree?

Issues for Essays and Discussion

The age of European expansion and religious wars was a period of both the breakdown and reconstruction of society. Describe this process of breakdown and reconstruction by discussing civil war, international war, and overseas expansion from about 1450 to about 1560. What were the causes of these events? What country (or countries) emerged from this era as the most powerful?

Interpretation of Visual Sources

Study the sixteenth-century print that has been reproduced on page 473 of your textbook. Describe the scene by identifying the precise actions of the participants. What specific types of offensive references are being destroyed? What are the ideas behind this "purification"?

Geography

1. On Outline Map 15.1 provided, and using maps 15.1 and 15.2 in the textbook as a reference, mark the following: the exploration routes of da Gama, Columbus, and Magellan, Cueta, the Cape of Good Hope, Amsterdam, Guinea, Calicut, Cape Horn, London, Lisbon, Goa, Antwerp, Mexico City, Moluccas.

2. Using Map 15.4 in the textbook as a reference, identify the areas that were the main sources of African slaves and the main areas of slave importation into the New World. Do the latter areas illustrate the economic origins of the slave trade?

3. On Outline Map 15.3 provided, and using Map 15.3 in the textbook as a reference, mark the following: the areas under Spanish Habsburg control, the areas under Austrian Habsburg control, Prussian lands, the United Netherlands, the German states, the boundary of the old Holy Roman Empire, Swedish possessions, Madrid, Lisbon, Vienna, Amsterdam.

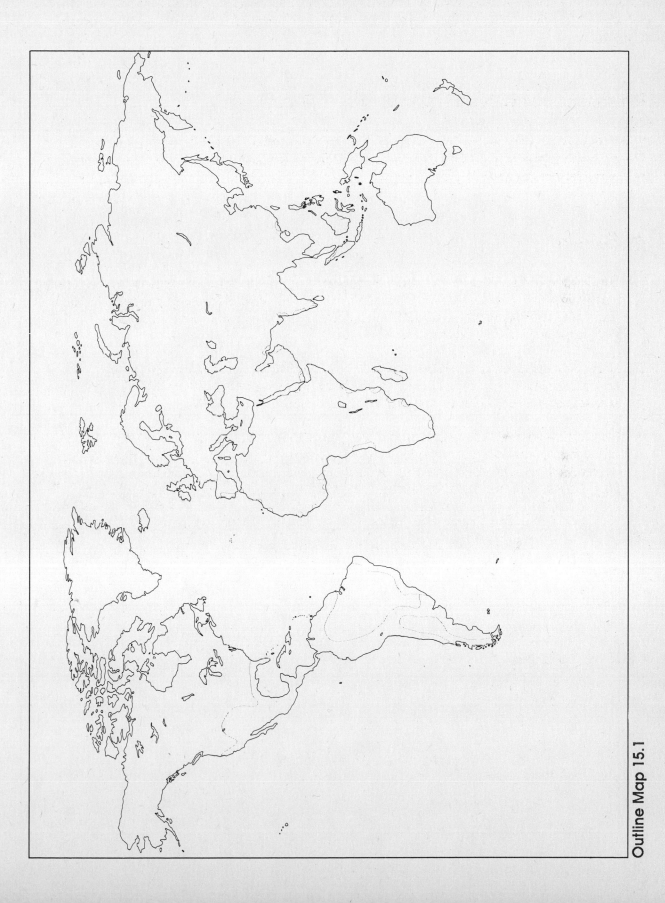

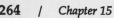

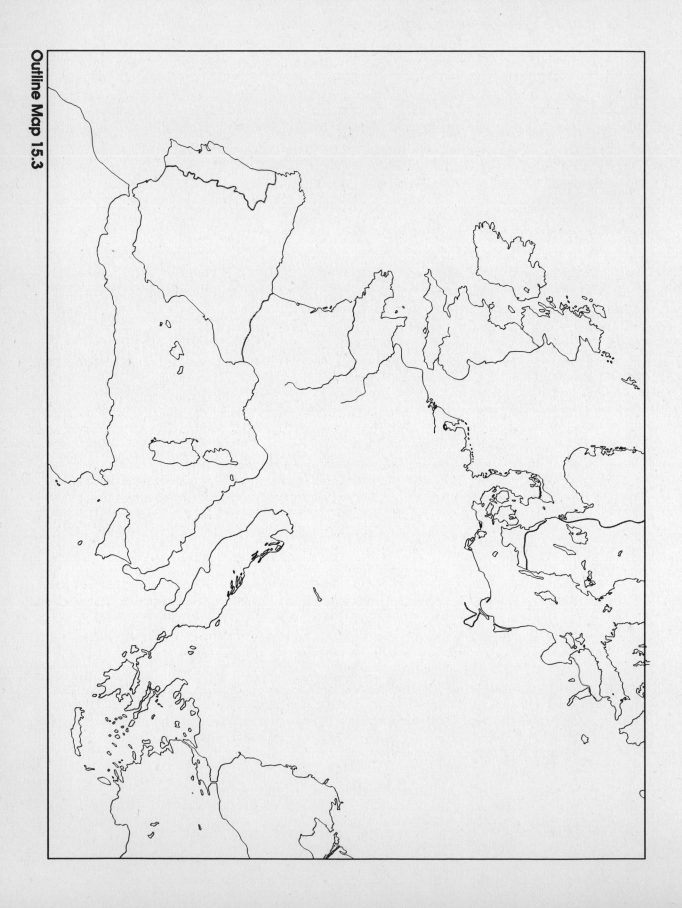

Understanding History Through the Arts

1. What did the Low Countries contribute to the arts? To investigate this subject, start with W. Gaunt, *Flemish Cities, Their History and Art* (1969), and O. Benesch, *The Art of the Renaissance in Northern Europe* (1945). See also E. Cammaerts, *The Treasure-House of Belgium* (1924).

2. What was the art of the New World like? For the arts of America prior to the European discoveries, see S. K. Lothorp, et al., *Pre-Columbian Art* (1957), and J. E. Thompson, *The Rise and Fall of Maya Civilization* (1954).

Problems for Further Investigation

1. In what ways is Montaigne representative of early modern skepticism? Those interested in skepticism and the life of its finest representative will want to read M. Lowenthal, ed., *Autobiography of Michel de Montaigne** (1935).

2. Who were the important women of this period? There were a number of extremely important and powerful sixteenth-century women whose biographies make for fascinating reading: R. Roeder, *Catherine de Medici and the Lost Revolution** (1937); J. E. Neal, *Queen Elizabeth I** (1934, 1966); and A. Fraser, *Mary Queen of Scots** (1969). An interesting seventeenth-century woman is Gustavus Adolphus's daughter, whose life is told in G. Masson, *Queen Christina* (1968). N. Harvey, *The Rose and the Thorn* (1977) is an account of the lives and times of Mary and Margaret Tudor.

3. What are the origins of mysogyny and racism? Begin with W. Monter's essay, "Protestant Wives, Catholic Saints, and Devil's Handmaid: Women in the Age of Reformations," in R. Bridenthal, C. Koonz, and S. Stuard, *Becoming Visible: Women in European History** (1987). To examine the sources of racism see D. B. Davis, *Slavery and Human Progress* (1984), and J. L. Watson, ed., *Asian and African Systems of Slavery* (1980).

4. Why were overseas empires formed in this period? Those interested in doing work in the area of European expansion should begin with D. L. Jensen, ed., *The Expansion of Europe: Motives, Methods, and Meaning* (1967). Students interested in understanding how the vast Spanish Empire worked will want to read C. H. Haring, *The Spanish Empire in America** (1947, 1963). This book includes an excellent bibliography on the subject.

5. Why were such severe religious wars fought in this era? Some of the problems faced in studying the religious conflict in France are discussed in J. H. M. Sahnon, *The French Wars of Religion** (1967). Anyone interested in research on the Thirty Years' War should begin with S. H. Steinberg, *The Thirty Years' War and the Conflict for European Hegemony, 1600–1660** (1966), and T. K. Rabb, *The Thirty Years' War** (1964).

---

*Available in paperback.

Chapter 16
Absolutism and Constitutionalism in Western Europe (ca 1589–1715)

Chapter Questions

After reading and studying this chapter you should be able to answer the following questions:

How did absolute monarchy and constitutionalism differ from the feudal and dynastic monarchies of earlier centuries? What social and economic factors limited absolute monarchs? Which countries best represent absolutism and constitutionalism?

Chapter Summary

The seventeenth century marks the development of two patterns of government in Europe: absolute monarchy and the constitutional state. This chapter examines how the political system of absolutism succeeded gloriously in France and faded dismally in England in the seventeenth century. Few kings have been as successful in establishing complete monarchial sovereignty as the great Sun King of France, Louis XIV. Louis gave Europe a masterful lesson on how to collaborate with the nobility to strengthen the monarchy and to reinforce the ancient aristocracy. He was a superb actor and propagandist, who built on the earlier achievements of Henry IV and Richelieu and used his magnificent palace of Versailles to imprison the French nobility in a beautiful golden cage. He succeeded in expanding France at the expense of the Habsburgs, and his patronage of the arts helped form the great age of French classicism. However, the economic progress he first made was later checked by his policy of revoking religious toleration.

While the France of Louis was the classic model of absolutism as the last phase of an historic feudal society, Spain was the classic case of imperial decline. By 1600 Spain was in trouble, and by 1700 it was no longer a major European power. Not only did the silver and labor of America run out, but this great American wealth ruined the Spanish economic and social structure. War with the Dutch, the English, and the French also helped turn Spain into a backwater of Europe.

England and the United Provinces of the Netherlands provide a picture of constitutionalism triumphing over absolutism. For England, the seventeenth century was a long period of political conflict, complete with a bitter civil war and a radical experiment with republicanism. The causes of this era of conflict were varied, but it is clear that by 1689 the English army and

Parliament had destroyed the Stuart quest for divine-right absolutism. The period that followed witnessed some important changes in the way the state is managed. The Netherlands was important not only because it became the financial and commercial center of Europe, but also because it provided the period's third model of political development—a loosely federated, middle-class constitutional state.

Study Outline

Use this outline to preview the chapter before you read a particular section in the textbook and then as a self-check to test your reading comprehension after you have read the chapter section.

I. Absolutism
    A. Absolutism defined
        1. In the absolutist state, sovereignty resided in kings—not the nobility or the parliament—who considered themselves responsible to God alone.
        2. Absolute kings created new state bureaucracies and standing armies, regulated all the institutions of government, and secured the cooperation of the nobility.
        3. The absolutist state foreshadowed the modern totalitarian state but lacked its total control over all aspects of its citizens lives.
    B. The foundations of French absolutism: Sully and Richelieu
        1. Henry IV achieved peace and curtailed the power of the nobility.
        2. His minister, Sully, brought about financial stability and economic growth.
        3. Cardinal Richelieu, the ruler of France under King Louis XIII, broke the power of the French nobility.
            a. His policy was total subordination of all groups and institutions to the French monarchy.
            b. He leveled castles and crushed aristocratic conspiracies.
            c. He established an efficient administrative system using intendants, who further weakened the local nobility.
            d. The Huguenot revolt of 1625 led to the destruction of fortified cities in France, eliminating another source of aristocratic power.
        4. Under Richelieu, France sought to break Habsburg power.
            a. He supported the struggle of the Swedish king, Gustavus Adolphus, against the Habsburgs.
            b. He acquired land and influence in Germany.
        5. Richelieu supported the new French Academy, which created a dictionary to standardize the French language.
        6. The French government's ability to tax was severely limited by local rights and the tax-exempt status of much of the nobility and the middle class.
        7. Mazarin continued Richelieu's centralizing policies, but these policies gave rise to a period of civil wars known as the Fronde.
            a. Many people of the aristocracy and the middle classes opposed the government policies of centralization and the huge debt.
            b. The conflicts hurt the economy and convinced the new king, Louis XIV, that civil war was destructive of social order and that absolute monarchy was the only alternative to anarchy.

II. The absolutism of Louis XIV
   A. Louis XIV, the "Sun King," was a devout Catholic who believed that God had established kings as his rulers on earth.
   B. He feared the nobility and was successful in collaboration with them to enhance both aristocratic prestige and royal power.
   C. He made the court at Versailles a fixed institution and used it as a means of preserving royal power and as the center of French absolutism.
      1. The architecture and art of Versailles were a means of carrying out state policy—a way to overawe his subjects and foreign powers.
      2. The French language and culture became the international style.
      3. The court at Versailles was a device to undermine the power of the aristocracy by separating power from status.
      4. A centralized state, administered by a professional class taken from the bourgeoisie, was formed.
   D. Economic management under Louis XIV: Colbert and mercantilism
      1. Mercantilism is a collection of governmental policies for the regulation of economic activities by and for the state.
      2. Louis XIV's finance minister, Colbert, tried to achieve a favorable balance of trade and make France self-sufficient so the flow of gold to other countries would be halted.
         a. Colbert encouraged French industry, enacted high foreign tariffs, and created a strong merchant marine.
         b. He hoped to make Canada part of a French empire.
         c. Though France's industries grew and the commercial classes prospered, its agricultural economy suffered under the burdens of heavy taxation, population decline, and poor harvests.
   E. The revocation of the Edict of Nantes
      1. In 1685, Louis revoked the Edict of Nantes, which had given religious freedom to French Protestants.
      2. This revocation caused many Protestants to flee the country, but it had little effect on the economy.
III. French classicism in art and literature
   A. French classicism imitated and resembled the arts of the ancients and the Renaissance.
   B. Poussin best illustrates classical idealism in painting.
   C. Louis XIV was a patron of the composers Lully, Couperin, and Charpentier.
   D. The comedies of Molière and the tragedies of Racine best illustrate the classicism in French theater.
IV. Louis XIV's wars
   A. The French army under Louis XIV was modern because the state, rather than the nobles, employed the soldiers.
      1. He appointed Louvois to create a professional army.
      2. Louis himself took personal command of the army.
   B. Louis continued Richelieu's expansionist policy.
      1. In 1667, he invaded Flanders and gained twelve towns.
      2. By the treaty of Nijmegen (1678) he gained some Flemish towns and all of Franche-Comté.

3. Strasbourg was taken in 1681 and Lorraine in 1684, but the limits of his expansion had been met.
4. Louis fought the new Dutch king of England, William III, and the League of Augsburg in a war.
   a. The Banks of Amsterdam and England financed his enemies.
   b. Louis's heavy taxes fell on the peasants, who revolted.
5. This led to the War of the Spanish Succession (1701–1713), which was over the issue of the succession to the Spanish throne: Louis claimed Spain but was opposed by the Dutch, English, Austrians, and Prussians.
   a. The war was also an attempt to preserve the balance of power in Europe and to check France's commercial power overseas.
   b. A Grand Alliance of the English, Dutch, Austrians, and Prussians was formed in 1701 to fight the French.
   c. Eugene of Savoy and Churchill of England led the alliance to victory over Louis.
   d. The war was concluded by the Peace of Utrecht in 1713, which forbade the union of France and Spain.
   e. The war ended French expansionism and left France on the brink of bankruptcy, with widespread misery and revolts.
V. The decline of absolutist Spain in the seventeenth century
   A. Factors contributing to Spain's decline
      1. Fiscal disorder, political incompetence, the lack of a strong middle class, population decline, intellectual isolation, and psychological malaise contributed to its decline.
      2. The defeat of the "Invincible Armada" in 1588 was a crushing blow to Spain's morale.
      3. Spain's economy began to decline by 1600.
         a. Royal expenditures increased, but income from the Americas decreased.
         b. Business and agriculture suffered.
      4. Spanish kings lacked force of character and could not deal with all these problems.
   B. The Treaty of the Pyrenees of 1659, which ended the French-Spanish wars, marked the end of Spain as a great power.
VI. Constitutionalism in England and the Netherlands
   A. Constitutionalism defined
      1. Under constitutionalism, the state must be governed according to law, not royal decree.
         a. It implies a balance between the power of the government and the rights of the subjects.
         b. A nation's constitution may be written or unwritten, but the government must respect it.
         c. Constitutional governments may be either republics or monarchies.
      2. Constitutional government is not the same as full democracy because not all of the people have the right to participate.
   B. The decline of royal absolutism in England (1603–1649)
      1. The Stuart kings of England lacked the political wisdom of Elizabeth I.
      2. James I was devoted to the ideal of rule by divine right.
      3. His absolutism ran counter to English belief.

4. The House of Commons wanted a greater say in the government of the state.
   a. Increased wealth had produced a better educated House of Commons.
   b. Between 1603 and 1640, bitter squabbles erupted between the Crown and the Commons.
C. The Protestant, or capitalist, ethic and the problem of religion in England
   1. Many English people, called Puritans, were attracted by the values of hard work, thrift, and self-denial implied by Calvinism.
   2. The Puritans, who were dissatisfied with the Church of England, saw James I as an enemy.
   3. Charles I and his archbishop, Laud, appeared to be pro-Catholic.
D. The English Civil War (1642–1649)
   1. Charles I had ruled without Parliament for eleven years.
   2. A revolt in Scotland over the religious issue forced him to call a new Parliament into session to finance an army.
      a. The Commons passed an act compelling the king to summon Parliament every three years.
      b. It also impeached Archbishop Laud and abolished the House of Lords.
      c. Religious differences in Ireland led to a revolt there, but Parliament would not trust Charles with an army.
   3. Charles initiated military action against Parliament.
      a. The civil war (1642–1649) revolved around the issue of whether sovereignty should reside in the king or in Parliament.
      b. The problem was not resolved, but Charles was beheaded in 1649.
E. Puritanical absolutism in England: Cromwell and the Protectorate
   1. Kingship was abolished in 1649 and a commonwealth proclaimed.
      a. A commonwealth is a government without a king whose power rests in Parliament and a council of state.
      b. In fact, the army controlled the government.
   2. Oliver Cromwell, leader of the "New Model Army" that defeated the royalists, came from the gentry class that dominated the House of Commons.
   3. Cromwell's Protectorate became a military dictatorship, absolutist and puritanical.
      a. Cromwell allowed religious toleration for all Christians, except Roman Catholics, and savagely crushed the revolt in Ireland.
      b. He censored the press and closed the theaters.
      c. He regulated the economy according to mercantilist principles.
      d. The mercantilist navigation act that required English goods to be transported on English ships was a boon to the economy and led to a commercial war with the Dutch.
F. The restoration of the English monarchy
   1. The restoration of the Stuart kings in 1660 failed to solve the problems of religion and the relationship between King and Parliament.
      a. According to the Test Act of 1673, those who refused to join the Church of England could not vote, hold office, preach, teach, attend the universities, or assemble, but these restrictions could not be upheld.
      b. Charles II appointed a council of five men (the "Cabal") to serve as both his major advisers and as members of Parliament.

     c. The Cabal was the forerunner of the cabinet system, and it helped create good relations with the Parliament.

    2. Charles's pro-French policies led to a Catholic scare.

    3. James II, an avowed Catholic, violated the Test Act by appointing Catholics to government and university positions.

    4. Fear of a Catholic monarchy led to the expulsion of James II and the Glorious Revolution.

G. The triumph of England's Parliament: constitutional monarchy and cabinet government

    1. The "Glorious Revolution" that expelled James II and installed William and Mary on the throne ended the idea of divine-right monarchy.

    2. The Bill of Rights of 1689 established the principal of Parliament's sovereignty.

       a. Locke maintained that people set up government to protect life, liberty, and property.

       b. Locke's ideas that there are natural, or universal, rights played a strong role in eighteenth-century Enlightenment thought.

    3. In the cabinet system, which developed in the eighteenth century, both legislative and executive power are held by the leading ministers, who form the government.

H. The Dutch republic in the seventeenth century

    1. The Dutch republic emerged from the sixteenth-century struggle against Spain and flowered in the seventeenth century.

    2. Power in the republic resided in the local Estates.

       a. The republic was a confederation: a weak union of strong provinces.

       b. The republic was based on middle-class ideas and values.

    3. Thrift, frugality, and religious toleration fostered economic growth.

    4. The province of Holland became the commercial and financial center of Europe—much of it based on transport of goods from all over the world.

       a. The Dutch East India Company was formed in 1602; it cut heavily into Portuguese trading in East Asia.

       b. The Dutch West India Company, founded in 1621, traded extensively in Latin America and Africa.

    5. War with France and England in the 1670s hurt the United Provinces.

Review Questions

Check your understanding of this chapter by answering the following questions.

1. In what way does the French minister Richelieu symbolize absolutism? What were his achievements?
2. Why can it be said that the palace of Versailles was used as a device to ruin the nobility of France? Was Versailles a palace or a prison?
3. Define mercantilism. What were the mercantilist policies of the French minister Colbert?
4. Why was the revocation of the Edict of Nantes a great error on the part of Louis XIV?
5. What were the reasons for the fall of the Spanish Empire?
6. Discuss the foreign policy goals of Louis XIV. Was he successful?
7. Define absolutism. How does it differ from totalitarianism?

8. What was the impact of Louis XIV's wars on the French economy and French society?
9. What were the causes of the War of the Spanish Succession? What impact did William III of England have on European events after about 1689?
10. What is constitutionalism? How does it differ from democratic form of government? From absolutism?
11. What were the attitudes and policies of James I that made him so unpopular with his subjects?
12. Who were the Puritans? Why did they come into conflict with James I?
13. What were the immediate and the long-range causes of the English Civil War of 1642–1649? What were the results?
14. Why did James II flee from England in 1688? What happened to the kingship at this point?
15. Were the events of 1688–89 a victory for English democracy? Explain.
16. Why is it said that Locke was the spokesman for the liberal English Revolution of 1689 and for representative government?
17. What accounts for the phenomenal economic success and political stability of the Dutch republic?
18. Describe the Dutch system of government. How was it different from that of other western European states? What was unusual about the Dutch attitudes toward religious beliefs?

Study-Review Exercises

Define the following key concepts and terms.

sovereign

totalitarianism

absolutism

mercantilism

republicanism

constitutionalism

cabinet government

French classicism

quixotic

commonwealth

Identify and explain the significance of each of the following people and terms.
Sully

paulette

Fronde

Cardinal Richelieu

Richelieu's *généralités*

The French Academy

Louis XIV of France

Versailles

Molière

Racine

Poussin

Dutch Estates General

intendants

Peace of Utrecht

Cabal of Charles II

Instrument of Government

Puritans

Oliver Cromwell

James II of England

English Bill of Rights

John Churchill

Philip II of Spain

Explain what each of these men believed about the placement of authority within society.
Cardinal Richelieu

James I of England

Thomas Hobbes

Louis XIV of France

John Locke

Sully

Explain what the following events were and why they were important.
revocation of the Edict of Nantes

Scottish revolt of 1640

War of the Spanish Succession

Glorious Revolution

English Civil War of 1642–1649

Test your understanding of the chapter by providing the correct answers.

1. The highest executive office of the Dutch republic. _____

2. Louis XIV's able minister of finance. _____

3. During the age of economic growth in Spain, a vast number of Spaniards *entered/left* religious orders.

4. For Louis XIV of France the War of the Spanish Succession was a *success/disaster*.

5. The Englishman who inflicted defeat on Louis XIV at Blenheim. _____

6. The archbishop whose goal was to enforce Anglican unity in England and Scotland.

   _____

7. He made the statement "From where do the merchant's profits come except from his own

   diligence and industry." _____

Multiple-Choice Questions

1. Mercantilism
   a. was a military system.
   b. insisted on a favorable balance of trade.
   c. was adopted in England but not in France.
   d. claimed that state power was based on land armies.

2. French Protestants tended to be
   a. poor peasants.
   b. the power behind the throne of Louis XIV.
   c. a financial burden for France.
   d. clever business people.

3. The War of the Spanish Succession began when Charles II of Spain left his territories to
   a. the French heir.
   b. the Spanish heir.
   c. Eugene of Savoy.
   d. the archduke of Austria.

4. Which of the following cities was the commercial and financial capital of Europe in the seventeenth century?
   a. London
   b. Hamburg
   c. Paris
   d. Amsterdam

5. Of the following, the country most centered on middle-class interests was
   a. England.
   b. Spain.
   c. France.
   d. the Netherlands.

6. Which of the following Englishmen was a Catholic?
   a. James II
   b. Oliver Cromwell
   c. Archbishop Laud
   d. William III

7. Which of the following is a characteristic of an absolute state?
   a. Sovereignty embodied in the representative assembly
   b. Bureaucracies solely accountable to the middle classes
   c. A strong voice expressed by the nobility
   d. Permanent standing armies

8. Cardinal Richelieu's most notable accomplishment was
   a. the creation of a strong financial system for France.
   b. the creation of a highly effective administrative system.
   c. winning the total support of the Huguenots.
   d. allying the Catholic church with the government.

9. The statement "There are no privileges and immunities which can stand against a divinely appointed king" forms the basis of the
   a. Stuart notion of absolutism.
   b. Stuart notion of constitutionalism.
   c. English Parliament's notion of democracy.
   d. English Parliament's notion of constitutionalism.

10. The English Long Parliament
    a. enacted legislation supporting absolutism.
    b. supported the Catholic tendencies of Charles I.
    c. supported Charles I as a military leader.
    d. enacted legislation against absolutism.

11. Cromwell's government is best described as a
    a. constitutional state.
    b. democratic state.
    c. military dictatorship.
    d. monarchy.

12. Absolute monarchs secured mastery over the nobility by all of the following *except*
    a. the creation of a standing army.
    b. the creation of a state bureaucracy.
    c. coercive actions.
    d. regulating religious groups.

13. Cardinal Richelieu consolidated the power of the French monarchy by doing all of the following *except*
    a. destroying the castles of the nobility.
    b. ruthlessly treating conspirators who threatened the monarchy.
    c. keeping nobles from gaining high government offices.
    d. eliminating the intendant system of local government.

14. One way in which Louis XIV controlled the French nobility was by
    a. maintaining standing armies in the countryside to crush noble uprisings.
    b. requiring the presence of the major noble families at Versailles for at least part of the year.
    c. periodically visiting the nobility in order to check on their activities.
    d. forcing them to participate in a parliamentary assembly.

15. The French army under Louis XIV
    a. had no standardized uniforms and weapons.
    b. lived off the countryside.
    c. had an ambulance corps to care for the troops.
    d. had no system for recruitment, training, or promotion.

16. The Peace of Utrecht in 1713
    a. shrunk the size of the British Empire significantly.
    b. represented the balance-of-power principle in action.
    c. enhanced Spain's position as a major power in Europe.
    d. marked the beginning of French expansionist policy.

17. The downfall of Spain in the seventeenth century can be blamed on
    a. weak and ineffective monarchs.
    b. an overexpansion of industry and trade.
    c. the growth of slave labor in America.
    d. the rise of a large middle class.

18. When Archbishop Laud tried to make the Presbyterian Scots accept the Anglican *Book of Common Prayer*, the Scots
    a. revolted.
    b. reluctantly accepted the archbishop's directive.
    c. ignored the directive.
    d. heartily adopted the new prayerbook.

19. Who among the following was a proponent of the idea that the purpose of government is to protect life, liberty, and property?
    a. Thomas Hobbes
    b. William of Orange
    c. John Locke
    d. Edmund Burke

20. After the United Provinces of the Netherlands won independence from Spain, their government could best be described as
    a. a strong monarchy.
    b. a centralized parliamentary system.
    c. a weak union of strong provinces.
    d. a democracy.

21. The Dutch economy was based on
    a. fishing, world trade, and banking.
    b. silver mining in Peru.
    c. export of textiles.
    d. a moral and religious disdain of wealth.

22. Dutch economic decline began with
    a. the end of the War of the Spanish Succession.
    b. the formation of the Dutch East India Company.
    c. its practice of religious toleration.
    d. the adoption of the ideas of John Calvin.

23. During the administration of Robert Walpole in Britain, the idea developed that
    a. the monarch was absolute.
    b. the cabinet should be replaced by a legislative parliament.
    c. the king's chief minister be known as the *stadholder*.
    d. the cabinet be responsible to the House of Commons.

24. The Amstel River was the major link between which of the following cities and its world trading system?
    a. London
    b. Amsterdam
    c. Paris
    d. Amiens

25. Which of the following is a book by Cervantes that has as its hero an idealistic but impractical soldier?
    a. *Don Quixote*
    b. *Tarfuffe*
    c. *Te Deum*
    d. *Phèdre*

Major Political Ideas

1. What are the major characteristics of absolutism and how does it, as a political system, differ from totalitarianism?

2. What is constitutionalism? What is the source of power within a constitutional state? How does constitutionalism differ from absolutism?

3. In 1649 England declared itself a commonwealth, or republican form of government. What is a republican state? Where does power reside in such a state?

Issues for Essays and Discussion

1. The seventeenth century saw great political instability and change, during which some modern forms of political organization emerged. Why did political turmoil exist, what new concepts of politics and power emerged, who were the most important participants in this process, and how was stability achieved?

2. Compare and contrast the political development of France, the Netherlands, and England in the seventeenth century. Of these three states, which is the most "modern"?

Interpretation of Visual Sources

Study the reproduction of the woodcut entitled *The Spider and the Fly* on page 508 of your textbook. What is the message the author of this illustration seeks to convey? Does it make a political statement? In your opinion, is there any historical evidence set forth in this chapter to suggest that this print represents historical truth?

Geography

1. On Outline Map 16.1 provided, and using Map 16.1 in the textbook as a reference, mark the territory added to France as a result of the wars and foreign policy of King Louis XIV.

2. Explain how each of the territories was acquired and from whom.

3. What changes in the balance of power occurred as a result of the Treaty of Utrecht in 1713?

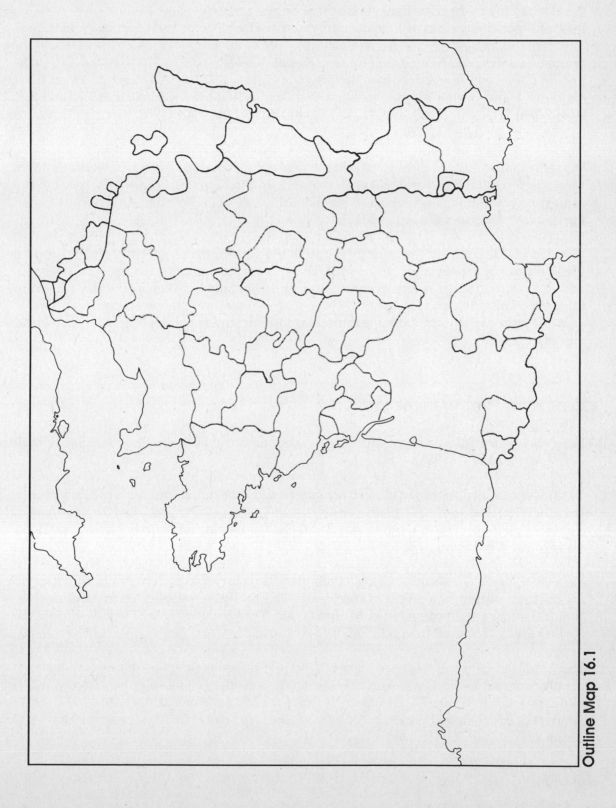

Understanding History Through the Arts

1. What was life at Versailles like? At the great English estates? Louis XIV and the magnificence of his court at Versailles are re-created with color and spirit in W. H. Lewis, *The Splendid Century** (1953). A vivid picture of life of the English upper classes—how they ran their estates, entertained, and influenced politics—is found in M. Girouard, *Life in the English Country House: A Social and Architectural History* (1979). The splendor of Versailles and French and British baroque painting and architecture are the subjects of Chapter 7, "The Baroque in France and England," in H. W. Janson, *History of Art* (1962). See also G. Walton, *Louis XIV's Versailles** (1986).

2. What are some of the architectural achievements of this period? The seventeenth century was a period of architectural splendor in France and in England. Some of the great achievements of this period are discussed in Chapter 7 of N. Pevsner, *An Outline Of European Architecture** (7th ed., 1963).

3. What can we learn from the great literature of the period? Much good reading is found in the literature of the seventeenth century. The great comic writer of the age was Molière, whose *Tartuffe* is still a source of entertainment. LaFontaine's fables are a lively reworking of tales from antiquity, and Cervantes's *Don Quixote* continues to inspire its readers. The greatest writer to emerge from the Puritan age in England was John Milton, whose *Paradise Lost* is a classic.

Problems for Further Investigation

1. Why was James Stuart a successful king in Scotland but a failure in England? See D. Willson, *King James VI and I** (1956).

2. What were the origins of the civil war in England? Some of the problems in interpretation of the crucial period 1642 to 1649 are considered in P. A. M. Taylor, ed., *The Origins of the English Civil War** (1960); L. Stone, ed., *Social Change and Revolution in England, 1540–1640** (1965); and B. Manning, *The English People and the English Revolution* (1976).

3. Was the Glorious Revolution of 1688 in England a victory for modern political democracy or a palace revolution by a group of aristocrats? This and other problems surrounding this political event are discussed in G. M. Straka, ed., *The Revolution of 1688 and the Birth of the English Political Nation** (rev. ed., 1973).

4. How did the Sun King create an absolutist state? Students interested in research on absolutism and Louis XIV in France will want to consider H. G. Judge, ed., *Louis XIV* (1965); William F. Church, ed., *The Greatness of Louis XIV: Myth or Reality?** (rev. ed., 1972); and R. F. Kierstead, ed., *State and Society in Seventeenth-Century France** (1975). The best biography of Louis XIV is *Louis XIV* (1968) by J. Wolf.

---

*Available in paperback.

5. What were the traditional patterns of military organization and strategy in this age of absolutism? In what ways did warfare change to reflect the political ambitions of Europe's monarchs and economic and social developments? Begin your investigation with M. van Creveld, *Technology and War, from 2000 B.C. to the Present* (1988). A helpful reference for the scholar of military history is R. Dupuy and T. Dupuy, *The Encyclopedia of Military History, from 3500 B.C. to the Present* (1982, 1990).

Chapter 17
Absolutism in Eastern Europe to 1740

Chapter Questions

After reading and studying this chapter you should be able to answer the following questions:

Why did the basic structure of society in eastern Europe move away from that in western Europe? How and why did the rulers of Austria, Prussia, and Russia manage to build more durable absolute monarchies than that of Louis XIV of France? How did the absolute monarchs' interactions with artists and architects contribute to the achievements of baroque culture?

Chapter Summary

This chapter discusses why monarchial absolutism developed with greater lasting strength in eastern Europe than in western Europe. In Russia, Prussia, and Austria monarchs became more powerful as the peasants were pushed back into serfdom. That is, peasants gradually lost the personal and economic freedoms they had built up over several hundred years during the Middle Ages. At the same time that eastern nobles gained greater social and economic control over the enserfed peasants, they lost political power to the rising absolute monarchs. Although there were some economic reasons for the re-emergence of serfdom in the east, it was essentially for political reasons that this strong authoritarian tradition emerged. As opposed to western Europe, it was the common people—the peasants—who were the great losers in the power struggle between nobility and monarchy. Absolutism in Russia, Austria, and Prussia emerged because of war, foreign invasion, and internal struggle. For example, the Austrian monarchs solved the problems arising from external conflicts and a multicultural state by building a strong, centralized military state. Prussian absolutism—intended to check the power of the nobility—was achieved by the Hohenzollern monarchs, while Russian absolutism was largely the outgrowth of the Mongol conquest and internal power struggles.

Some of the absolute monarchs were enlightened reformers, but their good intentions were often thwarted by internal problems. However, if reform from above was not very effective, the absolute monarchs' use of architecture and urban planning—much of it in the baroque style—to enhance their images was a noteworthy success. They created buildings and cities that reflected their growing power, and they hired baroque painters and musicians to glorify them and to fill their palaces with paintings and music.

Study Outline

Use this outline to preview the chapter before you read a particular section in your textbook and then as a self-check to test your reading comprehension after you have read the chapter section.

I. Lords and peasants in eastern Europe
    A. The medieval background (1400–1650)
        1. Personal and economic freedom for peasants increased between 1050 and 1300.
            a. Serfdom nearly disappeared.
            b. Peasants bargained freely with their landlords and moved about as they pleased.
        2. After 1300, powerful lords in eastern Europe revived serfdom to combat their economic problems.
            a. Laws that restricted the peasants' right of free movement were passed.
            b. Lords took more and more of the peasants' land and imposed heavier labor obligations.
    B. The consolidation of serfdom
        1. The re-establishment of hereditary serfdom took place in Poland, Prussia, and Russia between 1500 and 1650.
        2. The consolidation of serfdom was accompanied by the growth of estate agriculture.
            a. Lords seized peasant land for their own estates.
            b. They then demanded unpaid serf labor on those estates.
    C. Political reasons for changes in serfdom in eastern Europe
        1. Serfdom increased because of political, not economic, reasons.
        2. Weak monarchs could not resist the demands of the powerful noble landlords.
        3. The absence of the western concept of sovereignty meant that the king did not think in terms of protecting the people of the nation.
        4. Overall, the peasants had less political power in eastern Europe and less solidarity.
        5. The landlords systematically undermined the medieval privileges of the towns.
            a. The lords sold directly to foreign capitalists instead of to local merchants.
            b. Eastern towns lost their medieval right of refuge.
II. The rise of Austria and Prussia (1650–1750)
    A. Austria and the Ottoman Turks
        1. After the Thirty Years' War, the Austrian Habsburgs turned inward and eastward to unify their holdings.
            a. The Habsburgs replaced the Bohemian Czech (Protestant) nobility with their own warriors.
            b. Serfdom increased, Protestantism was wiped out, and absolutism was achieved.
            c. Ferdinand III created a standing army, centralized the government in Austria, and turned toward Hungary for land.
        2. This eastward turn led Austria to became absorbed in a war against the Turks over Hungary and Transylvania.
        3. Under Suleiman the Magnificent the Turks built the most powerful empire in the world, which included part of central Europe.
            a. The Turkish sultan was the absolute head of the state.

b. There was little private property, and a bureaucracy staffed by slaves.
4. The Turkish attack on Austria in 1683 was turned back, and the Habsburgs conquered all of Hungary and Transylvania by 1699.
5. The Habsburg possessions consisted of Austria, Bohemia, and Hungary, which were joined in a fragile union.
    a. The Pragmatic Sanction (1713) stated that the possessions should never be divided.
    b. The Hungarian nobility thwarted the full development of Habsburg absolutism, and Charles VI had to restore many of their traditional privileges after the rebellion led by Rákóczy in 1703.

B. Prussia in the seventeenth century
1. The Hohenzollern family ruled the electorate of Brandenburg but had little real power.
2. The Thirty Years' War weakened the representative assemblies of the realm and allowed the Hohenzollerns to consolidate their absolutist rule.
3. Frederick William (the Great Elector) used military force and taxation to unify his Rhine holdings, Prussia, and Brandenburg into a strong state.
    a. The traditional parliaments, or Estates, which were controlled by the Junkers (the nobles and the landowners), were weakened.
    b. War strengthened the elector, as did the Junkers' unwillingness to join with the towns to block absolutism.

C. The consolidation of Prussian absolutism
1. Frederick William I encouraged Prussian militarism and created the best army in Europe plus an efficient bureaucracy.
2. The Junker class became the military elite and Prussia a militarist state.

III. The development of Russia
A. The Vikings and the Kievan principality
1. Eastern Slavs moved into Russia between the fifth and ninth centuries.
2. Slavic-Viking settlements grew up in the ninth century.
3. The Vikings unified the eastern Slavs politically and religiously, creating a ruling dynasty and accepting Eastern Orthodox Christianity for themselves and the Slavs.
4. A strong aristocracy (the boyars) and a free peasantry made it difficult to strengthen the state.

B. The Mongol yoke and the rise of Moscow
1. The Mongols conquered the Kievan state in the thirteenth century and unified it under their harsh rule.
2. The Mongols used Russian aristocrats as their servants and tax collectors.
    a. The princes of Moscow served the Mongols well and became the hereditary great princes.
    b. Ivan I served the Mongols while using his wealth and power to strengthen the principality of Moscow.
    c. Ivan III stopped acknowledging the Mongol khan as the supreme ruler and assumed the headship of Orthodox Christianity.

C. Tsar and people to 1689
1. By 1505, the prince of Moscow—the tsar—had emerged as the single hereditary ruler of the eastern Slavs.

2. The tsars and the boyars struggled over who would rule the state; the tsars won and created a new "service nobility," who held the tsar's land on the condition that they serve in his army.

3. Ivan the Terrible was an autocratic tsar who expanded Muscovy and further reduced the power of the boyars.
   a. He murdered leading boyars and confiscated their estates.
   b. Many peasants fled his rule to the newly conquered territories, forming groups called Cossacks.
   c. Businessmen and artisans were bound to their towns and jobs; the middle class did not develop.

4. The Time of Troubles (1598–1613) was a period characterized by internal struggles and invasions.
   a. There was no heir, and relatives of the tsar fought against each other.
   b. Swedish and Polish armies invaded.
   c. Cossack bands slaughtered many nobles and officials.

5. Michael Romanov was elected tsar by the nobles in 1613, and he re-established tsarist autocracy.

6. The Romanovs brought about the total enserfment of the people, while the military obligations on the nobility were relaxed considerably.

7. A split in the church over religious reforms led to mass protests by the peasants, and the church became dependent on the state for its authority.

D. The reforms of Peter the Great

1. Peter wished to create a strong army for protection and expansion.
   a. He forced the nobility to serve in the army or in the civil service.
   b. He created schools to train technicians for his army.

2. Army and government became more efficient and powerful as an interlocking military-civilian bureaucracy was created and staffed by talented people.

3. Russian peasant life under Peter became more harsh.
   a. People replaced land as the primary unit of taxation.
   b. Serfs were arbitrarily assigned to work in the factories and mines.

4. Modest territorial expansion took place under Peter, and Russia became a European Great Power.
   a. Russia defeated Sweden in 1709 at Poltava to gain control of the Baltic Sea.
   b. Peter borrowed many Western ideas.

IV. Absolutism and the baroque

A. Palaces and power

1. Architecture played an important role in politics because it was used by kings to enhance their image and awe their subjects.

2. The royal palace was the favorite architectural expression of absolutist power.

3. The dominant artistic style of the age of absolutism was baroque—a dramatic and emotional style.

B. Royal cities and urban planning

1. The new St. Petersburg is an excellent example of the tie among architecture, politics, and urban development.
   a. Peter the Great wanted to create a modern, baroque city from which to rule Russia.

  b. The city became a showplace for the tsar paid for by the Russian nobility and built by the peasants.
C. The growth of St. Petersburg
  1. During the eighteenth century, St. Petersburg became one of the world's largest and most influential cities.
  2. The new city was Western and baroque in its layout and design.
    a. It had broad, straight avenues.
    b. Houses were built in a uniform line.
    c. There were parks, canals, and streetlights.
    d. Each social group was to live in a specific section.
  3. All social groups, especially the peasants, bore heavy burdens to construct the city.
  4. Tsarina Elizabeth and the architect Rastrelli crowned the city with great palaces.

Review Questions

Check your understanding of this chapter by answering the following questions.

1. What were the reasons for the re-emergence of serfdom in eastern Europe in the early modern period?
2. In western Europe the conflict between the king and his vassals resulted in gains for the common man. Why did this not happen in eastern Europe?
3. Why would the reign of the Great Elector be regarded as "the most crucial constitutional struggle in Prussian history for hundreds of years"? What did he do to increase royal authority? Who were the losers?
4. Prussia has traditionally been considered one of the most militaristic states in Europe. How do you explain this development? Who or what was responsible?
5. How did the Thirty Years' War and invasion by the Ottoman Turks help the Habsburgs consolidate power?
6. What was the Pragmatic Sanction and why were the Hungarian and Bohemian princes opposed to it?
7. What role, if any, did war play in the evolution of absolutism in eastern Europe?
8. What was the relationship between baroque architecture and European absolutism? Give examples.
9. It has been said that the common man benefited from the magnificent medieval cathedrals as much as the princes. Can the same be said about the common man and the building projects of the absolute kings and princes? Explain.
10. How did the Vikings influence Russian history?
11. How did the Mongols unify the eastern Slavs?
12. What role did Ivan the Terrible play in the rise of absolutism? Peter the Great?
13. Why was territorial expansion "the soul of tsardom"?

Study-Review Exercises

Define the following key concepts and terms.

absolutism

baroque

Prussian Junkers

Hohenzollern

kholops

Romanov

boyar

autocracy

Vikings

Habsburgs

Mongols

Pragmatic Sanction

Identify and explain the significance of the following people.

Suleiman the Magnificent

Frederick the Great

Charles VI of Austria

Prince Francis Rákóczy

Jenghiz Khan

Ivan the Terrible

Frederick William the Great Elector

Frederick William I

Great Prince Iaroslav the Wise

Ivan III

Peter the Great

Prince Eugene of Savoy

Bartolomeo Rastrelli

Explain what the following events were, who participated in them, and why they were important.
building of the Winter Palace of St. Petersburg

siege of Vienna, 1683

War of the Austrian Succession

Time of Troubles

Battle of Poltava

Test your understanding of the chapter by providing the correct answers.

1. The founder of the new Russian city on the coast of the Baltic Sea. _____

2. After 1500, serfdom in eastern Europe *increased/decreased*.

3. The Ottoman Turkish leader who captured Vienna in 1529. _____

4. In the struggle between the Hungarian aristocrats and the Austrian Habsburgs, the Hungarian aristocrats *maintained/lost* their traditional privileges.

5. This Prussian monarch doubled the size of Prussia in 1740 by taking Silesia from Austria.

   _____

6. The monarchs of eastern Europe were generally *stronger/weaker* than the kings of western Europe in the sixteenth and seventeenth centuries.

Place the following events in correct chronological order.

Election of the first Romanov tsar
Establishment of the Kievan state
Time of Troubles
Invasion by the Mongols
Building of St. Petersburg
Battle of Poltava

1.

2.

3.

4.

5.

6.

Multiple-Choice Questions

1. The unifiers and first rulers of the Russians were the
   a. Mongols.
   b. Turks.
   c. Romanovs.
   d. Vikings.

2. By the seventeenth century, commercial activity, manufacturing, and mining in Russia were owned or controlled by the
   a. rising urban capitalists.
   b. Cossacks.
   c. tsar.
   d. Russian church.

3. In eastern Europe the courts were largely controlled by
   a. the peasants.
   b. the monarchs.
   c. the church.
   d. the landlords.

4. The principality called the "sandbox of the Holy Roman Empire" was
   a. Brandenburg-Prussia.
   b. Hungary.
   c. Sweden.
   d. Austria.

5. Ivan the Terrible
   a. failed to conquer the khan.
   b. was afraid to call himself tsar.
   c. monopolized most mining and business activity.
   d. abolished the system of compulsory service for noble landlords.

6. Peter the Great's reforms included
   a. compulsory education away from home for the higher classes.
   b. a lessening of the burdens of serfdom for Russian peasants.
   c. an elimination of the merit-system bureaucracy.
   d. the creation of an independent parliament.

7. The dominant artistic style of the seventeenth and early eighteenth centuries was
   a. Gothic.
   b. romantic.
   c. impressionistic.
   d. baroque.

8. The noble landowners of Prussia were known as
   a. boyars.
   b. Junkers.
   c. Vikings.
   d. Electors.

9. Apparently the most important reason for the return to serfdom in eastern Europe from about 1500 to 1650 was
   a. political.
   b. economic.
   c. military.
   d. religious.

10. The Russian Cossacks were
    a. nobles created by Peter the Great.
    b. free groups and outlaw armies.
    c. private armies of the landlords.
    d. Turkish troops who settled in the Black Sea area.

11. After the disastrous defeat of the Czech nobility by the Habsburgs at the battle of White Mountain in 1618, the
    a. old Czech nobility accepted Catholicism in great numbers.
    b. majority of the Czech nobles' land was given to soldiers who had fought for the Habsburgs.
    c. conditions of the enserfed peasantry improved.
    d. Czech nobles continued their struggle effectively for many years.

12. After the Thirty Years' War and the creation of a large standing army, Austria turned its attention to control of
    a. northern Italy.
    b. Prussia.
    c. Hungary.
    d. Poland.

13. The result of the struggle of the Hungarian nobles against Habsburg oppression was that
    a. they suffered a fate similar to the Czech nobility.
    b. they gained a great deal of autonomy compared with the Austrian and Bohemian nobility.
    c. they won their independence.
    d. their efforts were inconclusive.

14. The monarch who established Prussian absolutism and who was named "the Soldiers' King" was
    a. Peter the Great.
    b. Frederick William I.
    c. Ivan IV.
    d. Elector Frederick III.

15. The Viking invaders of Russia were principally interested in
    a. controlling vast new lands politically.
    b. spreading their religion.
    c. establishing and controlling commercial interests.
    d. the conquest of Vienna.

16. The Muscovite princes gained their initial power through
    a. services rendered to the Vikings.
    b. strategic marriages.
    c. services rendered to the Mongols.
    d. defeat of the rival branches of the house of Ruiruk.

17. The rise of the Russian monarchy was largely a response to the external threat of the
    a. French monarchy.
    b. Asiatic Mongols.
    c. Prussian monarchy.
    d. English monarchy.

18. The Time of Troubles was caused by
    a. a dispute in the line of succession.
    b. Turkish invasions.
    c. Mongol invasions.
    d. severe crop failures resulting in starvation and disease.

19. In order to strengthen the Russian military, Peter the Great
    a. made the nobility serve in the civil administration or army for life.
    b. established a navy in the Atlantic.
    c. excluded foreigners from his service.
    d. turned over political power to the military.

20. The real losers in the growth of eastern Europe absolutism were the
    a. peasants.
    b. peasants and middle classes.
    c. nobility.
    d. nobility and the clergy.

21. The Siege of Vienna of 1683 was undertaken by
    a. the Hungarians under Prince Rákóczy.
    b. the Russians.
    c. the Turks.
    d. Frederick William of Prussia.

22. The Battle of Poltava marks a Russian victory over
    a. Sweden.
    b. Turkey.
    c. Prussia.
    d. Austria.

23. All of the following reflected the power and magnificence of royal absolutism *except*
    a. soaring Gothic cathedrals.
    b. baroque palaces.
    c. royal cities.
    d. broad, urban avenues.

24. The result of the Czech noble revolt of 1618 was
    a. their replacement by Habsburg loyalists.
    b. Czech independence.
    c. Czech autonomy within the Habsburg state.
    d. the rise of Protestantism in Bohemia.

25. The Habsburg state was made up of
    a. Austria, Bohemia, and Hungary.
    b. Austria, Prussia, and Hungary.
    c. Hungary, Brandenburg, and Silesia.
    d. Silesia, Bohemia, and Austria.

Major Political Ideas

1. Why do you think the history of Russia is more a history of servitude than of freedom? Was the major reason for the reinstatement of serfdom political or economic? Explain.

2. Compare and contrast the power of the nobility and the middle class in Russia with that of the nobility and the middle class in of western Europe.

Issues for Essays and Discussion

1. Trace the fortunes and political power of the noble classes in Russia, Austria, and Prussia from about 1300 to about the middle of the 1700s. How did the monarchs gain the upper hand?

2. Peter the Great of Russia and Frederick William the Great Elector of Prussia are often viewed as heroes and reformers in the histories of their own countries. How valid is this assessment?

Interpretation of Visual Sources

Study the print entitled *Molding the Prussian Spirit* on page 543 of the textbook. Describe the scene. Why would this print have been included in a book for children? What were the reasons for Prussia's "obsessive bent for military organization and military scales of value"?

Geography

1. On Outline Map 17.3 provided, and using Map 17.3 in the textbook for reference, mark the following: the area covered by the principality of Moscow in 1300, the territories acquired by the principality of Moscow from 1300 to 1689, the acquisitions of Peter the Great.

2. Looking at Map 17.2 in the textbook, identify the three territorial parts of the Habsburg (Austrian) state and explain how they came to be united.

Outline Map 17.3

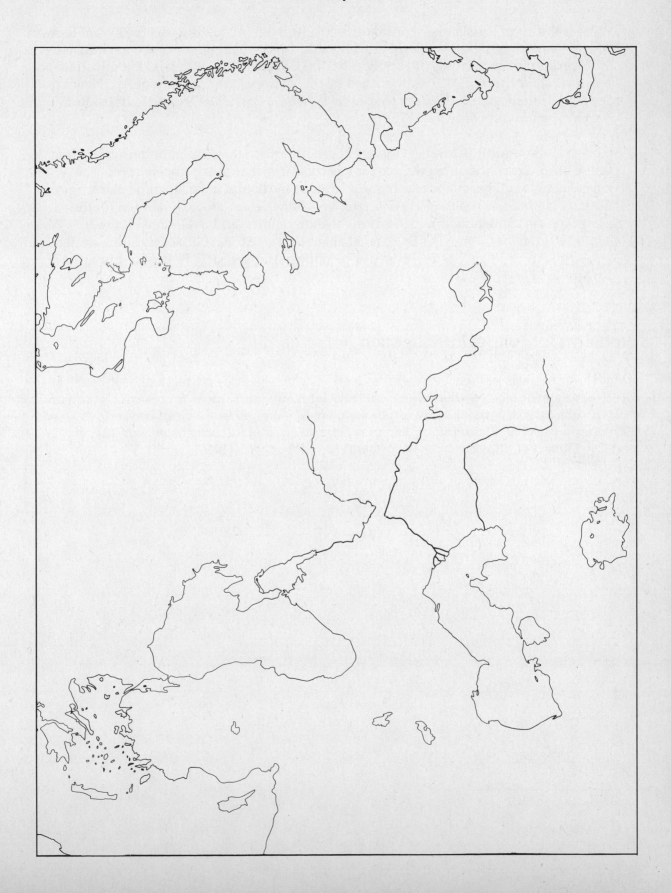

Understanding History Through the Arts

1. What is the art of Russia like? For centuries the Kremlin in Moscow was the axis of Russian culture—the place where works of great historical and artistic significance were amassed. Many examples of painting and applied art of the Kremlin are discussed and illustrated in *Treasures of the Kremlin** (1979), published by the Metropolitan Museum of Art, New York. See also, T. Froncek, ed., *The Horizon Book of the Arts of Russia* (1970), and G. Hamilton, *The Art and Architecture of Russia* (1975).

2. How does baroque music reflect the age? Baroque music, the dominant musical style in the age of absolutism, was often written for a particular monarch or princely court. The mathematical and harmonic emphasis of baroque music and its aristocratic patronage are illustrated in the six *Brandenburg Concertos* by Johann Sebastian Bach, written for the margrave of Brandenburg in the early eighteenth century, and in George F. Handel's *Water Music*, written for George I of England at about the same time. Both of these are available on numerous recordings. For the history of baroque music, see M. F. Bukofzer, *Music in the Baroque Era* (1947).

Problems for Further Investigation

What Western ideas influenced Peter the Great? The personality and reign of Tsar Peter the Great have generated considerable controversy for many years. Ideas for research in this and related subjects in Russian history can be found in M. Raeff, *Peter the Great* (rev. ed., 1972); V. Klyuchevsky and N. Riasanovsky, *Images of Peter the Great in Russian History and Thought* (1985); and L. J. Oliva, ed., *Russia and the West from Peter to Khrushchev* (1965).

---

*Available in paperback.

Chapter 18
Toward a New World-View

Chapter Questions

After reading and studying this chapter you should be able to answer the following questions:

Why did the world-view of the educated classes change from a primarily religious one to one that was primarily secular and scientific? How did this new outlook on life affect society and politics?

Chapter Summary

In the course of the seventeenth and eighteenth centuries the educated classes of Europe moved from a world-view that was basically religious to one that was primarily secular. The development of scientific knowledge was the key cause of this intellectual change. Until about 1500, scientific thought reflected the Aristotelian-medieval world-view, which taught that a motionless earth was at the center of a universe made up of planets and stars in ten crystal spheres. These and many other beliefs showed that science was primarily a branch of religion. Beginning with Copernicus, who taught that the earth revolved around the sun, Europeans slowly began to reject Aristotelian-medieval scientific thought. They developed a new conception of a universe based on natural laws, not on a personal God. Isaac Newton formulated the great scientific synthesis: the law of universal gravitation. This was the culminating point of the scientific revolution.

The new science was more important for intellectual development than for economic activity or everyday life, for above all it promoted critical thinking. Nothing was to be accepted on faith; everything was to be submitted to the rational, scientific way of thinking. This critical examination of everything, from religion and education to war and politics, was the program of the Enlightenment and the accomplishment of the philosophes, a group of thinkers who propagandized the new world-view across Europe and the North American colonies. These writers and thinkers, among them Voltaire, Montesquieu, and Diderot, produced books and articles that influenced all classes and whose primary intent was teaching people how to think critically and objectively about all matters.

The philosophes were reformers, not revolutionaries. Their "enlightened" ideas were adopted by a number of monarchs who sought to promote the advancement of knowledge and improve the lives of their subjects. Most important in this group were Frederick II of Prussia and Catherine II of Russia and the Habsburgs, Maria Theresa and Joseph II. Despite some reforms, particularly in the area of law, Frederick and Catherine's role in the Enlightenment was in the abstract rather than the practical. The Habsburgs were more successful in legal and tax reform, control of the church, and improvement of the lot of the serfs, although much of Joseph's spectacular peasant reform was later undone. Yet reform of society from the top down, that is, by the absolute monarchs through "enlightened absolutism," proved to be impossible because the enlightened monarchs could not ignore the demands of their conservative nobilities. In the end, it was revolution, not enlightened absolutism, that changed and reformed society.

The chapter closes with a discussion of how the middle class of France used the Parlement of Paris and its judgeships as a counterweight to absolutism and the revival of aristocratic power. This opposition was crushed by Louis XV's chancellor Maupeou, only to reappear with the new King Louis XVI.

Study Outline

Use this outline to preview the chapter before you read a particular section and than as a self-check to test your reading comprehension after you have read the chapter section.

  I. The scientific revolution: the origin of the modern world
   A. The scientific revolution of the seventeenth century was the major cause of the change in world-view and one of the key developments in the evolution of Western society.
   B. Scientific thought in the early 1500s
     1. European ideas about the universe were based on Aristotelian-medieval ideas.
       a. Central to this view was the belief in a motionless earth fixed at the center of the universe.
       b. Around the earth moved ten crystal spheres, and beyond the spheres was heaven.
     2. Aristotle's scheme suited Christianity because it positioned human beings at the center of the universe and established a home for God.
     3. Science in this period was primarily a branch of theology.
   C. The Copernican hypothesis
     1. Copernicus, a Polish clergyman and astronomer, claimed that the earth revolved around the sun and that the sun was the center of the universe.
     2. This heliocentric theory was a departure from medieval thought and created doubts about traditional Christianity.
   D. From Tycho Brahe to Galileo
     1. Brahe set the stage for the modern study of astronomy by building an observatory and collecting data.
     2. His assistant, Kepler, formulated three laws of planetary motion that proved the precise relationships among planets in a sun-centered universe.
     3. Galileo discovered the laws of motion using the experimental method—the cornerstone of modern science.
       a. He also applied the experimental method to astronomy, using the newly invented telescope.

b. Galileo was tried by the Inquisition for heresy in 1633 and forced to recant his views.

E. Newton's synthesis
1. Newton integrated the astronomy of Copernicus and Kepler with the physics of Galileo.
    a. He formulated a set of mathematical laws to explain motion and mechanics.
    b. The key feature in his synthesis was the law of universal gravitation.
2. Henceforth, the universe could be explained through mathematics.

F. Causes of the scientific revolution
1. Medieval universities provided the framework for the new science.
2. The Renaissance stimulated science by rediscovering ancient mathematics and supporting scientific investigations.
3. The navigational problems of sea voyages generated scientific research and new instruments.
4. Better ways of obtaining knowledge about the world improved scientific methods.
    a. Bacon advocated empirical, experimental research.
    b. Descartes stressed mathematics and deductive reasoning.
5. After about 1630 the Catholic church discouraged science while Protestantism tended to favor it.

G. Some consequences of the scientific revolution
1. A scientific community emerged whose primary goal was the expansion of knowledge.
2. A modern scientific method arose that was both theoretical and experimental and refused to base its conclusions on tradition and established sources.
3. Because the link between pure science and applied technology was weak, the scientific revolution had little effect on daily life before the nineteenth century.

II. The Enlightenment
A. Enlightenment ideas made up a new world-view.
1. Natural science and reason can explain all aspects of life.
2. The scientific method can explain the laws of human society.
3. Progress—the creation of better societies and better people—is possible.

B. The emergence of the Enlightenment
1. Many writers made scientific thought understandable to a large nonscientific audience.
    a. Fontenelle stressed the idea of progress.
    b. He was also cynical about organized religion and absolute religious truth.
2. Skeptics such as Bayle concluded that nothing can be known beyond all doubt and stressed open-mindedness.
3. The growth of world travel led Europeans to look at truth and morality in relative, not absolute, terms.
4. In his *Essay Concerning Human Understanding,* Locke insisted that all ideas are derived from experience—the human mind at birth is like a blank table (*tabula rasa*).

C. The philosophes and their ideas
1. The philosophes asked fundamental philosophical questions and were committed to the reformation of society and humanity, although they often had to cloak attacks on church and state in satire.

a. Montesquieu's theory of the separation of powers was extremely influential.
b. Voltaire challenged traditional Catholic theology and exhibited a characteristic philosophe belief in a distant God who let human affairs take their own course.
c. Diderot and d'Alembert edited the *Encyclopedia*, which examined all of human knowledge and attempted to teach people how to think critically and rationally.

2. The later Enlightenment writers built rigid and dogmatic systems.
a. D'Holbach argued that humans were completely controlled by outside forces.
b. Hume argued that the mind is nothing but a bundle of impressions that originate in sense experiences.
c. Rousseau attacked rationalism and civilization; he claimed that children must develop naturally and spontaneously, and in *The Social Contract* argued that the general will of the people is sacred and absolute.

D. The social setting of the Enlightenment
1. Enlightenment ideas—including new ideas about women's rights—were spread by salons of the upper classes.
2. The salons were often presided over by women.
3. These salons seemed to have functioned as informal "schools" for women.

III. The development of absolutism
A. Many philosophes believed that "enlightened" reform would come by way of "enlightened" monarchs.
1. The philosophes believed that a benevolent absolutism offered the best chance for improving society.
2. The rulers seemed to seek the philosophes' advice.
3. The philosophes distrusted the masses and felt that change had to come from above.

B. The "Greats": Frederick II of Prussia and Catherine II of Russia
1. Frederick II used the War of the Austrian Succession (1740–1748) to expand Prussia into a great power by seizing Silesia.
2. The Seven Years' War (1756–1763) saw an attempt by Maria Theresa, with the help of France and Russia, to regain Silesia, but it failed.
3. Frederick allowed religious freedom and promoted education, legal reform, and economic growth but never tried to change Prussia's social structure.
4. Catherine II imported Western culture to Russia, supported the philosophes, and began a program of domestic reform.
5. The Pugachev uprising in 1773 led her to reverse the trend toward reform of serfdom and give nobles absolute control of their serfs.
6. She engaged in a policy of territorial expansion and, with Prussia and Austria, carved up Poland.

C. Absolutism in France and Austria
1. Favored by the duke of Orléans, who governed as a regent until 1723, the French nobility regained much of the power it had lost under Louis XIV.
a. The Parlement of Paris won two decisive victories against taxation.
b. It then asserted that the king could not levy taxes without its consent.
2. Under Louis XV the French minister Maupeou began the restoration of royal absolutism by abolishing the Parlement of Paris.

3. Louis XVI reinstated the Parlement of Paris, and the country drifted toward renewed financial and political crises.
4. Maria Theresa of Austria introduced reforms that limited church power, revised the tax system and the bureaucracy, and reduced the power of the lords over the serfs.
5. Her successor, Joseph II, was a dedicated reformer who abolished serfdom, taxed all equally, and granted religious freedom.
6. Because of opposition from both the nobles and the peasants, Joseph's reforms were short-lived.

D. An overall evaluation of absolutism and the influence of the Enlightenment
1. In France, the rise of judicial and aristocratic opposition combined with liberalism put absolutism on the defensive.
2. In eastern Europe the results of enlightened absolutism were modest and absolutism remained strong.
3. By combining state building with the culture and critical thinking of the Enlightenment, absolute monarchs succeeded in expanding the role of the state in the life of society.

Review Questions

Check your understanding of this chapter by answering the following questions.

1. Contrast the old Aristotelian-medieval world-view with that of the sixteenth and seventeenth centuries. What were the contributions of Copernicus, Brahe, Kepler, Galileo, and Newton? What is meant by Newton's "synthesis"?
2. How did the new scientific theory and discoveries alter the concept of God and religion? Did science, in fact, come to dictate humanity's concept of God?
3. What were the scientific and religious implications of Copernicus's theory?
4. Discuss the origins and the momentum of the scientific revolution in terms of (a) its own "internal logic" and (b) external and nonscientific causes.
5. How did Bacon and Descartes contribute to the development of the modern scientific method?
6. Did the Catholic and Protestant churches retard or foster scientific investigation? Explain.
7. What were the consequences of the rise of modern science?
8. What were the central concepts of the Enlightenment?
9. Who were the philosophes and what did they believe?
10. In what ways were Frederick of Prussia and Catherine of Russia enlightened monarchs?
11. What was the effect of Catherine's reign on (a) the Russian nobility, (b) the Russian serfs, and (c) the position of Russia in the European balance of power?
12. What was the nature of the power struggle between the aristocrats and Louis XV of France?

Study-Review Exercises

Define the following key concepts and terms.
Aristotelian world-view

empirical method

Copernican hypothesis

deductive reasoning

rationalism

progress

secular

skepticism

tabula rasa

Parlement of Paris

Enlightenment

enlightened absolutism

philosophes

Gresham College

Identify and explain the significance of each of the following people.

Diderot

Bayle

Kepler

Galileo

Bacon

Descartes

D'Holbach

Newton

Montesquieu

Voltaire

Copernicus

Brahe

Catherine the Great

Frederick the Great

Maria Theresa

Louis XV

Joseph II

Explain the new ideas of each the following books. What were some of the consequences of these ideas?
On the Revolutions of the Heavenly Spheres

New Astronomy or Celestial Physics

Two New Sciences

Principia

Conversations on the Plurality Of Worlds of 1686

Historical and Critical Dictionary

The Spirit of the Laws

Essay Concerning Human Understanding

Philosophical Dictionary

Encyclopedia: The Rational Dictionary of the Sciences, the Arts, and the Crafts

The Social Contract

Test your understanding of the chapter by providing the correct answers.

1. According to Aristotle, the sublunar world was made up of four elements: air, fire,

   _____ , and _____ .

2. Copernicus *did/did not* attempt to disprove the existence of God.

3. Galileo claimed that *motion/rest* is the natural state of all objects.

4. The key feature in Newton's synthesis was the law of _____ .

5. In the medieval universities, science emerged as a branch of _____ .

6. The method of finding latitude came out of study and experimentation in the country of

   _____ .

7. The idea of "progress" *was/was not* widespread in the Middle Ages.

8. In the seventeenth and eighteenth centuries a close link between pure (theoretical) science and applied technology *did/did not* exist.

9. A _____ is one who believes that nothing can ever be known beyond all doubt.

10. Voltaire believed that _____ was history's greatest man because he used his genius to benefit humanity.

11. Overall, Joseph II of Austria *succeeded/failed* as an enlightened monarch.

Place the following ideas in correct chronological order.

Copernicus's idea that the sun is the center of the universe
Montesquieu's theory of the separation of powers
D'Holbach's theory that human beings were machines
Aristotle's view of a motionless earth at the center of the universe
Newton's law of universal gravitation

1.

2.

3.

4.

5.

Multiple-Choice Questions

1. Catherine the Great accomplished which of the following?
   a. Annexed part of Poland
   b. Freed the Russian serfs
   c. Denied any sort of religious toleration
   d. Persecuted the philosophes of France

2. "Enlightened" monarchs believed in all of the following *except*
   a. reform.
   b. democracy.
   c. cultural values of the Enlightenment.
   d. secularism.

3. Geoffrin and Deffand were
   a. scientific writers.
   b. religious leaders in France.
   c. leaders of the Enlightenment salons.
   d. leaders of the serf uprising in France.

4. The philosophes were
   a. mainly university professors.
   b. generally hostile to monarchial government.
   c. enthusiastic supporters of the Catholic church.
   d. satirists who wished to reform society and humanity.

5. The social setting of the Enlightenment
   a. excluded women.
   b. was characterized by poverty and boredom.
   c. was dominated by government officials.
   d. was characterized by witty and intelligent conversation.

6. Catherine the Great
   a. believed the philosophes were dangerous revolutionaries.
   b. freed the serfs to satisfy Diderot.
   c. increased the size of the Russian Empire.
   d. established a strong constitutional monarchy.

7. According to medieval thought, the center of the universe was the
   a. sun.
   b. earth.
   c. moon.
   d. heaven.

8. The Aristotelian world-view placed emphasis on the idea of
   a. the sun as the center of the universe.
   b. the rejection of Christian theology.
   c. an earth that moves in space.
   d. crystal spheres moving around the earth.

9. Copernicus's theory of a sun-centered universe
   a. suggested the universe was small and closed.
   b. questioned the idea that crystal spheres moved the stars around the earth.
   c. suggested that the worlds of heaven and earth were radically different from each other.
   d. suggested an enormous and possibly infinite universe.

10. The first astronomer to prove his theories through the use of mathematical equations was
    a. Galileo.
    b. Kepler.
    c. Brahe.
    d. Newton.

11. D'Holbach, Hume, and Rousseau are examples of the later Enlightenment trend toward
    a. rigid systems.
    b. social satire.
    c. religion.
    d. the idea of absolutism.

12. The French philosopher who rejected his contemporaries and whose writings influenced the romantic movement was
    a. Rousseau.
    b. Voltaire.
    c. Diderot.
    d. Condorcet.

13. The gathering ground for many who wished to discuss the ideas of the French Enlightenment was the
    a. salon.
    b. lecture hall.
    c. palace at Versailles.
    d. University of Paris.

14. Frederick II is considered an enlightened monarch because he
    a. regained Silesia from Prussia.
    b. wrote poetry and improved the legal and bureaucratic systems.
    c. kept the aristocrats in a dominant position socially and politically.
    d. avoided war.

15. Catherine the Great of Russia hardened her position on serfdom after the
    a. Pugachev rebellion.
    b. Moscow rebellion.
    b. Polish rebellion.
    c. "Five Year" rebellion.

16. After Louis XIV's death
    a. the nobility lost considerable power.
    b. the lower classes secured judicial positions in the Parlement.
    c. the French government struggled with severe economic difficulties.
    d. absolutism remained firmly entrenched during the succeeding reign.

17. Which of the following used the War of the Austrian Succession to expand Prussia into a great power?
    a. Joseph II
    b. Frederick II
    c. Frederick William I
    d. Louis XIV

18. The aggressiveness of Prussia, Austria, and Russia led to the disappearance of which eastern European kingdom from the map after 1795?
    a. Hungary
    b. Sweden
    c. Brandenburg
    d. Poland

19. Francis Bacon's great contribution to scientific methodology was
    a. the geocentric theory.
    b. the notion of logical speculation.
    c. the philosophy of empiricism.
    d. analytic geometry.

20. Which of the following men set the stage for the modern study of astronomy by building an observatory and collecting data?
    a. Darwin
    b. Hume
    c. Newton
    d. Brahe

21. The Parlement of Paris was
    a. a high court dominated by nobles who were formerly middle class.
    b. a center of royal absolutism.
    c. used by Maupeou to strengthen the king's position.
    d. not interested in tax reform or finance.

22. Maria Theresa was a devout Catholic who
    a. sought to limit the church's influence in Austria.
    b. was not interested in the Enlightenment.
    c. did nothing to improve the lot of the agricultural population.
    d. was a weak monarch unable to hold the Austrian Empire together.

23. After 1715 in France, the direction of political change was
    a. toward greater absolutism.
    b. away from Enlightenment political thought.
    c. in favor of opposition forces—largely the nobility and the Parlement of Paris.
    d. toward "enlightened absolutism."

24. In his famous book *Emile*, Rousseau argued that
    a. children are born with corrupting ideas and must be tamed.
    b. women should be taught the same subjects as men.
    c. boys and girls should be taught to operate in separate spheres.
    d. children should be exposed to corruption at an early age so that they know how to reject it.

25. Descartes' idea was that the world consists of two fundamental entities or substances, which we can call
    a. the physical and the spiritual.
    b. water and air.
    c. reason and passion.
    d. deduction and induction.

Major Political Ideas

1. Describe the concept of enlightened absolutism in terms of its political and legal goals. Did it work? What was the response of the aristocracy to this political concept?

2. This chapter emphasizes the difference between a secular and religious view of the world. What is meant by *secular* and what effect did a secular world-view have on political loyalties?

Issues for Essays and Discussion

In the course of the eighteenth century the basic outlook on life and society held by many men and women changed dramatically. In what ways did this transformation affect scientific, political, religious, social, and economic thought? In working out your argument explain how specific new scientific ideas and methods of reasoning led directly to new political and social ideas.

Interpretation of Visual Sources

Study the print of Louis XIV's visit to the Royal Academy in 1671 on page 571 of the textbook. Write a paragraph on how this print illustrates the relationship between science and politics. Did the scientific revolution have a great effect on how kings ran their states? Why were some monarchs interested in science? Does this print give any clues?

Geography

Compare Map 18.1 to Map 17.2. Describe what the "partition of Poland" was, when it took place, why, and who benefited.

Understanding History Through the Arts

How did the Enlightenment affect the arts? This period is often referred to as the age of the baroque style, and the achievements of its great artists are discussed in M. Kitson, *The Age of the Baroque* (1966). See also Chapter 6 in N. Pevsner, *An Outline of European Architecture* (7th ed., 1963), and E. Kaufmann, *Architecture in the Age of Reason—Baroque and Post-Baroque in England, Italy, and France* (1955, *1968). On the subject of the Scottish Enlightenment see T. A. Markus, ed., *Order and Space: Architectural Form and Its Context in the Scottish Enlightenment* (1982). Few artists captured English life as well as the painter Hogarth, whose *Rake's Progress* and *Harlot's Progress* point to the consequences of moral decay. Hogarth's paintings can be seen and studied in W. Gaunt, *The World of William Hogarth* (1978), and D. Bindman, *Hogarth** (1981). For a description of French life by painters of the time, see T. E. Crow, *Painters and Public Life in Eighteenth-Century Paris* (1985).

Problems for Further Investigation

1. Write an essay in which you describe and analyze an important work of the Enlightenment. What were the ideas set forth by the author and how do these ideas reflect or illustrate Enlightenment thought and change? The two greatest philosophes of the age of Enlightenment were Rousseau and Voltaire. Rousseau's ideas on education and natural law are set forth in *Emile*, and Voltaire's most-praised work is *Candide*, a funny and sometimes bawdy parody of eighteenth-century life and thought. Selections from the great *Encyclopedia* are found in S. Gendzier, ed., *Denis Diderot: The Encyclopedia: Selections* (1967). Much of the fiction of the eighteenth century reflects, often in satire, the spirit of the new world-view—Jonathan Swift, *Gulliver's Travels*; Daniel Defoe, *Moll Flanders*; and Henry Fielding, *Tom Jones*, are just a few of the many novels of this period. In Germany, the *Sturm und Drang* (storm and stress) movement embraced the ideas of the Enlightenment and

*Available in paperback.

romanticism and produced works such as Lessing's *Nathan the Wise,* which stressed a universal religion.

2. How have historians interpreted the meaning and impact of the Enlightenment? Students interested in this topic will want to begin with two books that set forth some of the major issues and schools of interpretation on the subject: B. Tierney et al., eds., *Enlightenment—The Age of Reason** (1967), and R. Wines, ed., *Enlightened Despotism** (1967).

3. Why was it not until the seventeenth century that rational science emerged? What has been the relationship between science and religion in Western society? What ideas did Darwin and modern biologists draw from the scientific revolution of 1500–1800? These are just a few of the questions asked by scholars of the subject. Begin your investigation with H. Butterfield, *The Origins of Modern Science* (1951); A. R. Hall, *From Galileo to Newton, 1630–1720* (1963); G. Sarton, *Introduction to the History of Science* (1927–1948, 5 vols.); or L. Thorndike, *History of Magic and Experimental Science* (1923–1958). On particular figures in science see F. S. Taylor, *Galileo and the Freedom of Thought* (1938); A. Armitage, *Copernicus, the Founder of Modern Astronomy* (1938); M. Casoar, *Johannes Kepler,* C. Hettman, trans. (1959); L. T. More, *Isaac Newton* (1934); and I. Cohen, *Franklin and Newton* (1956).

*Available in paperback.

Studying Effectively—Exercise 4

Learning to Classify Information According to Sequence

As you know, a great deal of historical information is classified by sequence, in which things follow each other in time. This kind of *sequential order* is also known as *time order* or *chronological order*.

Attention to time sequence is important in the study of history for at least two reasons.

1. It helps you organize historical information effectively.

2. It promotes historical understanding. If you know the order in which events happen, you can think intelligently about questions of cause and effect. You can begin to evaluate conflicting interpretations.

Since time sequences are essential in historical study, the authors have placed a number of timelines in the text to help you organize the historical information.

Two Fallacies Regarding Time Sequences

One common fallacy is often known by the famous Latin phrase *post hoc, ergo propter hoc:* "after this, therefore because of this." This fallacy assumes that one happening that follows another *must* be caused by the first happening. Obviously, some great development (such as the Protestant Reformation) could come after another (the Italian Renaissance) without being caused by it. *Causal relationships must be demonstrated, not simply assumed on the basis of the "after this, therefore because of this" fallacy.*

A second common, if old-fashioned, fallacy assumes that time sequences are composed only of political facts with precise data. But in considering social, intellectual, and economic developments, historians must often speak with less chronological exactitude—in terms of decades or even centuries, for example. Yet they still use time sequences, and students of history must recognize them. For example, did you realize that the sections on "The Scientific Revolution" and "The Enlightenment" in Chapter 18 are very conscientious about time sequence, even though they do not deal with political facts?

Exercise

Reread the large section in Chapter 18 on "The Scientific Revolution" with an eye for dates and sequential order. Then take a sheet of notebook paper and with the book open make a "Timeline for the Scientific Revolution." Pick out at least a dozen important events and put them in the time sequence, with a word or two to explain the significance when possible.

Suggestion: Do not confine yourself solely to specific events with specific dates. Also, integrate some items from the subsection on the causes of the scientific revolution into the sequence. You may find that constructing timelines helps you organize your study.

After you have completed your timeline, compare it with the one on the following page, which shows how one of the authors of the text did this assignment.

Timeline on the Scientific Revolution

(1300–1500)	Renaissance stimulates development of mathematics
early 1500s	Aristotle's ideas on movement and universe still dominant
1543	Copernicus publishes *On the Revolution of the Heavenly Spheres*
1572, 1577	New star and comet create more doubts about traditional astronomy
1546–1601	Tycho Brache—famous astronomer, creates mass of observations
1571–1630	Johannes Kepler—his three laws prove Copernican theory and demolish Aristotle's beliefs
1589	Galileo Galilei (1564–1642) named professor of mathematics
1610	Galileo studies moon with telescope and writes of experience
1561–1626	Francis Bacon—English scientific enthusiast, advocates experimental (inductive) method
1596–1650	René Descartes—French philosopher, discovers analytical geometry in 1619 and advocates theoretical (deductive) method
to about 1630	All religious authorities oppose Copernican theory
about 1632	Galileo tried by papal inquisition
1622	Royal Society of London founded—brings scientists and practical men together
1687	Isaac Newton publishes his *Principia*, synthesizing existing knowledge around idea of universal gravitation
to late 1700s	Consequences of scientific revolution primarily intellectual, not economic

Chapter 19
The Expansion of Europe in the Eighteenth Century

Chapter Questions

After reading and studying this chapter you should be able to answer the following questions:

How did the European economy expand and change in the eighteenth century? What were the causes of this expansion? How did these changes affect people and their work?

Chapter Summary

How did our "modern" world begin? This chapter discusses the important economic and demographic changes of the eighteenth century, which led up to the Industrial Revolution. It also prepares us for understanding the life of ordinary people in the eighteenth century, which is the subject of the following chapter.

The chapter covers four important and interrelated subjects. First, the centuries-old open-field system of agricultural production, a system that was both inefficient and unjust, is described. This system was gradually transformed into a more productive system of capitalistic farming, first in the Low Countries and then in England. Some English peasants suffered in the process, but on the whole the changes added up to a highly beneficial agricultural revolution. The second topic is the explosive growth of European population in the eighteenth century. This growth, still imperfectly understood, was probably due largely to the disappearance of the plague and to new and better foods, such as the potato. Doctors and organized medicine played a very minor role in the improvements in health. Third, the chapter discusses the movement of manufacturing from urban shops to cottages in the countryside. Rural families worked there as units in the new domestic system, which provided employment for many in the growing population. The domestic system was particularly effective in the textile industry, which this chapter examines in detail.

Finally, the chapter shows how the mercantilist economic philosophy of the time resulted in wars for trade and colonies. Mercantilism also led to the acquisition of huge markets for manufactured goods, especially cloth. The demand from these new markets fostered the growth of the domestic system and put pressure on it. This eventually led to important inventions and the development of the more efficient factory system. Thus the modern world was born. It is important to look for the interrelatedness of these changes and to keep in mind that it was in only one country, Great Britain, that all of these forces were fully at work.

Study Outline

Use this outline to preview the chapter before you read a particular section in your textbook and then as a self-check to test your reading comprehension after you have read the chapter section.

I. Agriculture and the land
   A. The hazards of an agrarian economy
      1. The agricultural yields in seventeenth-century Europe were not much higher than in ancient Greece.
      2. Frequent poor harvests and bad weather led to famine and disease.
   B. The open-field system
      1. The open-field system, developed during the Middle Ages, divided the land into a few large fields, which were then cut up into long, narrow strips.
      2. The fields were farmed jointly by the community, but a large portion of the arable land was always left fallow.
      3. Common lands were set aside for community use.
      4. The labor and tax system throughout Europe was unjust, but eastern European peasants suffered the most.
         a. There were few limitations on the amount of forced labor the lord could require.
         b. Serfs could be sold.
      5. By the eighteenth century most peasants in western Europe were free from serfdom, and many owned some land.
   C. The agricultural revolution of the late seventeenth and eighteenth centuries
      1. The use of idle fallow land by crop rotation increased cultivation, which meant more food.
         a. The secret was in alternating grain crops with nitrogen-storing crops, such as peas and beans, root crops, and grasses.
         b. This meant more fodder for animals, which meant more meat for the people and more manure for fertilizer.
         c. These improvements necessitated ending the open-field system by "enclosing" the fields.
      2. Enclosure of the open fields to permit crop rotation also meant the disappearance of common land.
         a. Many peasants and noble landowners opposed these changes.
         b. The enclosure process was slow, and enclosed and open fields existed side by side for a long time.
   D. The leadership of the Low Countries and England
      1. By the middle of the seventeenth century, the Low Countries led in intensive farming.
         a. This Dutch lead was due largely to the need to feed a growing population.

       b. The growth of the urban population provided good markets for the produce.

  2. Dutch engineers such as Vermuyden helped England drain its marshes to create more arable land.

       a. Townsend was one of the pioneers of English agricultural improvement.

       b. Tull advocated the use of horses for plowing and drilling equipment for sowing seeds.

E. The cost of enclosure

  1. Some historians argue that the English landowners were more efficient than continental owners, and that enclosures were fair.

  2. Others argue that the enclosure acts forced small peasants and landless cottagers off the land.

  3. In reality, the enclosure and the exclusion of cottagers and laborers had begun as early as the sixteenth century.

       a. It was the independent peasant farmers who could not compete, and thus began to disappear.

       b. The tenant farmers, who rented land from the big landlords, benefited from enclosure.

       c. By 1815 a tiny minority of English and Scottish landlords held most of the land—which they rented to tenants, who hired laborers.

  4. The eighteenth-century enclosure movement marked the completion of the rise of market-oriented estate agriculture and the emergence of a landless rural proletariat.

II. The beginning of the population explosion

A. The limitations on population growth up to 1700

  1. The traditional checks on growth were famine, disease, and war.

  2. These checks kept Europe's population growth rate fairly low.

B. The new pattern of population growth in the eighteenth century

  1. The basic cause of population growth was fewer deaths, partly owing to the disappearance of the plague.

       a. Stricter quarantine measures helped eliminate the plague.

       b. The elimination of the black rat by the brown rat was a key reason for the disappearance of the disease.

  2. Advances in medicine, such as inoculation against smallpox, did little to reduce the death rate in Europe.

  3. Improvements in sanitation promoted better public health.

  4. An increase in the food supply meant fewer famines and epidemics, especially as transportation improved.

  5. The growing population often led to overpopulation and increased rural poverty.

III. The growth of cottage industry

A. Rural industry

  1. The rural poor took in manufacturing work to supplement their income.

  2. By the eighteenth century this cottage industry challenged the monopoly of the urban craft industry.

B. The putting-out system

  1. The putting-out system was based on rural workers producing cloth in their homes for merchant-capitalists, who supplied the raw materials and paid for the finished goods.

    2. This capitalist system reduced the problem of rural unemployment and provided cheap goods.

    3. England led the way in the conversion from urban to rural textile production.

C. The textile industry in England as an example of the putting-out system

    1. The English textile industry was a family industry: the women would spin and the men would weave.

    2. A major problem was that there were not enough spinners to make yarn for the weaver.

    3. Strained relations often existed between workers and capitalist employers.

    4. The capitalist found it difficult to control the worker and the quality of the product.

IV. Building the Atlantic economy in the eighteenth century

A. Mercantilism and colonial wars

    1. Mercantilism is a system of economic regulations aimed at increasing the power of the state, particularly by creating a favorable balance of trade.

    2. English mercantilism was further characterized by the use of government regulations to serve the interests of private individuals.

    3. The Navigation Acts were a form of economic warfare.

       a. They required that most goods exported to England be carried on British ships.

       b. These acts gave England a virtual trade monopoly with its colonies.

    4. The French quest for power in Europe and North America led to international wars.

       a. The loss of the War of the Spanish Succession forced France to cede parts of Canada to Britain.

       b. The Seven Years' War (1756–1763) was the decisive struggle in the French-British competition for colonial empire, and France ended up losing all its North American possessions.

B. Land and wealth in North America

    1. Colonies helped relieve European poverty and surplus population as settlers eagerly took up farming on the virtually free land.

       a. The availability of land made labor expensive in the colonies.

       b. Cheap land and scarce labor were critical factors in the growth of slavery.

    2. The English mercantilist system benefited American colonists.

       a. They exported food to the West Indies to feed the slaves and sugar and tobacco to Britain.

       b. The American shipping industry grew.

    3. The population of the North American colonies grew very quickly during the eighteenth century, and the standards of living were fairly high.

C. The growth of foreign trade

    1. Trade with the English colonists compensated for a decline in English trade on the Continent.

    2. The colonies also encouraged industrial growth in England.

D. Revival in colonial Latin America

    1. Spain's political revitalization was matched by economic improvement in its colonies.

       a. Silver mining recovered in Mexico and Peru.

       b. Trade grew, though industry remained weak.

2. In much of Latin America, Creole landowners dominated the economy and the Indian population by means of debt peonage.
3. Compared to North America, racial mixing was more frequent in Spanish America.

Review Questions

Check your understanding of the chapter by answering the following questions.

1. How did the open-field system work? Why was much of the land left uncultivated while the people sometimes starved?
2. What changes brought the open-field system to an end?
3. Where did the modern agricultural revolution originate? Why?
4. What is meant by *enclosure*? Was this movement a great swindle of the poor by the rich, as some have claimed?
5. Was the dramatic growth of population in the eighteenth century due to a decreasing death rate or an increasing birthrate? Explain.
6. How was the grip of the deadly bubonic plague finally broken?
7. What improvements in the eighteenth century contributed to the decline of disease and famine?
8. How did the putting-out system work and why did it grow?
9. What were the advantages and disadvantages of the putting-out system for the merchant-capitalist? For the worker?
10. What was mercantilism? How could it have been a cause of war? Of economic growth?
11. The eighteenth century witnessed a large number of expensive and drawn-out wars. Who was attempting to alter the balance of power? Were the causes of these wars economic or political?
12. Did the American colonists and the American colonial economy benefit or suffer from the British mercantilistic colonial system?
13. What role did the Creoles play in colonial Latin America? The *mestizos*? The Indians?

Study-Review Exercises

Define the following key concepts and terms.

agrarian economy

famine foods

common land

open-field system

enclosure

mercantilism

cottage industry

putting-out system

fallow fields

agricultural revolution

crop rotation

asiento

mestizos

primogeniture

Creole elite

Identify and explain the significance of each of the following people and terms.
Jethro Tull

Charles Townsend

Cornelius Vermuyden

bubonic plague

Asiatic brown rat

British Navigation Acts

Treaty of Paris

Peace of Utrecht

spinning jenny

turnips

potatoes

Explain the following wars in the age of mercantilism by filling in the appropriate information in the table.

Name of War	Dates	Participants	Causes	Outcome
Anglo-Dutch wars				
War of the Spanish Succession				
War of the Austrian Succession				
Seven Years' War				

Fill in the blank with the letter of the correct answer.

_____ 1. Its disappearance encouraged population growth.

_____ 2. Agricultural land set aside for general village use.

_____ 3. The area with the highest average standard of living in the world.

_____ 4. After 1763 the major power in India.

_____ 5. West African slave trade.

_____ 6. Led Europe in agriucltural improvement.

_____ 7. Offspring of racial intermarriage.

_____ 8. The most important new eighteenth-century food.

a. Low Countries
b. *mestizos*
c. commons
d. Thirty Years' War
e. American colonies
f. potato
g. *asiento*
h. France
i. bubonic plague
j. Britain

Multiple-Choice Questions

1. Dutch agricultural innovation in the eighteenth century was due to
   a. the movement of people from cities to rural areas.
   b. British examples.
   c. population growth and extensive urbanization.
   d. the discovery of the open-field system.

2. Which of the following was a weakness of the cottage textile industry?
   a. An imbalance between spinning and weaving
   b. Shortage of labor
   c. Rigid control of the quality of the product
   d. Not enough demand for the product

3. Which of the following is a characteristic of eighteenth-century economic change?
   a. Decreased world trade
   b. The decline of the cottage system of textile production
   c. The creation of more common lands and open fields for production
   d. The increase in both population and food supply

4. The English enclosure movement ultimately resulted in
   a. more land for a greater number of farmers.
   b. fewer opportunities for the well-off tenant farmers.
   c. the concentration of landowning in the hands of a tiny minority.
   d. opportunity for the landless laborer to purchase small farms.

5. The agricultural improvements of the mid-eighteenth century were based on the elimination of
   a. livestock farming.
   b. the open-field system.
   c. rotation of fields.
   d. nitrogen-producing plants, such as peas and beans.

6. Which of the following prevented eighteenth-century peasants from earning a profit on their land?
   a. The combination of oppressive landlords and poor harvests
   b. The plague
   c. The relatively light taxes imposed on them by landlords
   d. Their reliance on crop rotation

7. The mercantilist attitude toward the state was that
   a. the government should regulate the economy.
   b. governmental power should be increased at the expense of private profit.
   c. using governmental economic power to help private interests is unethical.
   d. the economy should be left to operate according to its natural laws.

8. The new farming system consisting of crop rotation and the use of nitrogen-fixing crops caught on quickly in
   a. the Low Countries and England.
   b. Russia.
   c. eastern Europe as a whole.
   d. Scandinavia.

9. The rapid development of Dutch farming was the result of all of the following *except*
   a. the increasing number of cities and towns.
   b. Dutch reluctance to accept agricultural innovations.
   c. an unencumbered political and economic system.
   d. a dense population.

10. A fair description of the European population before 1700 would be that it
    a. was remarkably uniform in its growth.
    b. increased steadily on account of very young marriages and large families.
    c. decreased slightly on account of war, famine, and disease.
    d. grew slowly and erratically.

11. After 1720, the plague did not reappear because of all of the following *except*
    a. the development of an effective vaccination against the disease in 1718.
    b. the practice of isolating carriers of the dread disease.
    c. the invasion of the Asiatic brown rat.
    d. quarantine in Mediterranean ports.

12. In the mid-seventeenth century, England's major maritime competitor was
    a. France.
    b. the Netherlands.
    c. Spain.
    d. Denmark.

13. The Seven Years' War between France and Britain resulted in
    a. British dominance in North America and India.
    b. French dominance in North America and India.
    c. a stalemate.
    d. British dominance only in North America.

14. The slow growth of industry in North America during the colonial period was caused by
    a. the availability of land and the high cost of labor.
    b. a lack of capital for investment.
    c. a scorn for industry.
    d. British settlers in America had no use for manufactured goods.

15. The black-to-white ratio in America by 1774 was
    a. one to four.
    b. one to eight.
    c. one to ten.
    d. one to two.

16. The abundance of land in the American colonies encouraged all of the following *except*
    a. increased population through natural increase and immigration.
    b. a higher standard of living.
    c. the growth of slavery in the southern colonies.
    d. economic inequality.

17. Which of the following resulted from British mercantilist policies?
    a. A reduction of exports to the Continent
    b. A serious decline of Dutch shipping and commerce
    c. British colonists no longer purchasing all of their goods from Britain
    d. A decline of trade with colonial plantation owners

18. The group that used the new farming methods to the fullest in England was
    a. independent farmers.
    b. well-financed, profit-minded tenant farmers.
    c. large landowners.
    d. small landowning wage laborers.

19. The group who formed the aristocratic elite in Spanish America was the
    a. Creoles.
    b. Indians.
    c. *mestizos.*
    d. Habsburgs

20. The landowners who dominated the economy and the Indian population of Spain's Latin American empire are known as
    a. *mestizos.*
    b. Creoles.
    c. mercantilists.
    d. warlords.

21. Vermuyden's famous "Dutch river" canal was located in
    a. Cambridgeshire, England.
    b. the swampland south of Amsterdam.
    c. the province of Groningen in the Netherlands.
    d. eastern Germany.

22. The initial target of the English Navigation Acts was
    a. France.
    b. Spain.
    c. the American colonists.
    d. the Dutch.

23. As a result of British victory in the War of the Spanish Succession, Spain was forced to give up the *asiento,* meaning
    a. the Isthmus of Panama.
    b. Nova Scotia fishing rights.
    c. Mexico.
    d. the West African slave trade.

24. The Seven Years' War, which ended in 1763, was a victory for
    a. France, who received Louisiana.
    b. Spain, who won the *asiento* back.
    c. Britain, who won territory in North America and India.
    d. the colonists in America, who won free trade rights.

25. British men and women, by the workings of the mercantilist system, were able to purchase goods such as sugar, tobacco, and dried fish
    a. only from plantations within the empire, such as America.
    b. from any country in the world.
    c. from the Continent, largely the Dutch, because of cheapness.
    d. from the Spanish merchants of Central and South America.

Major Political Ideas

1. What was agricultural enclosure? One of the most popular political ramifications of the agricultural revolution was the notion that the rich landowners used their power, including political influence, to swindle the poor cottagers and push farm laborers off the land. Do you agree? What are the arguments on both sides, and which is most convincing?

2. Mercantilism was a form of economic capitalism. Define it in full. What is the impact of mercantilism on political thought and political policy? Did mercantilism lead to war?

Issues for Essays and Discussion

From the late seventeenth century into the eighteenth century, western Europe (particularly the Netherlands and Britain) experienced an agricultural change, population explosion, and a growth of rural industry. Explain these changes. Make reference to specific events. In what way, if any, are these three interrelated?

Interpretation of Visual Sources

Study the photograph entitled *Enclosing the Fields* on page 600 of your textbook. What country do you suspect this is? Distinguish the traditional "open field" from the new "enclosed" organization. Identify the old ridges and furrows. Compare this to the print on page 597 and the illustration on page 599. Why were fields such as these enclosed?

Geography

On Outline Map 19.3 provided, and using Map 19.2 in the textbook as reference, mark the colonial holdings of the European countries in North America in 1755. What territorial changes took place in North America after 1763? Which European country gained most territory after 1763? Which country lost the most territory after 1763? Did the largest colonial holdings go to the largest European countries—or was a position on the Atlantic the key factor?

Outline Map 19.3

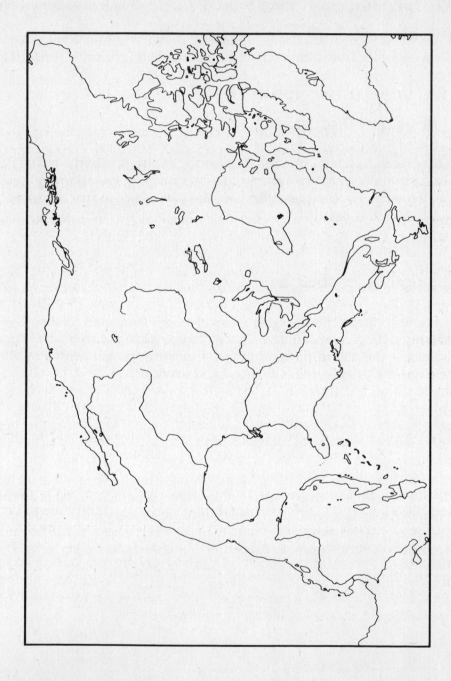

Understanding History Through the Arts

What influence did the culture of East have on the imperialist westerners? Begin your inquiry with R. Schwab, *The Oriental Renaissance: Europe's Rediscovery of India and the East, 1680–1880* (1987). Conversely, a study of how the West influenced the architecture of India is found in G. H. R. Tillotson, *The Tradition of Indian Architecture: Continuity, Controversy, and Change Since 1850* (1990), and N. Evenson, *Indian Metropolis: A View Toward the West* (1990).

Problems for Further Investigation

1. What were the motives of those who carved out great new empires in South and North America? Why did the northern Europeans settle in North American and the southern Europeans concentrate on South America? Begin your study with D. K. Fieldhouse, *The Colonial Empires* (1971), and R. Davies, *The Rise of Atlantic Economies* (1973). Students interested in Scottish history will find the subject of how Scotland came to dominate the North American tobacco trade covered in T. Devine, *The Tobacco Lords: A Study of the Tobacco Merchants of Glasgow and Their Trading Activities, 1740–1850* (1975).

2. What were the new patterns of urbanization in this age of population growth and agricultural change? An important work on this subject that shows where urbanization took place over a 350-year period is J. De Vries, *European Urbanisation, 1500–1800* (1987).

3. Why did the agricultural revolution take place? How did agricultural change and rural life differ from place to place within Europe? For more on agricultural life in Britain, start with J. D. Chambers and G. E. Mingay, *The Agricultural Revolution (1750–1880)* (1966), and for the Netherlands, with J. de Vries, *The Dutch Rural Economy in the Golden Age, 1500–1700* (1974). On the subject of soil, climate, land tenure, and the routine of peasant life in Russia before 1917 turn to R. Pipes, *Russia Under the Old Regime** (1974, 1982). For Europe in general, F. Huggett, *The Land Question and European Society Since 1650** (1975), presents a picture of how agricultural changes affected the development of European society.

4. Was enclosure a blessing or a great swindle for the British farmer? This question has been debated by historians and social commentators since the movement toward business agriculture began in sixteenth-century England. The general argument against enclosure was first set out in the sixteenth century by Sir Thomas More, who claimed (in his book *Utopia*) that it resulted in rural unemployment and rural crime. It is the enclosures between 1750 and 1850, however, that are the most controversial. The best contemporary coverage of the debate is G. E. Mingay, *Enclosure and the Small Farmer in the Age of the Industrial Revolution** (1968), which also contains a useful bibliography.

---

*Available in paperback.

Chapter 20
The Life of the People

Chapter Questions

After reading and studying this chapter you should be able to answer the following questions:

How did the peasant masses and the urban poor live in western Europe prior to the late-eighteenth-century age of revolution? Why did traditional marriage and sex practices begin to change in the late eighteenth century? What was it like to be a child in preindustrial society? How adequate was the diet and health care of the people of the eighteenth century? Were there any signs of improvement? What influence did religion hold in everyday life and what was pietism?

Chapter Summary

Until recently scholars have not been very interested in how men and women lived in preindustrial society. The aspects of everyday life, such as family relations, sex, marriage, health, and religion, took a secondary place in history. As a result, much of our understanding of these subjects is often based on myth rather than on solid historical research and interpretations. This chapter corrects some of the long-standing myths and provides a close look at the life of the people.

Contrary to early belief, for example, it appears that in western Europe the nuclear rather than the extended family was very common among preindustrial people. Furthermore, preindustrial people did not marry in their early teens, and illegitimacy was not as common as usually thought, and certainly less so than today. The concept of childhood as we know it hardly existed. The author also shows that when the poor got enough to eat their diet was probably almost as nutritionally sound as that of rich people. As for medical science, it probably did more harm than good in the eighteenth century. Also explained in this chapter are the reasons for a kind of "sexual revolution," particularly for women, beginning in the mid-eighteenth century, when young people began engaging in sex at an earlier age and illegitimacy began to rise. These changes accompanied new patterns of marriage and work—much of which were connected to the growth of new economic opportunities for men and women.

Education and literacy improved significantly, particularly in countries such as Prussia and Scotland. In the area of religion the eighteenth century witnessed a tug of war between the Enlightenment's attempt to demystify Christianity and place it on a more rational basis and a popular movement to retain traditional ritual, superstition, and religious mysteries. In Protestant and Catholic countries alike, rulers and religious leaders sought to purify religion by eliminating many ritualistic practices. The response to this reform by the common people in Catholic countries was a resurgence of religious ritual and mysticism, while in Protestant Germany and England there occurred a popular religious revival based on piety and emotional conversion. Meanwhile, most of Europe—Catholic and Protestant—saw the state increase its control over the church.

Study Outline

Use this outline to preview the chapter before you read a particular section in your textbook and then as a self-check to test your reading comprehension after you have read the chapter section.

I. Marriage and the family
   A. Extended and nuclear families
      1. The nuclear family, not the extended family, was most common in preindustrial western and central Europe.
      2. Early marriage was not common prior to 1750, and many women (perhaps as much as half) never married at all.
      3. Marriage was commonly delayed because of poverty and/or local law and tradition.
   B. Work away from home
      1. Many boys left home to work as craftsmen or laborers.
      2. Girls left to work as servants—where they often were physically and sexually mistreated.
   C. Premarital sex and birth-control practices
      1. Illegitimate children were not common in preindustrial society.
      2. Premarital sex was common, but marriage usually followed.
      3. Coitus interruptus was the most common form of birth control.
   D. New patterns of marriage and illegitimacy
      1. The growth of cottage industry (and later, the factory) resulted in people marrying earlier and for love.
      2. The explosion of births and the growth of prostitution from about 1750 to 1850 had several causes.
         a. Increasing illegitimacy signified rebellion against laws that limited the right of the poor to marry.
         b. Pregnant servant girls often turned to prostitution, which also increased illegitimacy.
   E. The question of sexual emancipation for women
      1. Women in cities and factories had limited economic independence.
      2. Poverty caused many people to remain single—leading to premarital sex and illegitimate births.

II. Infants and children in preindustrial society
   A. Child care and nursing
      1. Infant mortality was very high.
      2. Breast-feeding of children was common among poor women.
      3. Middle- and upper-class women hired wet nurses.
      4. The occupation of wet-nursing was often exploitative of lower-class women.
   B. Foundlings and infanticide
      1. "Killing nurses" and infanticide were forms of population control.
      2. Foundling hospitals were established but could not care for all the abandoned babies.
         a. Some had as many as 25,000 children.
         b. In reality, many were simply a form of legalized infanticide.
   C. Attitudes toward children
      1. Attitudes toward children were different from those of today, partly because of the frequency of death.
         a. Parents and doctors were generally indifferent to children.
         b. Children were often neglected or treated brutally.
      2. The Enlightenment brought about more humane treatment of children.
         a. Critics like Rousseau called for more love and understanding of children.
         b. The practice of swaddling was discouraged.
   D. Schools and education
      1. The beginnings of education for common people were in the seventeenth and eighteenth centuries.
      2. Protestantism encouraged popular education.
      3. Literacy increased, especially in France and Scotland, between 1700 and 1800.
III. The European's food
   A. The life span of Europeans increased from twenty-five years to thirty-five years between 1700 and 1800, partly because diet improved and plagues disappeared.
   B. Diet and nutrition
      1. The diet of ordinary people improved.
         a. Poor people ate mainly grains and vegetables.
         b. Milk and meat were rarely eaten.
      2. Rich people ate quite differently from the poor.
         a. Their diet was rich in meat and wine.
         b. They spurned fruits and vegetables.
   C. The impact of diet on health
      1. There were nutritional advantages and disadvantages to the diet of the poor.
         a. Their breads were very nutritious.
         b. Their main problem was getting enough green vegetables and milk.
      2. The rich often ate too much rich food.
   D. New foods and new knowledge about diet
      1. The potato substantially improved the diet of the poor.
         a. For some poor people, particularly in Ireland, the potato replaced grain as the primary food in the eighteenth century.
         b. Elsewhere in Europe, the potato took hold more slowly, but became a staple by the end of the century.

2. There was a growth in market gardening and an improvement in food variety in the eighteenth century.
3. There was some improvement in knowledge about diet, and Galen's influence declined.
4. Greater affluence caused many to turn to less nutritious food such as white bread and sugar.

IV. Medical science and the sick
   A. The medical professionals
     1. The demonic view of disease was common, and faith healers were used to exorcise the demons.
     2. Pharmacists sold drugs that were often harmful to their patients.
     3. Surgeons often operated without anesthetics and in the midst of dirt.
     4. Physicians frequently bled or purged people to death.
   B. The terrible conditions at hospitals
     1. Patients were crowded together, often several to a bed.
     2. There was no fresh air or hygiene.
     3. Hospital reform began in the late eighteenth century.
   C. Mental illness
     1. Mental illness was misunderstood and treated inhumanely.
     2. Some attempts at reform occurred in the late eighteenth century.
   D. Medical experiments and research
     1. Much medical experimentation was creative quackery.
     2. The conquest of smallpox was the greatest medical triumph of the eighteenth century.
       a. Montague and Jenner's work on inoculation was the beginning of a significant decline in smallpox.
       b. Jenner's work laid the foundation for the science of immunology in the nineteenth century.

V. Religion and Christian churches
   A. The institutional church
     1. Despite the critical spirit of the Enlightenment, the local parish church remained important in daily life, and the priest or pastor was the link between the people and the church hierarchy.
     2. The Protestant belief in individualism in religion was tempered by increased state control over the church and religious life.
     3. Catholic monarchs also increased state control over the church, making it less subject to papal influence.
       a. Spain took control of ecclesiastical appointments and the Inquisition and, with France, pressured Rome to dissolve the Jesuits.
       b. In Austria, Maria Theresa and Joseph II greatly reduced the size and influence of the monasteries and convents.
   B. Catholic piety
     1. In Catholic countries the old religious culture of ritual and superstition remained popular.
     2. Catholic clergy reluctantly allowed traditional religion to survive.

C. Protestant revival
   1. Pietism stressed religious enthusiasm, popular education, and individual religious development.
   2. In England, Wesley was troubled by religious corruption, decline, and uncertainty.
      a. His Methodist movement rejected the Calvinist idea of predestination and stressed salvation through faith.
      b. Wesley's ministry brought on a religious awakening, particularly among the lower classes.

Review Questions

Check your understanding of this chapter by answering the following questions.

1. Did the typical preindustrial family consist of an extended or a nuclear family? What evidence can you cite to support your answer?
2. In *Romeo and Juliet*, Juliet was just fourteen and Romeo was not too many years older. Is this early marriage typical of preindustrial society? Why did so many people not marry at all?
3. When did the custom of late marriage begin to change? Why?
4. Did preindustrial men and women practice birth control? What methods existed?
5. How do you explain that prior to 1750 there were few illegitimate children but there was a growth of illegitimacy thereafter?
6. It is often claimed that factory women, as opposed to their rural counterparts, were sexually liberated. Is this claim correct? Explain.
7. How and why did life expectancy improve in the eighteenth century?
8. What were the differences in the diets of the rich and the poor in the eighteenth century? What nutritional deficiencies existed?
9. How important was the potato in the eighteenth century? Is it important enough to merit more attention from historians?
10. How important were the eighteenth-century advances in medical science in extending the life span?
11. What was the demonic view of disease?
12. It is said that when it came to medical care, the poor were better off than the rich because they could not afford doctors or hospitals. Why might this have been true?
13. Why was there so much controversy over the smallpox inoculation? Was it safe? What contribution did Edward Jenner make to the elimination of this disease?
14. How was mental illness regarded and treated in the eighteenth century?
15. What effect did changes in church-state relations have on the institutions of the church?
16. Describe the forms in which popular religious culture remained in Catholic Europe.
17. Define pietism and describe how it is reflected in the work and life of John Wesley.

Study-Review Exercises

Define the following key concepts and terms.
extended family

demonic view of disease

nuclear family

preindustrial childhood

illegitimacy explosion

Methodists

coitus interruptus

purging

"killing nurses"

Jesuits

Identify and explain the significance of each of the following people.
Lady Mary Montague

Edward Jenner

James Graham

Joseph II

John Wesley

Test your understanding of the chapter by providing the correct answers.

1. It is apparent that the practice of breast-feeding *increased/limited* the fertility of lower-class women.

2. The teenage bride *was/was not* the general rule in preindustrial Europe.

3. Prior to about 1750, premarital sex usually *did/did not* lead to marriage.

4. In the eighteenth century, the _____ was the primary new food in Europe.

5. People lived *longer/shorter* lives as the eighteenth century progressed.

6. The key to Jenner's discovery was the connection between immunity from smallpox and

    _____ , a mild and noncontagious disease.

7. In Catholic countries it was largely *the clergy/the common people* who wished to hold on to traditional religious rituals and superstitions.

8. The Englishman who brought religious "enthusiasm" to the common folk of England.

    _____

Multiple-Choice Questions

1. One of the chief deficiencies of the diet of both rich and poor Europeans was the absence of sufficient
    a. meat.
    b. fruit and vegetables.
    c. white bread.
    d. wine.

2. A family in which three or four generations live under the same roof under the direction of a patriarch is known as a(n)
    a. nuclear family.
    b. conjugal family.
    c. industrial household.
    d. extended family.

3. Prior to about 1750, marriage between two persons was more often than not
   a. undertaken freely by the couple.
   b. controlled by law and parents.
   c. based on romantic love.
   d. undertaken without economic considerations.

4. The establishment of foundling hospitals in the eighteenth century was an attempt to
   a. prevent the spread of the bubonic plague.
   b. isolate children from smallpox.
   c. prevent willful destruction and abandonment of newborn children.
   d. provide adequate childbirth facilities for rich women.

5. All but which of the following sentences about preindustrial society's attitudes toward children is true?
   a. Parents often treated their children with indifference and brutality.
   b. Poor children were often forced to work in the early factories.
   c. Doctors were the only people interested in the children's welfare.
   d. Killing of children by parents or nurses was common.

6. It appears that the role of doctors and hospital care in bringing about improvement in health in the eighteenth century was
   a. very significant.
   b. minor.
   c. helpful only in the area of surgery.
   d. helpful only in the area of preventive medicine.

7. In the seventeenth and early eighteenth centuries people usually married
   a. surprisingly late.
   b. surprisingly early.
   c. almost never.
   d. and divorced frequently.

8. Which of the following was *not* a general characteristic of the European family of the eighteenth century?
   a. The nuclear family
   b. Late marriages
   c. Many unmarried relatives
   d. The extended family

9. The overwhelming reason for postponement of marriage was
   a. that people didn't like the institution of marriage.
   b. lack of economic independence.
   c. the stipulation of a legal age.
   d. that young men and women valued the independence of a working life.

10. In the second half of the eighteenth century, the earlier pattern of marriage and family life began to break down. Which of the following was *not* a result of this change?
    a. A greater number of illegitimate births
    b. Earlier marriages
    c. Marriages exclusively for economic reasons
    d. Marriages for love

11. The "illegitimacy explosion" of the late eighteenth century was encouraged by all but which one of the following?
    a. The laws, especially in Germany, concerning the right of the poor to marry
    b. The mobility of young people needing to work off the farm
    c. The influence of the French Revolution, which repressed freedom in sexual and marital behavior
    d. The decreasing influence of parental pressure and village tradition.

12. Which of the following statements best describes the attitude toward children in the first part of the eighteenth century?
    a. They were protected and cherished.
    b. They were never disciplined.
    c. They were treated as they were—children living in a child's world.
    d. They were ignored, often brutalized, and often unloved.

13. Most of the popular education in Europe of the eighteenth century was sponsored by
    a. the church.
    b. the state.
    c. private individuals.
    d. parents, in the home.

14. Which of the following would most likely be found in an eighteenth-century hospital?
    a. Isolation of patients
    b. Sanitary conditions
    c. Uncrowded conditions
    d. Uneducated nurses and poor nursing practices

15. The greatest medical triumph of the eighteenth century was the conquest of
    a. starvation.
    b. smallpox.
    c. scurvy.
    d. cholera.

16. The practice of sending one's newborn baby to be suckled by a poor woman in the countryside was known as
    a. the cottage system.
    b. infanticide.
    c. wet-nursing.
    d. overlaying.

17. Which of the following was *not* a common food for the European poor?
    a. Vegetables
    b. Beer
    c. Dark bread
    d. Milk

18. It appears that the chief dietary problem of European society was the lack of an adequate supply of
    a. vitamins A and C.
    b. vitamin B complex.
    c. meat.
    d. sugar.

19. Most probably the best thing an eighteenth-century sick person could do with regard to hospitals would be to
    a. enter only if an operation was suggested by a doctor.
    b. enter only if in need of drugs.
    c. enter only a hospital operating under Galenic theory.
    d. stay away.

20. The country that led the way in the development of universal education was
    a. Britain.
    b. Prussia.
    c. France.
    d. Austria.

21. In which of the following countries did a religious conviction that the path to salvation lay in careful study of the Scriptures led to an effective network of schools and a very high literacy rate by 1800?
    a. Austria
    b. England
    c. France
    d. Scotland

22. The desire for "bread as white as snow" led to
    a. a decline in bacterial diseases.
    b. a significant nutritional advance.
    c. an increase in the supply of bread.
    d. a nutritional decline.

23. The general eighteenth-century attitude toward masturbation was that it
    a. was harmless and perhaps healthy.
    b. unacceptable for women but okay for men.
    c. caused insanity and thereby must be prevented.
    d. did not exist.

24. The general trend in Catholic countries was for monarchs to follow the Protestant lead in
   a. limiting the power and influence of the church.
   b. adopting the idea of predestination.
   c. casting off all allegiance to the papacy.
   d. protecting the poor.

25. During the eighteenth century the Society of Jesus
   a. found its power and position in Europe rise.
   b. gained considerable land in Portugal and France.
   c. was ordered out of France and Spain.
   d. avoided politics and property accumulation altogether.

Major Political Ideas

1. Do you believe that the material circumstances of preindustrial life had any affect on the way people thought and acted politically?

2. Does this chapter suggest that there was a cultural or economic division of society?

3. Was society more or less divided in terms of gender roles? In terms of class?

Issues for Essays and Discussion

1. Did the common people of preindustrial Europe enjoy a life of simple comfort and natural experiences? Or was theirs a life of brutal and cruel exploitation? Discuss this in terms of the nature of family life, childhood, diet and health, and education and religion.

2. In general, was life, by the late eighteenth century, getting better or worse?

Interpretation of Visual Sources

Study the reproduction of the print entitled *The Five Senses* on page 638 of your textbook. What is the theme of this print? What does it tell us about the treatment of children? Is this typical of how society treated children? How does the illustration mirror some of the ideas of the Enlightenment? (Refer to Chapter 18.)

Understanding History Through the Arts

1. What can art tell us about childhood in the preindustrial era? Painting is one of the major sources of information for the history of childhood. Preindustrial childhood is the subject of

Children's Games by Pieter Brueghel the Elder, a lively, action-packed painting of over two hundred children engaged in more than seventy different games. The painting is the subject of an interesting article by A. Eliot, "Games Children Play," *Sports Illustrated* (January 11, 1971): 48–56.

2. How is preindustrial life portrayed in literature and film? Samuel Richardson wrote a novel about the life of a household servant who became the prey of the lecherous son of her master, *Pamela, or Virtue Rewarded** (1740). Tom Jones, eighteenth-century England's most famous foundling, was the fictional hero of Henry Fielding's *Tom Jones* and the subject and title of director Tony Richardson's highly acclaimed, award-winning film version of Fielding's novel. Starring Albert Finney, Susannah York, and Dame Edith Evans, the film re-creates, in amusing and satirical fashion, eighteenth-century English life. A more recent film adaptation is Richardson's *Joseph Andrews*, based on another Fielding novel.

3. Was urban life more comfortable than rural life? What was the great attraction of the city? London was the fastest-growing city in the eighteenth century. How people lived in London is the subject of two highly readable and interesting books: M. D. George, *London Life in the Eighteenth Century** (3rd ed., 1951), and R. J. Mitchell and M. D. R. Leys, *A History of London Life** (1963).

Problems for Further Investigation

1. What was daily life like for poor women in this period? Few men in preindustrial society earned enough to support a family. This, in part, explains why and when women married, and why most women worked. The preindustrial woman, therefore, was not in any modern sense a homemaker. The subject of women and the family economy in eighteenth-century France is discussed by O. Hufton in *The Poor of Eighteenth-Century France* (1974).

2. What was the cause of the so-called population explosion? Did medical science contribute to an improvement in eighteenth-century life? Until about twenty years ago, it was fashionable to believe that the population explosion was due to improvements made by medical science. Although this theory is generally disclaimed today, it appears to be enjoying a slight revival. For both sides of the argument, begin your study with M. Anderson, *Population Change in North-Western Europe, 1750–1850** (1988), and then read the following journal articles (which also have bibliographies): T. McKeown and R. G. Brown, "Medical Evidence Related to English Population Change," *Population Studies 9* (1955); T. McKeown and R. G. Record, "Reasons for the Decline in Mortality in England and Wales During the Nineteenth Century," *Population Studies 16* (1962); and P. Razzell, "Population Change in Eighteenth-Century England: A Reinterpretation," *Economic History Review*, 2nd series, 18-2 (1965). For the history of disease, see D. Hopkins, *Princes and Peasants: Smallpox in History* (1977).

*Available in paperback.

Chapter 21
The Revolution in Politics, 1775–1815

Chapter Questions

After reading and studying this chapter you should be able to answer the following questions:

What were the causes of the political revolutions between 1775 and 1815 in America and France? What were the ideas and objectives of the revolutionaries in America and France? Who won and who lost in these revolutions?

Chapter Summary

The French and American revolutions were the most important political events of the eighteenth century. They were also a dramatic conclusion to the Enlightenment, and both revolutions, taken together, form a major turning point in human history. This chapter explains what these great revolutions were all about.

The chapter begins by describing classical liberalism, the fundamental ideology of the revolution in politics. Liberalism, which had deep roots, called for freedom and equality at a time when monarchs and aristocrats took their great privileges for granted. The immediate cause of the American Revolution, the British effort to solve the problem of war debts, was turned into a political struggle by the American colonists, who already had achieved considerable economic and personal freedom. The American Revolution stimulated reform efforts throughout Europe.

It was in France that the ideas of the Enlightenment and liberalism were put to their fullest test. The bankruptcy of the state gave the French aristocracy the chance to grab power from a weak king. This move backfired, however, because the middle class grabbed even harder. It is significant that the revolutionary desires of the middle class depended on the firm support and violent action of aroused peasants and poor urban workers. It was this action of the common people that gave the revolution its driving force.

In the first two years of the French Revolution, the middle class, with its allies from the peasantry and urban poor, achieved unprecedented reforms. The outbreak of an all-European war against France in 1792 then resulted in a reign of terror and a dictatorship by radical moralists, of whom Robespierre was the greatest. By 1795, this radical patriotism wore itself out. The revolutionary momentum slowed, and the Revolution deteriorated into a military dictatorship under the opportunist Napoleon. Yet, until 1815 the history of France was that of war, and that war spread liberalism to the rest of Europe. French conquests also stimulated nationalism. The world of politics was turned upside down.

Study Outline

Use this outline to preview the chapter before you read a particular section in your textbook and then as a self-check to test your reading comprehension after you have read the chapter section.

I. Liberty and equality
  A. In the eighteenth century, liberty meant human rights and freedoms and the sovereignty of the people.
  B. Equality meant equal rights and equality of opportunity.
  C. The roots of liberalism
    1. The Judeo-Christian tradition of individualism, reinforced by the Reformation, supported liberalism.
    2. Liberalism's modern roots are found in the Enlightenment's concern for freedom and legal equality, as best expressed by Locke and Montesquieu.
    3. Liberalism was attractive to both the aristocracy and the middle class, but it lacked the support of the masses.
II. The American Revolution (1775–1789)
  A. Some argue that the American Revolution was not a revolution at all but merely a war for independence.
  B. The origins of the Revolution
    1. The British wanted the Americans to pay their share of imperial expenses.
      a. Americans paid very low taxes.
      b. Parliament passed the Stamp Act (1765) to raise revenue.
      c. Vigorous protest from the colonies forced its repeal (1766).
    2. Although no less represented than Englishmen themselves, many Americans believed they had the right to make their own laws.
      a. Americans have long exercised a great deal of independence.
      b. Their greater political equality was matched by greater social and economic equality—there was no hereditary noble or serf class.
    3. The issue of taxation and representation ultimately led to the outbreak of fighting.
  C. The independence movement was encouraged by several factors.
    1. The British refused to compromise, thus losing the support of many colonists.
    2. The radical ideas of Thomas Paine, expressed in the best-selling *Common Sense,* greatly influenced public opinion in favor of independence.
    3. The Declaration of Independence, written by Thomas Jefferson and passed by the Second Continental Congress (1776), further increased the desire of the colonists for independence.
    4. Although many Americans remained loyal to Britain, the independence movement had wide-based support from all sections of society.
    5. European aid, especially from the French government and from French volunteers, contributed greatly to the American victory in 1783.

D. Framing the Constitution and the Bill of Rights
1. The federal, or central, government was given important powers—the right to tax, the means to enforce its laws, and the regulation of trade—but the states had important powers too.
2. The executive, legislative, and judicial branches of the government were designed to balance one another.
3. The Anti-Federalists feared that the central government had too much power; to placate them, the Federalists wrote the Bill of Rights, which spells out the rights of the individual.
   a. Liberty did not, however, necessarily mean democracy.
   b. Equality meant equality before the law, not equality of political participation or economic well-being.
E. The American Revolution reinforced the Enlightenment idea that a better world was possible, and Europeans watched the new country with fascination.
III. The French Revolution (1789–1791)
A. The influence of the American Revolution
1. Many French soldiers, such as Lafayette, served in America and were impressed by the ideals of the Revolution.
2. The American Revolution influenced the French Revolution, but the latter was more violent and more influential; it opened the era of modern politics.
B. The breakdown of the old order
1. By the 1780s, the government was nearly bankrupt.
2. The French banking system could not cope with the fiscal problems, leaving the monarchy with no choice but to increase taxes.
C. Legal orders and social realities: the three estates
1. The first estate, the clergy, had many privileges and much wealth, and it levied an oppressive tax (the tithe) on landowners.
2. The second estate, the nobility, also had great privileges, wealth, and power, and it taxed the peasantry for its own profit.
3. The third estate, the commoners, was a mixture of a few rich members of the middle class, urban workers, and the mass of peasants.
D. Revisionist historians challenge the traditional interpretation of the origins of the French Revolution.
1. They argue that the bourgeoisie were not locked in conflict with the nobility, that both groups were highly fragmented.
   a. The nobility remained fluid and relatively open.
   b. Key sections of the nobility were liberal.
   c. The nobility and the bourgeoisie were not economic rivals.
2. Nevertheless, the old interpretation, that a new social order was challenging the old, is still convincing and valid.
E. The formation of the National Assembly of 1789
1. Louis XVI's plan to tax landed property was opposed by the Assembly of Notables and the Parlement of Paris.
2. Louis then gave in and called for a meeting of the Estates General, the representative body of the three estates.
   a. Two-thirds of the delegates from the clergy were parish priests.

       b. A majority of the noble representatives were conservative, but fully a third were liberals committed to major change.

       c. The third estate representatives were largely lawyers and government officials.

       d. The third estate wanted the three estates to meet together to ensure the passage of fundamental reforms.

       e. According to Sieyès in *What Is the Third Estate?*, the third estate constituted the true strength of the French nation.

   3. The dispute over voting in the Estates General led the third estate to break away and form the National Assembly, which pledged, in the Oath of the Tennis Court, not to disband until they had written a new constitution.

   4. Louis tried to reassert his monarchical authority and assembled an army.

F. The revolt of the poor and the oppressed

   1. Rising bread prices in 1788–89 stirred the people to action.

   2. Fearing attack by the king's army, angry Parisians stormed the Bastille on July 14, 1789.

       a. The people took the Bastille, and the king was forced to recall his troops.

       b. This uprising of the masses saved the National Assembly.

       c. All across France peasants began to rise up against their lords.

       d. The Great Fear seized the countryside.

   3. The peasant revolt forced the National Assembly to abolish feudal obligations.

G. A limited monarchy established by the bourgeoisie

   1. The National Assembly's Declaration of the Rights of Man (1789) proclaimed the rights of all citizens and guaranteed equality before the law and a representative government.

   2. Meanwhile, the poor women of Paris marched on Versailles and forced the royal family and the government to move to Paris.

   3. The National Assembly established a constitutional monarchy and passed major reforms.

       a. The nobility was abolished as a separate legal order.

       b. All lawmaking power was placed in the hands of the National Assembly.

       c. The jumble of provinces was replaced by 83 departments.

       d. The metric system was introduced.

       e. Economic freedom was promoted.

   4. The National Assembly nationalized the property of the church and abolished the monasteries.

   5. This attack on the church turned many people against the Revolution.

IV. World war and republican France (1791–1799)

A. Foreign reactions and the beginning of war

   1. Outside France, liberals and radicals hoped that the revolution would lead to a reordering of society everywhere, but conservatives such as Burke (in *Reflections on the Revolution in France*) predicted it would lead to chaos and tyranny.

   2. Wollstonecraft challenged Burke (in *A Vindication of the Rights of Woman*), arguing that it was time for women to demand equal rights.

   3. Fear among European kings and nobility that the revolution would spread resulted in the Declaration of Pillnitz (1791), which threatened the invasion of France by Austria and Prussia.

4. In retaliation, the patriotic French deputies, most of them Jacobins, declared war on Austria in 1792.
   a. France was soon retreating before the armies of the First Coalition.
   b. A war of patriotic fervor swept France.
5. In 1792 a new National Convention proclaimed France a republic and imprisoned the king.
B. The "second revolution" and rapid radicalization in France
   1. The National Convention proclaimed France a republic in 1792.
   2. However, the convention was split between the Girondists and the Mountain, led by Robespierre and Danton.
   3. Louis XVI was tried and convicted of treason by the National Convention and guillotined in early 1793.
   4. French armies continued the "war against tyranny" by declaring war on nearly all of Europe.
   5. In Paris, the struggle between the Girondists and the Mountain for political power led to the political rise of the laboring poor.
   6. The sans-culottes—the laboring poor—allied with the Mountain and helped Robespierre and the Committee of Public Safety gain power.
C. Total war and the Terror (1793–1794)
   1. Robespierre established a planned economy to wage total war and aid the poor.
      a. The government fixed prices on key products and instituted rationing.
      b. Workshops were nationalized to produce goods for the war effort, and raw materials were requisitioned.
   2. The Reign of Terror was instituted to eliminate opposition to the Revolution, and many people were jailed or executed.
   3. The war became a national mission against evil within and outside of France, and not a class war.
      a. The danger of foreign and internal foes encouraged nationalism.
      b. A huge army of patriots was led by young generals who relied on mass attack.
D. The Thermidorian reaction and the Directory (1794–1799)
   1. Fear of the Reign of Terror led to the execution of its leader, Robespierre.
   2. The period of the Thermidorian reaction following Robespierre's death was marked by a return to bourgeois liberalism.
      a. Economic controls were abolished.
      b. Riots by the poor were put down.
      c. The Directory, a five-man executive body, was established.
   3. The poor lost their fervor for revolution.
   4. A military dictatorship was established in order to prevent a return to peace and monarchy.
V. The Napoleonic era (1799–1815)
   A. Napoleon's rule
      1. Napoleon appealed to many, like Abbé Sieyès, who looked for a strong military leader to end the country's upheaval.
      2. Napoleon was named first consul of the republic in 1799.
      3. He maintained order and worked out important compromises.
         a. His Civil Code of 1804 granted the middle class equality under the law and safeguarded their right to own property.

      b. He confirmed the gains of the peasants.

      c. He centralized the government, strengthened the bureaucracy, and granted amnesty to nobles.

      d. He signed the Concordat of 1801, which guaranteed freedom of worship for Catholics.

   4. Napoleon brought order and stability to France but betrayed the ideals of the Revolution by violating the rights of free speech and press and free elections.

      a. Women had no political rights.

      b. There were harsh penalties for political offenses.

B. Napoleon's wars and foreign policy

   1. He defeated Austria (1801) and made peace with Britain (1802), the two remaining members of the Second Coalition.

   2. Another war (against the Third Coalition—Austria, Russia, Sweden, and Britain) resulted in British naval dominance at the Battle of Trafalgar (1805).

   3. Napoleon used the fear of a conspiracy to return the Bourbons to power to get himself proclaimed emperor in 1804.

   4. The Third Coalition collapsed at Austerlitz (1805), and Napoleon reorganized the German states into the Confederation of the Rhine.

   5. In 1806, Napoleon defeated the Prussians at Jena and Auerstädt.

      a. In the Treaty of Tilsit (1807), Prussia lost half its population, while Russia accepted Napoleon's reorganization of western and central Europe.

      b. Russia also joined with France in a blockade against British goods.

   6. Napoleon's Grand Empire in Europe meant French control of continental Europe.

      a. Napoleon introduced many French laws, abolishing feudal dues and serfdom in the process.

      b. However, he also levied heavy taxes.

   7. The beginning of the end for Napoleon came with the Spanish revolt (1808) and the British blockade.

   8. The French invasion of Russia in 1812 was a disaster for Napoleon.

   9. Napoleon was defeated by the Fourth Coalition (Austria, Prussia, Russia, and Great Britain) and abdicated his throne in 1814, only to be defeated again at Waterloo in 1815.

  10. The Bourbon dynasty was restored in France under Louis XVIII.

Review Questions

Check your understanding of the chapter by answering the following questions.

1. The ideas of liberty and equality were the central ideas of classical liberalism. Define these ideas. Are they the same as democracy?
2. According to Locke, what is the function of government?
3. Did the Americans or the British have the better argument with regard to the taxation problem?
4. Why is the Declaration of Independence sometimes called the world's greatest political editorial?
5. What role did the European powers play in the American victory? Did they gain anything?

6. What was the major issue in the debate between the Federalists and the Anti-Federalists?
7. Did the American Revolution have any effect on France?
8. Describe the three estates of France. Who paid the taxes? Who held the wealth and power in France?
9. With the calling of the Estates General, "the nobility of France expected that history would repeat itself." Did it? What actually did happen?
10. What were the reforms of the National Assembly. Do they display the application of liberalism to society?
11. What were the cause and the outcome of the peasants' uprising of 1789?
12. What role did the poor women of Paris play in the Revolution?
13. Why were France and Europe overcome with feelings of fear and mistrust?
14. Why did the Revolution turn into war in 1792?
15. Who were the sans-culottes? Why were they important to radical leaders such as Robespierre? What role did the common people play in the Revolution?
16. Why did the Committee of Public Safety need to institute a Reign of Terror?
17. Describe the Grand Empire of Napoleon in terms of its three parts. Was Napoleon a liberator or a tyrant?
18. What caused Napoleon's downfall? Was it inevitable?

Study-Review Exercises

Define the following key concepts and terms.

liberalism

checks and balances

natural or universal rights

republican

popular sovereignty

tithe

Identify and explain the significance of each of the following people and terms.

Stamp Act

Battle of Trafalgar

American Bill of Rights

Loyalists

Constitutional Convention of 1787

Jacobins

Girondists

Mountain

Reign of Terror

National Assembly

Declaration of the Rights of Woman

Bastille

sans-culottes

Girondists

Mountain

"the baker, the baker's wife, and the baker's boy"

Lord Nelson

Mary Wollstonecraft

Edmund Burke

Marie Antoinette

Marquis de Lafayette

Thomas Jefferson

Robespierre

John Locke

Abbé Sieyès

Test your understanding of the chapter by providing the correct answers.

1. Napoleon's plan to invade England was made impossible by the defeat of the French and

   Spanish navies in the Battle of _____ in 1805.

2. Overall, the common people of Paris played *a minor/an important* role in the French Revolution.

3. The author of the best-selling radical book *Common Sense.* _____

4. Prior to the crisis of the 1760s, American colonists had exercised *little/a great deal of* political and economic independence from Britain.

5. The peasant uprising of 1789 in France ended in *victory/defeat* for the peasant class.

6. By the 1790s, people like Sieyès were increasingly looking to *the people/a military ruler* to bring order to France.

Multiple-Choice Questions

1. Eighteenth-century liberals stressed
   a. economic equality.
   b. equality in property holding.
   c. equality of opportunity
   d. racial and sexual equality.

2. Which came first?
   a. Formation of the French National Assembly
   b. Execution of King Louis XVI
   c. American Bill of Rights
   d. Seven Years' War

3. The French Jacobins were
   a. aristocrats who fled France.
   b. monarchists.
   c. priests who supported the Revolution.
   d. revolutionary radicals.

4. The French National Assembly was established by
   a. the middle class of the Third Estate.
   b. King Louis XVI.
   c. the aristocracy.
   d. the sans-culottes.

5. The National Assembly did all but which of the following?
   a. Nationalized church land
   b. Issued the Declaration of the Rights of Man
   c. Established the metric system of weights and measures
   d. Brought about the Reign of Terror

6. In 1789 the influential Abbé Sieyès wrote a pamphlet in which he argued that France should be ruled by the
   a. nobility.
   b. clergy.
   c. people.
   d. king.

7. In 1799 Sieyès argued that authority in society should come from
   a. the people.
   b. the leaders of the Third Estate.
   c. a strong military leader.
   d. the Directory.

8. In the first stage of the Revolution the French established
   a. a constitutional monarchy.
   b. an absolutist monarchy.
   c. a republic.
   d. a military dictatorship.

9. Edmund Burke's *Reflections on the Revolution in France* is a defense of
   a. the Catholic church.
   b. Robespierre and the Terror.
   c. the working classes of France.
   d. the English monarchy and aristocracy.

10. Generally, the people who did not support eighteenth-century liberalism were the
    a. elite.
    b. members of the middle class.
    c. masses.
    d. intellectuals.

11. Most eighteenth-century demands for liberty centered on
    a. the equalization of wealth.
    b. a classless society.
    c. better welfare systems.
    d. equality of opportunity.

12. Americans objected to the Stamp Act because the tax it proposed
    a. was exorbitant.
    b. was not required of people in Britain.
    c. would have required great expense to collect.
    d. was imposed without their consent.

13. The American Revolution
    a. had very little impact on Europe.
    b. was supported by the French monarchy.
    c. was not influenced by Locke or Montesquieu.
    d. was supported by almost everyone living in the United States.

14. Which of the following was a cause of the outbreak of revolution in France in 1789?
    a. Peasant revolt in the countryside
    b. The death of Louis XVI
    c. The demand of the nobility for greater power and influence
    d. The invasion of France by foreign armies

15. The first successful revolt against Napoleon began in 1808 in
    a. Spain.
    b. Russia.
    c. Germany.
    d. Italy.

16. Prior to about 1765, the American people were
    a. fairly independent of the British government.
    b. subject to heavy and punitive British controls.
    c. paying a majority share of British military costs.
    d. under the direct control of the East India Company.

17. The major share of the tax burden in France was carried by the
    a. peasants.
    b. bourgeoisie.
    c. clergy.
    d. nobility.

18. The participation of the common people of Paris in the revolution was initially attributable to
    a. their desire to be represented in the Estates General.
    b. the soaring price of food.
    c. the murder of Marat.
    d. the large number of people imprisoned by the king.

19. For the French peasants, the Revolution of 1789 meant
    a. a general movement from the countryside to urban areas.
    b. greater landownership.
    c. significant political power.
    d. few, if any, gains.

20. The group that announced that it was going to cut off Marie Antoinette's head, "tear out her heart, and fry her liver" was the
    a. National Guard.
    b. Robespierre radicals.
    c. revolutionary committee.
    d. women of Paris.

21. The group that had the task of ridding France of any internal opposition to the revolutionary cause was the
    a. Revolutionary Army.
    b. secret police.
    c. republican mob of Paris.
    d. Committee of Public Safety.

22. In her writings, Mary Wollstonecraft argues that
    a. the liberating promise of the French Revolution must be extended to women.
    b. British life is threatened by the revolutionary chaos in France.
    c. Burke is correct in his defense of inherited privilege.
    d. women should devote themselves to education, not politics.

23. Some historians have questioned the traditional interpretation of the French Revolution by arguing that
    a. the Revolution was solely the result of a clash of economic classes.
    b. the key to the Revolution was the social and economic isolation of the nobility.
    c. fundamental to the Revolution was the clash between the bourgeois and noble classes.
    d. the nobility and the bourgeois had common political and economic interests.

24. The abolition of many tiny German states and the old Holy Roman Empire and the reorganization of fifteen German states into a Confederation of the Rhine was the work of
    a. the Congress of Vienna.
    b. Frederick William III of Prussia.
    c. the Continental system.
    d. Napoleon.

25. Napoleon's plan to invade Britain was scrapped as a result of
    a. the Treaty of Amiens.
    b. the Battle of Trafalgar.
    c. the fall of the Third Coalition.
    d. economic restraints in France.

Major Political Ideas

1. Define liberalism. What did it mean to be a liberal in the eighteenth and nineteenth century sense? How does this liberalism compare to twentieth-century liberalism? To democracy? What is the relationship between liberalism and the Enlightenment idea of natural law?

2. How did Americans interpret the term *equality* in 1789? Has it changed since then? Are the definitions of *liberalism* and *equality* unchangeable, or do they undergo periodic redefinition?

Issues for Essays and Discussion

1. What were the causes, both immediate and long term, of the French Revolution? Was it basically an economic event? A social or political struggle? Support your argument by making reference to specific events and ideas.

2. Why did the French Revolution become violent? Is it inevitable that all revolutions turn into violence and dictatorship?

3. Was the American Revolution a true revolution or a war of independence? Support your argument with reference to specific events and ideas.

Interpretation of Visual Sources

Study the reproduction of the print *To Versailles* on page 673 of your textbook. Who are the participants and what are their motives? Is a recognizable social class represented here? Did demonstrations such as this have any impact on the course of the Revolution?

Geography

1. On Outline Map 21.1 provided, and using Map 21.1 in the textbook as a reference, mark the following: the boundaries of France before the outbreak of war in 1792, and the areas acquired by France by 1810.

2. Look closely at Map 21.1 in the text. Can you find the four small British outposts scattered throughout Europe? How were these outposts necessary to and a reflection of Britain's military power? What did these outposts mean for smugglers and Napoleon's efforts to stop British trade with continental countries?

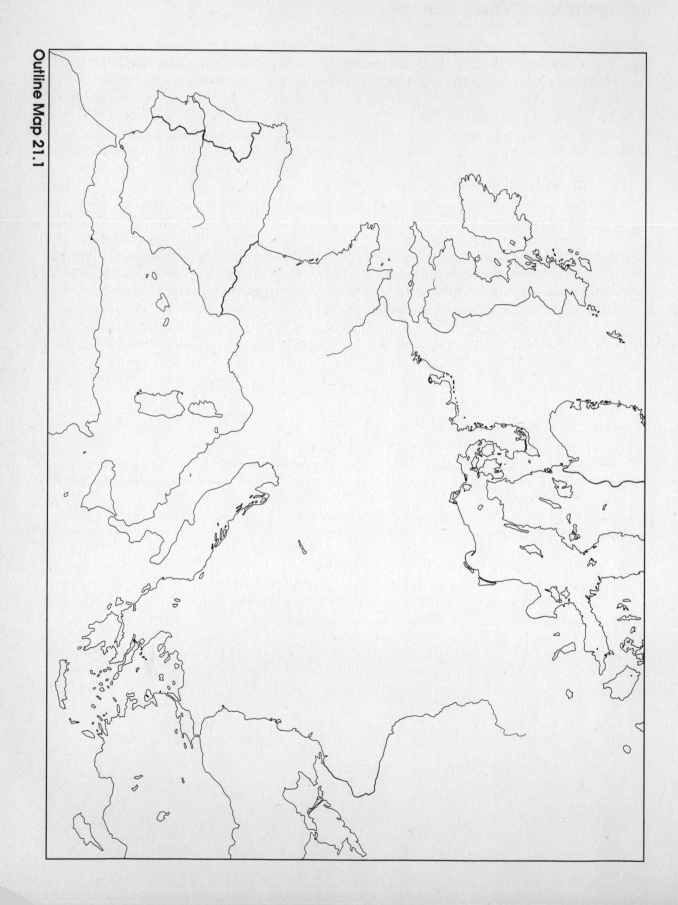

Understanding History Through the Arts

1. How did the era of revolution affect architecture? Out of the Enlightenment and the upheaval of the Revolution, and in response to the desire to create a new social order based on principles of natural law, French architects took traditional classical and baroque features and merged them with an interest in natural geometrical shapes. The result was an original architecture of bold and gigantic buildings. The leading architects in this movement were Etienne-Louis Boullée and Claude-Nicolas Ledoux. Their work can be found in most general histories of architecture, but the student may wish to begin with E. Kaufmann, *Architecture in the Age of Reason** (1954), and A. Vidler, *Claude-Nicolas Ledoux, Architecture and Social Reform at the End of the Ancien Régime* (1990).

2. What was the impact of the French Revolution on art? The Revolution in France forced art to become a statement of politics and political ideals. The style was a "new classicism" based on simplicity and rationality, with references to Roman civic virtue. This new style, whose goal was to inspire patriotism, was made popular by Jacques Louis David. David, a member of the National Convention, painted a number of emotional masterpieces that glorified first the Revolution—such as *Oath in the Tennis Court* and *The Death of Marat*—and later the patriotic aims of Napoleon. For a view of David and other revolutionary artists of the late eighteenth century, see E. Kennedy, *A Cultural History of the French Revolution* (1989), and R. Paulson, *Representations of Revolution, 1789–1820** (1987).

Problems for Further Investigation

1. Do individuals determine history, or is history the product of the environment? The various arguments of scholars over the motives and contributions of Napoleon are brought together in D. H. Pinkney, ed., *Napoleon: Historical Enigma** (1969). The story of Admiral Lord Nelson, Britain's hero and victor of great sea battles, is interestingly told in R. Hough, *Nelson, A Biography* (1980).

2. King George III of Britain has often been viewed, in American history, as the archenemy of liberty and constitutionalism. Is this a fair assessment? The debate over his role has gone on for a number of years and is the subject of a book of collected opinions, *George III: Tyrant or Constitutional Monarch?** (1964), edited by E. A. Reitan.

3. How important were women in the French Revolution? Did the people of Paris play a role in determining the Revolution's political ideas? Group action in a revolution makes for an interesting study. The role of women in the Revolution in France (and in other times) is well handled in E. Boulding, *The Underside of History: A View of Women Through Time* (1976). The people (which includes the Paris mob) who participated in the Revolution in France are the subject of the interesting study by George Rude, *The Crowd in the French Revolution** (1959).

---

*Available in paperback.

4. How did the French Revolution start? Students interested in the origins of the French Revolution will want to check R. W. Greenlaw, ed., *The Economic Origins of the French Revolution** (1958), and those interested in political theory may want to consider a study of liberalism, beginning with H. Schultz, ed., *English Liberalism and the State: Individualism or Collectivism** (1972).

*Available in paperback.

Primary Sources
The Rights of Man and of Woman

Drawing upon the ideas of the Enlightenment, particularly those of John Locke and Jean-Jacques Rousseau, the bourgeois-dominated French National Assembly issued on August 26, 1789, *The Declaration of the Right of Man and of the Citizen*. Thousands of copies of this document circulated in France, and it became the ideological manifesto of the Revolution. Its influence on the rest of Europe and the world was equally noteworthy. In 1792 an English woman, Mary Wollstonecraft, wrote *A Vindication of the Rights of Woman*, which was a reply to Edmund Burke's attack on the French Revolution and the starting point for the debate over whether the natural rights of man should apply, in full, to women.

What, according to these documents, are the principle rights of man and woman? In what principles are these rights grounded? What Enlightenment views do these documents illustrate?

Declaration of the Rights of Man and of the Citizen, 1789

The representatives of the French people, organized as a National Assembly, believing that the ignorance, neglect, or contempt of the rights of man are the sole cause of public calamities and of the corruption of governments, have determined to set forth in a solemn declaration the natural, unalienable, and sacred rights of man, in order that this declaration, being constantly before all the members of the Social body, shall remind them continually of their rights and duties; in order that the acts of the legislative power, as well as those of the executive power, may be compared at any moment with the objects and purposes of all political institutions and may thus be more respected, and, lastly, in order that the grievances of the citizens, based here-after upon simple and incontestable principles, shall tend to the maintenance of the constitution and redound to the happiness of all. Therefore the National Assembly recognizes and proclaims, in the presence and under the auspices of the Supreme Being, the following rights of man and of the citizen:

Article

1. Men are born and remain free and equal in rights. Social distinctions may be founded only upon the general good.

2. The aim of all political association is the preservation of the natural and imprescriptible rights of man. These rights are liberty, property, security, and resistance to oppression.

3. The principle of all sovereignty resides essentially in the nation. No body nor individual may exercise any authority which does not proceed directly from the nation.

4. Liberty consists in the freedom to do everything which injures no one else; hence the exercise of the natural rights of each man has no limits except those which assure to the other members of the society the enjoyment of the same rights. These limits can only be determined by law.

5. Law can only prohibit such actions as are hurtful to society. Nothing may be prevented which is not forbidden by law, and no one may be forced to do anything not provided for by law.

6. Law is the expression of the general will. Every citizen has a right to participate personally, or through his representative, in its foundation. It must be the same for all, whether it protects or punishes. All citizens, being equal in the eyes of the law, are equally eligible to all dignities and to all public positions and occupations, according to their abilities, and without distinction except that of their virtues and talents.

7. No person shall be accused, arrested, or imprisoned except in the cases and according to the forms prescribed by law. Any one soliciting, transmitting, executing, or causing to be executed, any arbitrary order, shall be punished. But any citizen summoned or arrested in virtue of the law shall submit without delay, as resistance constitutes an offense.

8. The law shall provide for such punishments only as are strictly and obviously necessary, and no one shall suffer punishment except it be legally inflicted in virtue of a law passed and promulgated before the commission of the offense.

9. As all persons are held innocent until they shall have been declared guilty, if arrest shall be deemed indispensable, all harshness not essential to the securing of the prisoner's person shall be severely repressed by law.

10. No one shall be disquieted on account of his opinions, including his religious views, provided their manifestation does not disturb the public order established by law.

11. The free communication of ideas and opinions is one of the most precious of the rights of man. Every citizen may, accordingly, speak, write, and print with freedom, but shall be responsible for such abuses of this freedom as shall be defined by law.

12. The security of the rights of man and of the citizen requires public military forces. These forces are, therefore, established for the good of all and not the personal advantage of those to whom they shall be intrusted.

13. A common contribution is essential for the maintenance of the public forces and for the cost of administration. This should be equitably distributed among all the citizens in proportion to their means.

14. All the citizens have a right to decide, either personally or by their representatives, as to the necessity of the public contribution; to grant this freely; to know to what uses it is put; and to fix the proportion, the mode of assessment and of collection and the duration of the taxes.

15. Society has the right to require of every public agent an account of his administration.

16. A society in which the observance of the law is not assured, nor the separation of powers defined, has no constitution at all.

17. Since property is an inviolable and sacred right, no one shall be deprived thereof except where public necessity, legally determined, shall clearly demand it, and then only on condition that the owner shall have been previously and equitably indemnified.

Mary Wollstonecraft, *The Vindication of the Rights of Woman*, 1792*

Contending for the rights of woman, my main argument is built on this simple principle, that if she be not prepared by education to become the companion of man, she will stop the progress of knowledge and virtue; for truth must be common to all, or it will be inefficacious with respect to its influence on general practice. And how can woman be expected to co-operate unless she know why she ought to be virtuous? Unless freedom strengthen her reason till she comprehend her duty, and see in what manner it is connected with her real good? If children are to be educated to understand the true principle of patriotism, their mother must be a patriot; and the love of mankind, from which an orderly train of virtues spring, can only be produced by considering the moral and civil interest of mankind; but the education and situation of woman, at present, shuts her out from such investigations.

In this work I have produced many arguments, which to me were conclusive, to prove that the prevailing notion respecting a sexual character was subversive of morality, and I have contended, that to render the human body and mind more perfect, chastity must more universally prevail, and that chastity will never be respected in the male world till the person of woman is not, as it were, idolized, when little virtue sense embellish it with the grand traces of mental beauty, or the interesting simplicity of affection.

Consider, sir, dispassionately, these observations—for a glimpse of this truth seemed to open before you when you observed, "that to see one half of the human race excluded by the other from all participation of government, was a political phenomenon that, according to abstract principles, it was impossible to explain." If so, on what does your constitution rest? If the abstract rights of man will bear discussion and explanation, those of woman, by a parity of

---

Source: Mary Wollstonecraft, from the Dedication of the first edition, *The Vindication of the Rights of Woman* (1792).

reasoning, will not shrink from the same test: though a different opinion prevails in this country, built on the very arguments which you use to justify the oppression of woman—prescription.

Consider—I address you as a legislator—whether, when men contend for their freedom, and to be allowed to judge for themselves respecting their own happiness, it be not inconsistent and unjust to subjugate women, even though you firmly believe that you are acting in the manner best calculated to promote their happiness? Who made man the exclusive judge, if woman partake with him the gift of reason?

But, if women are to be excluded, without having a voice, from a participation of the natural rights of mankind, prove first, to ward off the charge of injustice and inconsistency, that they want reason—else this flaw in your NEW CONSTITUTION will ever show that man must, in some shape, act like a tyrant; and tyranny, in whatever part of society it rears its brazen front, will ever undermine morality.

I have repeatedly asserted, and produced what appeared to me irrefragable arguments drawn from matters of fact, to prove my assertion, that women cannot, by force, be confined to domestic concerns; for they will, however ignorant, intermeddle with more weighty affairs, neglecting private duties only to disturb, by cunning tricks, the orderly plans of reason which rise above their comprehension.

Besides, whilst they are only made to acquire personal accomplishments, men will seek for pleasure in variety, and faithless husbands will make faithless wives: such ignorant beings, indeed, will be very excusable when, not taught to respect public good, nor allowed any civil rights, they attempt to do themselves justice by retaliation.

The box of mischief thus opened in society, what is to preserve private virtue, the only security of public freedom and universal happiness?

Let there be then no coercion established in society, and the common law of gravity prevailing, the sexes will fall into their proper places. And, now that more equitable laws are forming your citizens, marriage may become more sacred: your young men may choose wives from motives of affection, and your maidens allow love to root out vanity.

The father of a family will not then weaken his constitution and debase his sentiments by visiting the harlot, nor forget, in obeying the call of appetite, the purpose for which it was implanted. And, the mother will not neglect her children to practise the arts of coquetry, when sense and modesty secure her the friendship of her husband.

But, till men become attentive to the duty of a father, it is vain to expect women to spend that time in their nursery which they, "wise in their generation," choose to spend at their glass; for this exertion of cunning is only an instinct of nature to enable them to obtain indirectly a little of that power of which they are unjustly denied a share: for, if women are not permitted to enjoy legitimate rights, they will render both men and themselves vicious, to obtain illicit privileges.

I wish, sir, to set some investigations of this kind afloat in France; and should they lead to a confirmation of my principles, when your constitution is revised the Rights of Woman may be respected, if it be fully proved that reason calls for this respect, and loudly demands JUSTICE for one half of the human race.—I am, sir, your respectfully,

M. W.

Appendixes: Answers to Objective Questions
Outline Maps

Chapter 1

Study-Review Exercises

Test your understanding.

1. Charles Darwin
2. Hammurabi
3. pharaoh
4. Hyksos
5. Akhenaten
6. Egyptian and Hittite
7. Babylon
8. were
9. could
10. Neolithic
11. Tigris, Euphrates
12. was
13. Herodotus

Place the following events in chronological order.

1. 6
2. 3
3. 5
4. 2
5. 4
6. 1

Multiple-Choice Questions

1. b
2. b
3. c
4. b
5. c
6. a
7. b
8. d
9. a
10. a
11. b
12. d
13. b
14. b
15. a
16. c
17. b
18. c
19. d
20. a
21. b
22. c
23. b
24. d
25. a

Chapter 2

Study-Review Exercises

Test your understanding.

1. a
2. more
3. Yahweh
4. did
5. Medes, Persians
6. east
7. satrapies

Multiple-Choice Questions

1. b
2. d
3. b
4. b
5. b
6. c
7. c
8. a
9. d
10. c
11. b
12. c
13. d
14. a
15. d
16. c
17. a
18. b
19. d
20. d
21. a
22. d
23. c
24. c
25. b

Chapter 3

Study-Review Exercises

Fill in the blank lines.

1. g
2. d
3. b
4. a
5. c
6. e
7. i
8. f

Test your understanding.

1. Athens, Sparta, Thebes
2. were
3. did
4. Philip of Macedonia
5. divine law
6. were
7. supported
8. Thebes

Multiple-Choice Questions

1. b
2. c
3. c
4. d
5. b
6. d
7. a
8. b
9. d
10. d
11. b
12. a
13. d
14. b
15. a
16. d
17. d
18. d
19. c
20. d
21. b
22. b
23. c
24. a
25. b

Chapter 4

Study-Review Exercises

Test your understanding.

1. no
2. Stoicism
3. discard
4. Diogenes
5. did not
6. 330 B.C.
7. did not
8. Antigonid, Ptolemaic, Seleucid, Pergamene
9. increase
10. fate or chance
11. tolerant
12. Isis

Multiple-Choice Questions

1. c
2. d
3. b
4. b
5. b
6. c
7. c
8. a
9. d
10. a
11. d
12. d
13. b
14. b
15. c
16. c
17. c
18. a
19. d
20. d
21. d
22. a
23. d
24. d
25. d

Chapter 5

Study-Review Exercises

Test your understanding.

1. Carthage
2. did
3. Sicily, North Africa
4. did not
5. more
6. Jupiter
7. realistic
8. did not
9. patrician

Place the following events in chronological order.

1. 3
2. 6
3. 1
4. 4
5. 5
6. 2

Multiple-Choice Questions

1. c
2. b
3. a
4. d
5. a
6. b
7. c
8. b
9. d
10. b
11. a
12. b
13. c
14. d
15. b
16. c
17. b
18. b
19. d
20. b
21. d
22. c
23. d
24. d
25. a

Chapter 6

Study-Review Exercises

Test your understanding.

1. did
2. Byzantium (Constantinople)
3. Livy
4. increase
5. A.D. 380
6. did
7. increase
8. minor
9. expansion

Place the following events in chronological order.

1. 5
2. 3
3. 2
4. 1
5. 4
6. 6

Multiple-Choice Questions

1. d
2. d
3. b
4. d
5. b
6. d
7. d
8. a
9. a
10. d
11. b
12. b
13. c
14. b
15. c
16. a
17. d
18. d
19. d
20. d
21. a
22. d
23. d
24. b
25. d

Chapter 7

Study-Review Exercises

Test your understanding.

1. did
2. Constantine
3. wergeld
4. east
5. was
6. Augustine of Hippo
7. German chieftains
8. *City of God*
9. emperor

Multiple-Choice Questions

1. c
2. d
3. b
4. b
5. a
6. b
7. b
8. c
9. b
10. a
11. d
12. d
13. d
14. a
15. b
16. d
17. c
18. b
19. c
20. a
21. b
22. d
23. b
24. a
25. d

Chapter 8

Study-Review Exercises

Test your understanding.

1. Einhard
2. increase
3. less
4. good
5. Alcuin
6. Salerno

Place the following events in chronological order.

1. 6
2. 4
3. 2
4. 8
5. 5
6. 3
7. 7
8. 1

Multiple-Choice Questions

1. c
2. c
3. c
4. c
5. b
6. d
7. b
8. a
9. c
10. b
11. c
12. d
13. a
14. c
15. d
16. c
17. c
18. b
19. c
20. a
21. d
22. a
23. b
24. c
25. a

Chapter 9

Study-Review Exercises

Test your understanding.

1. increase/eroded
2. warmer
3. decrease, increase
4. Cluny
5. clergy, emperor
6. Gorze

Multiple-Choice Questions

1. d
2. c
3. a
4. d
5. a
6. b
7. b
8. c
9. a
10. b
11. b
12. d
13. b
14. b
15. a
16. c
17. d
18. c
19. d
20. a
21. d
22. c
23. a
24. c
25. d

Chapter 10

Study-Review Exercises

Test your understanding.

1. uncertain
2. greater
3. did
4. manor
5. never
6. bride
7. late
8. knighthood
9. was not
10. horse

Multiple-Choice Questions

1. d
2. c
3. c
4. b
5. c
6. d
7. a
8. b
9. b
10. d
11. c
12. a
13. c
14. c
15. c
16. c
17. c
18. d
19. a
20. d
21. c
22. d
23. d
24. c.
25. c

Chapter 11

Study-Review Exercises

Test your understanding.

1. *Unam Sanctam*
2. Exchequer
3. Frederick Barbarossa
4. *Domesday Book*
5. England
6. Sicily
7. Magna Carta
8. Scholastic
9. Romanesque
10. *summa*
11. Hanseatic League
12. Peter Abelard
13. Thomas Becket
14. Parlement of Paris

Multiple-Choice Questions

1. d
2. b
3. c
4. c
5. b
6. b
7. d
8. b
9. c
10. d
11. b
12. d
13. a
14. a
15. c
16. c
17. a
18. c
19. d
20. c
21. a
22. d
23. c
24. a
25. d

Chapter 12

Study-Review Exercises

Test your understanding.

1. did not
2. bad
3. England, France
4. Lollards
5. economic
6. decrease

Place the following events in chronological order.

1. 2
2. 7
3. 3
4. 5
5. 1
6. 6
7. 8
8. 4

Multiple-Choice Questions

1. d
2. d
3. a
4. c
5. b
6. a
7. c
8. b
9. b
10. d
11. b
12. c
13. a
14. c
15. b
16. b
17. b
18. a
19. b
20. c
21. c
22. d
23. b
24. d
25. a

Chapter 13

Study-Review Exercises

Test your understanding.

1. Niccolò Machiavelli
2. less
3. increased
4. Thomas More
5. declined
6. is not

Multiple-Choice Questions

1. a
2. d
3. d
4. b
5. b
6. b
7. c
8. d
9. a
10. d
11. d
12. d
13. c
14. b
15. b
16. b
17. b
18. b
19. a
20. d
21. a
22. b
23. d
24. d
25. a

Chapter 14

Study-Review Exercises

Test your understanding.

1. did
2. king
3. political
4. Martin Luther
5. Alexander VI
6. was
7. weaken
8. Protestant

Multiple-Choice Questions

1. c
2. d
3. b
4. a
5. b
6. b
7. c
8. c
9. a
10. b
11. a
12. c
13. a
14. d
15. c
16. b
17. b
18. c
19. a
20. c
21. c
22. a
23. d
24. b
25. c

Chapter 15

Study-Review Exercises

Test your understanding.

1. Thirty Years' War
2. Cortez
3. Edict of Nantes
4. sixteenth
5. Gustavus Adolphus
6. the United Provinces of the Netherlands
7. Amsterdam
8. Elizabeth I
9. skepticism
10. Charles V
11. Concordat of Bologna
12. Portugal

Multiple-Choice Questions

1. a
2. b
3. d
4. d
5. d
6. b
7. a
8. b
9. a
10. c
11. a
12. b
13. c
14. c
15. b
16. b
17. b
18. d
19. d
20. c
21. d
22. b
23. c
24. a
25. c

Chapter 16

Study-Review Exercises

Test your understanding.

1. stadholder
2. Colbert
3. entered
4. disaster
5. John Churchill
6. Laud
7. Calvin

Multiple-Choice Questions

1. b
2. d
3. a
4. d
5. d
6. a
7. d
8. b
9. a
10. d
11. c
12. d
13. d
14. b
15. c
16. b
17. a
18. a
19. c
20. c
21. a
22. a
23. d
24. b
25. a

Chapter 17

Study-Review Exercises

Test your understanding.

1. Peter the Great
2. increased
3. Suleiman the Magnificent
4. maintained
5. Frederick II (the Great)
6. weaker

Place the following events in chronological order.

1. 4
2. 1
3. 3
4. 2
5. 5
6. 6

Multiple-Choice Questions

1. d
2. c
3. d
4. a
5. c
6. a
7. d
8. b
9. a
10. b
11. b
12. c
13. b
14. b
15. c
16. c
17. b
18. a
19. a
20. b
21. c
22. a
23. a
24. a
25. a

Chapter 18

Study-Review Exercises

Test your understanding.

1. water, earth
2. did not
3. motion
4. universal gravitation
5. philosophy
6. Portugal
7. was not
8. did not
9. skeptic
10. Newton
11. failed

Place the following events in chronological order.

1. 4
2. 1
3. 5
4. 2
5. 3

Multiple-Choice Questions

1. a
2. b
3. c
4. d
5. d
6. c
7. b
8. d
9. d
10. b
11. a
12. a
13. a
14. b
15. a
16. c
17. b
18. d
19. c
20. d
21. a
22. a
23. c
24. c
25. a

Chapter 19

Study-Review Exercises

Fill in the blank line.

1. i
2. c
3. e
4. j
5. g
6. a
7. b
8. f

Multiple-Choice Questions

1. c
2. a
3. d
4. c
5. b
6. a
7. a
8. a
9. b
10. d
11. a
12. b
13. a
14. a
15. a
16. d
17. b
18. b
19. a
20. b
21. a
22. d
23. d
24. c
25. a

Chapter 20

Study-Review Exercises

Test your understanding.

1. limited	3. did	5. longer	7. the common people
2. was not	4. potato	6. cowpox	8. Wesley

Multiple-Choice Questions

1. b	8. d	15. b	22. d
2. d	9. b	16. c	23. c
3. b	10. c	17. d	24. a
4. c	11. c	18. a	25. c
5. c	12. d	19. d	
6. b	13. a	20. b	
7. a	14. d	21. d	

Chapter 21

Study-Review Exercises

Test your understanding.

1. Trafalgar	3. Thomas Paine	5. victory
2. an important	4. a great deal of	6. a military ruler

Multiple-Choice Questions

1. c	8. a	15. a	22. a
2. d	9. d	16. a	23. d
3. d	10. c	17. a	24. d
4. a	11. d	18. b	25. b
5. d	12. d	19. b	
6. c	13. a	20. d	
7. c	14. c	21. d	

Outline Map 1.1

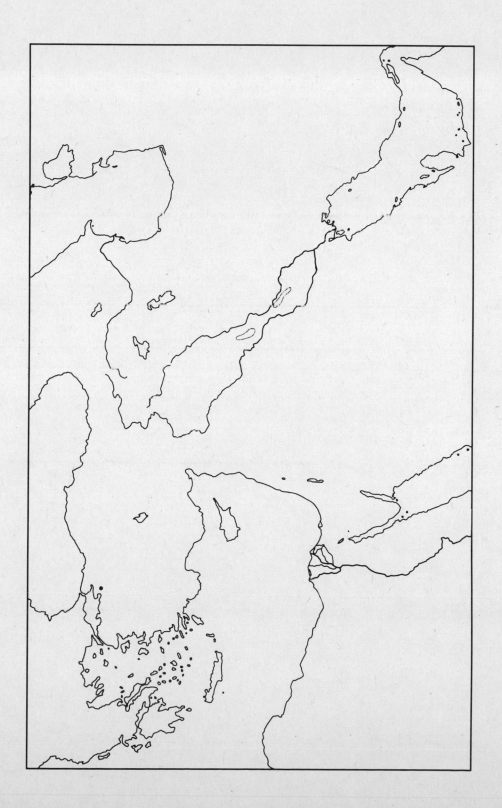

Outline Map 2.3

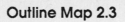

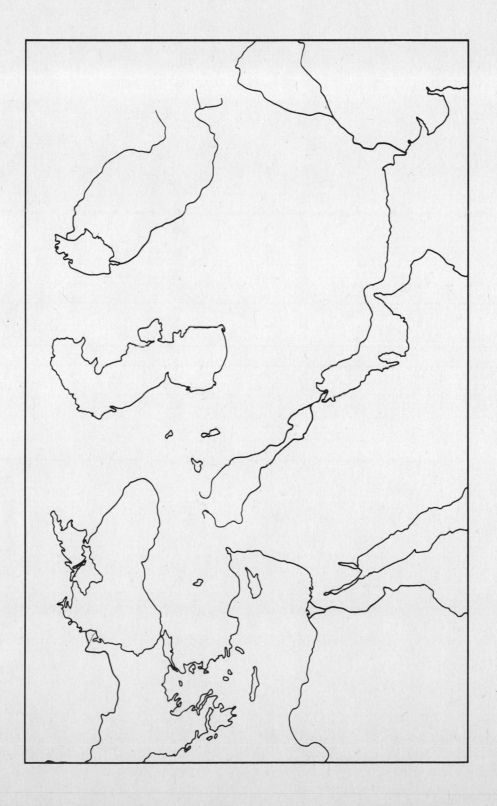

Outline Map 3.1

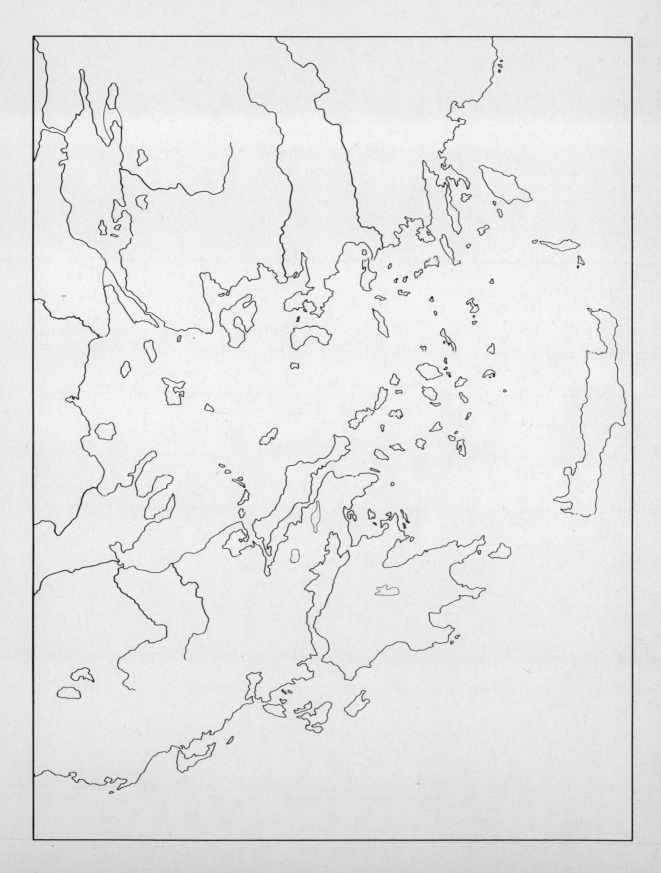

Outline Map 4.1

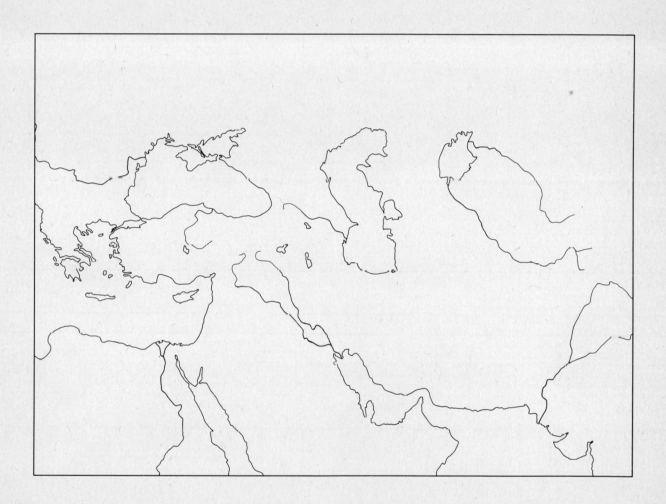

Outline Map 5.2

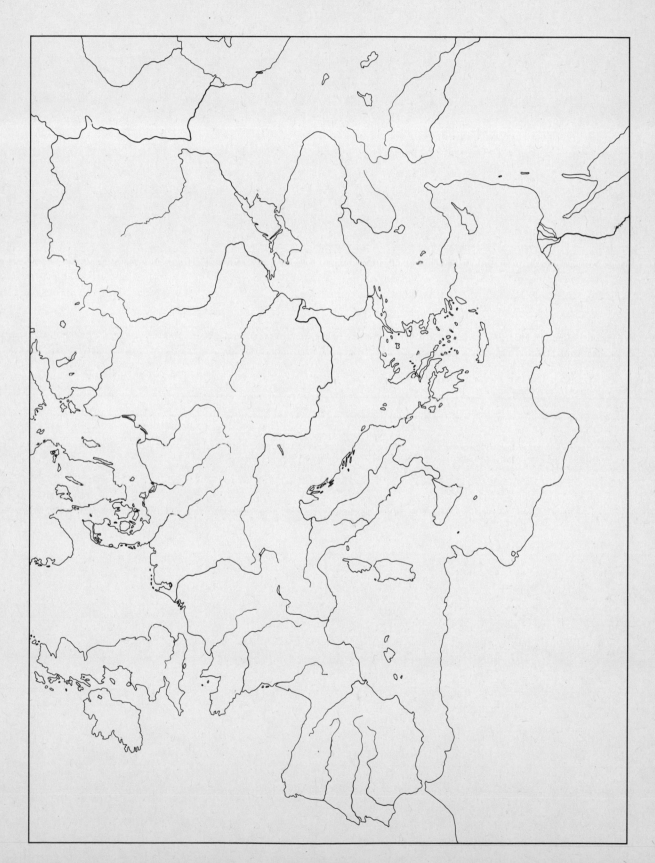

Outline Map 6.1

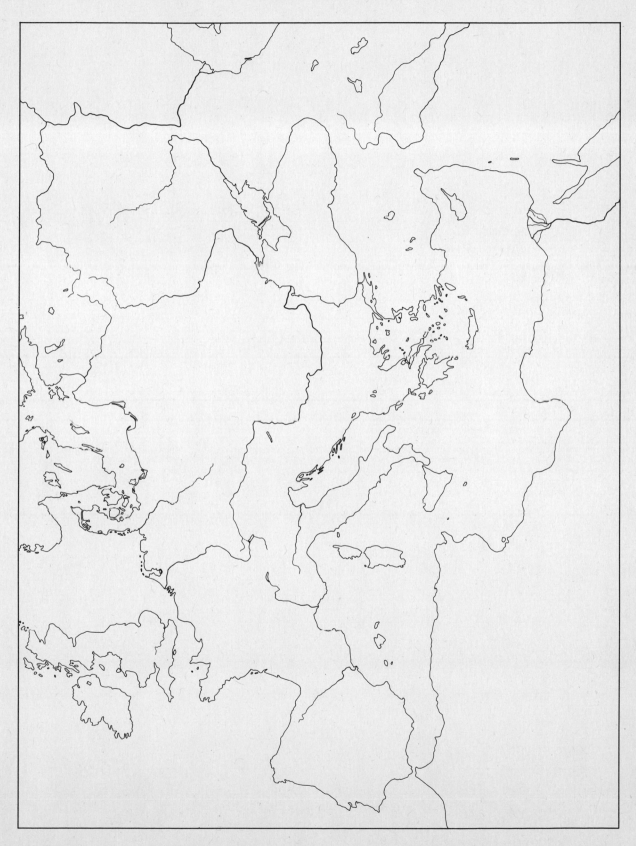

Outline Map 7.3

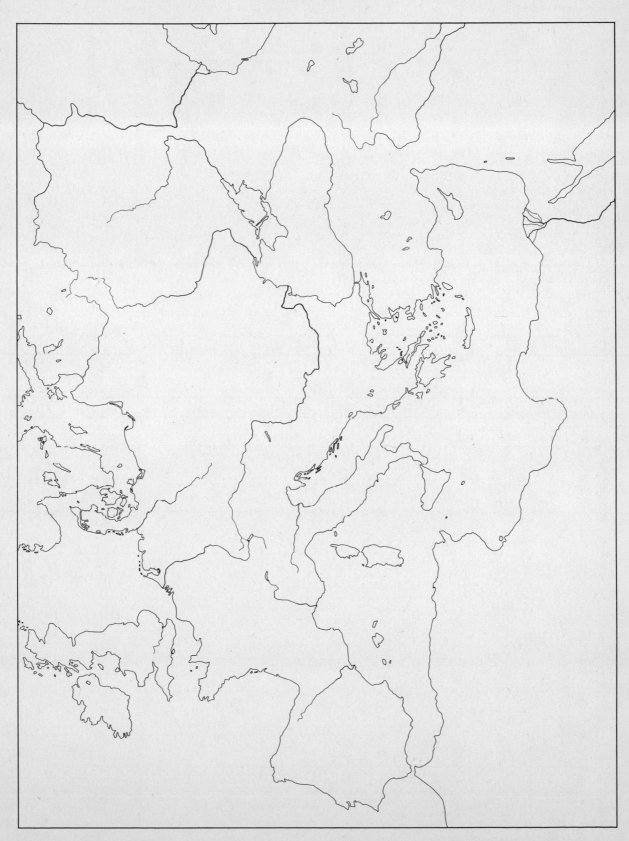

Outline Map 8.1

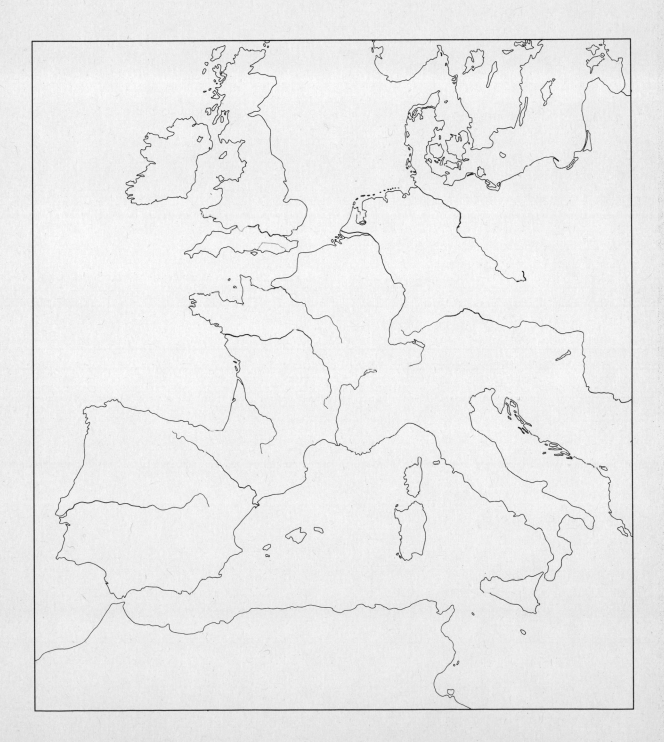

Outline Map 11.2

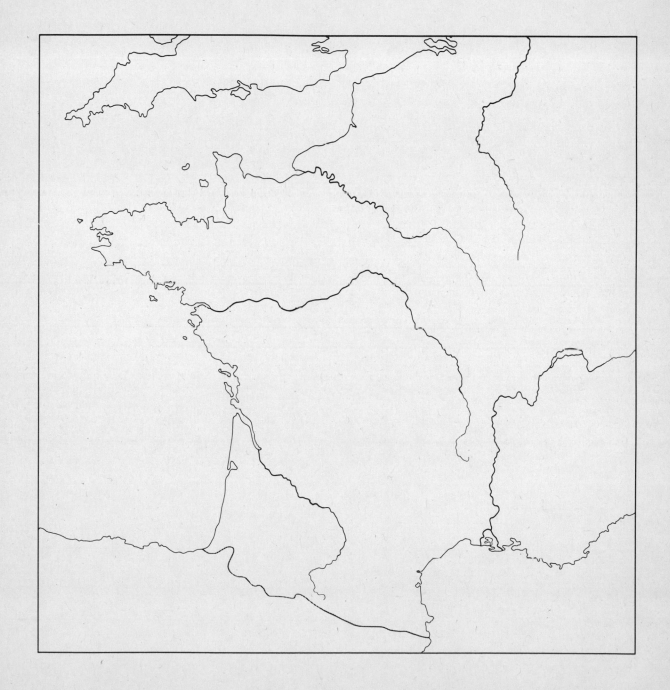

Outline Map 13.1

Outline Map 14.1

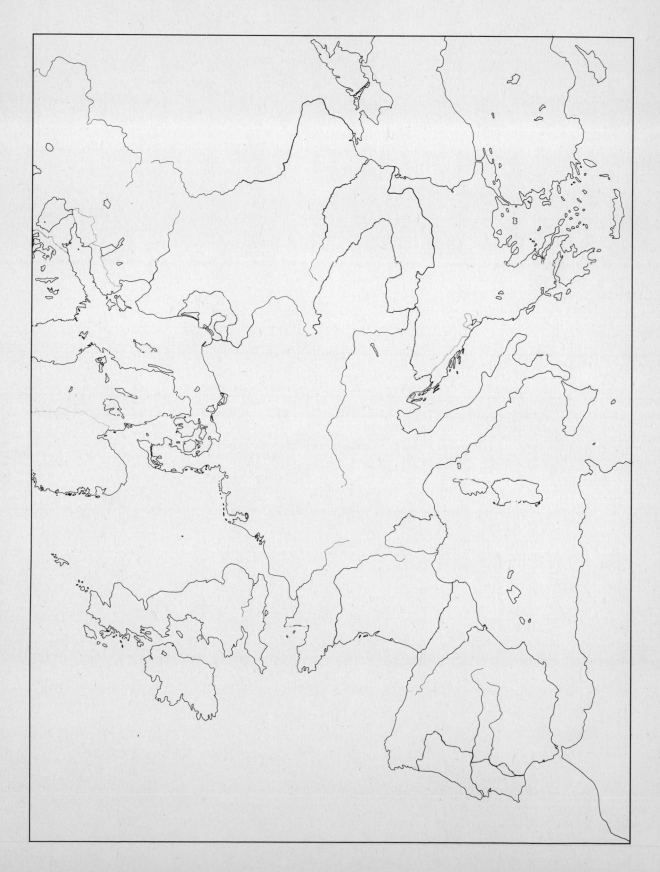

Outline Map 15.1

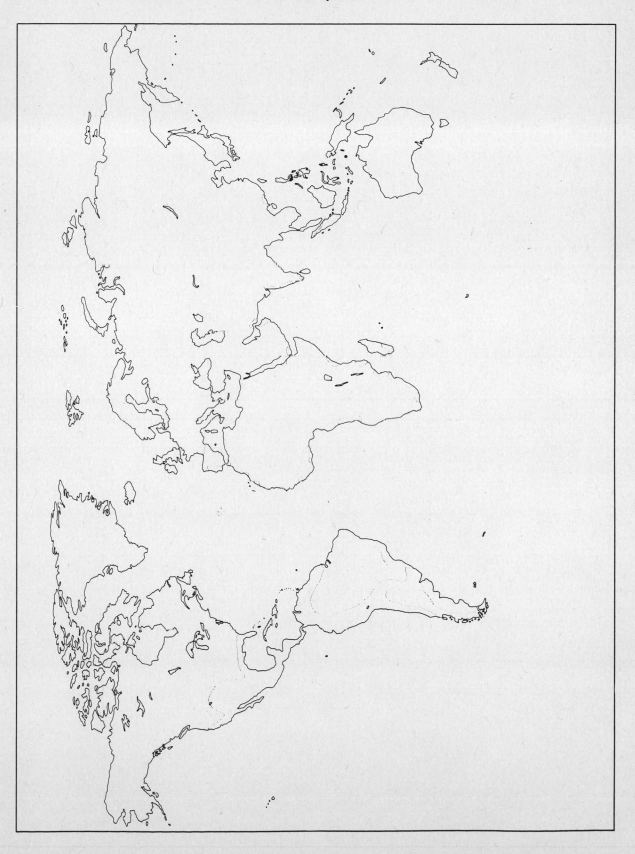

Outline Map 15.3

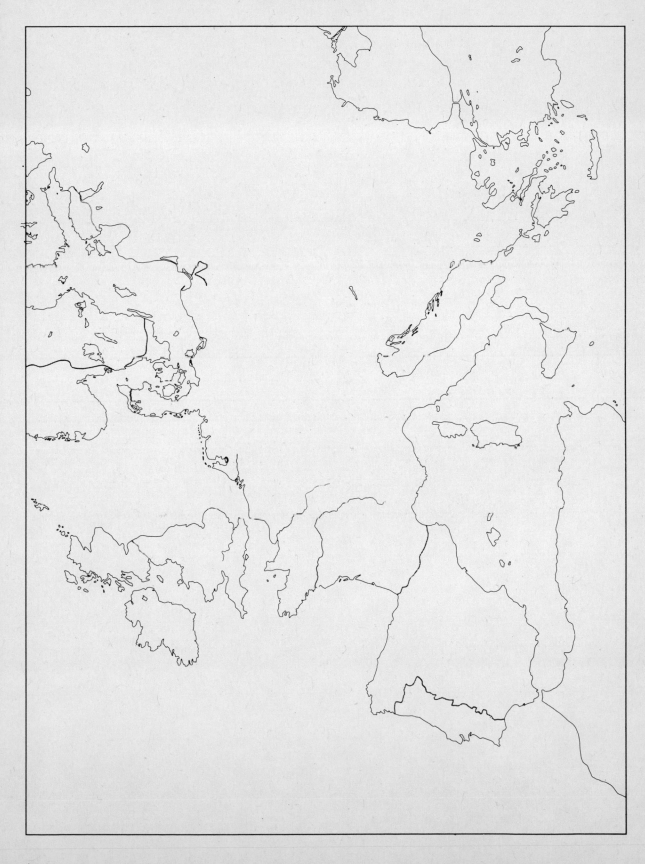

Outline Map 16.1

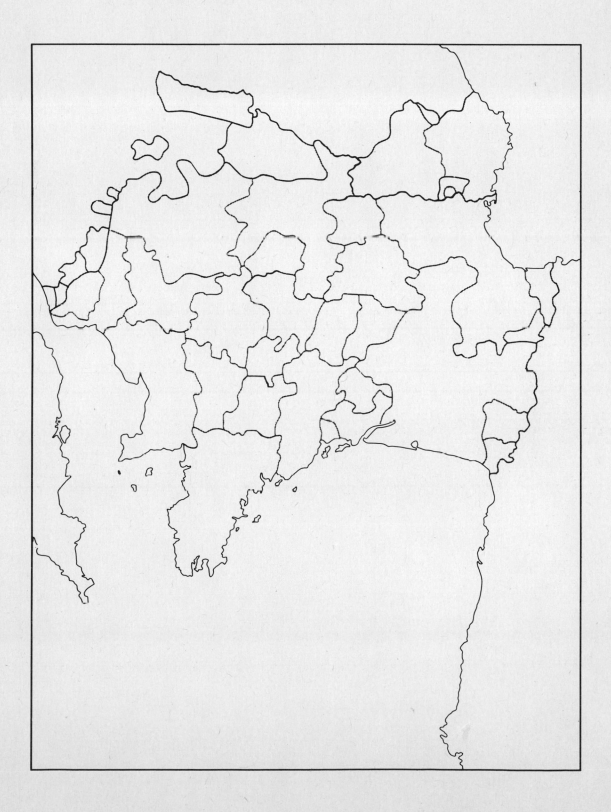

Outline Map 17.3

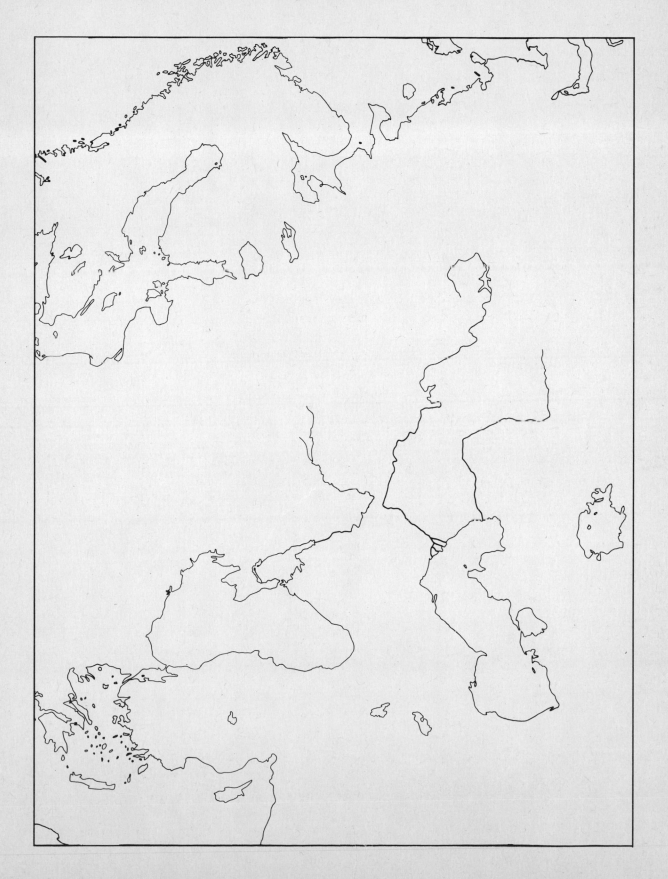

Outline Map 19.3

Outline Map 21.1

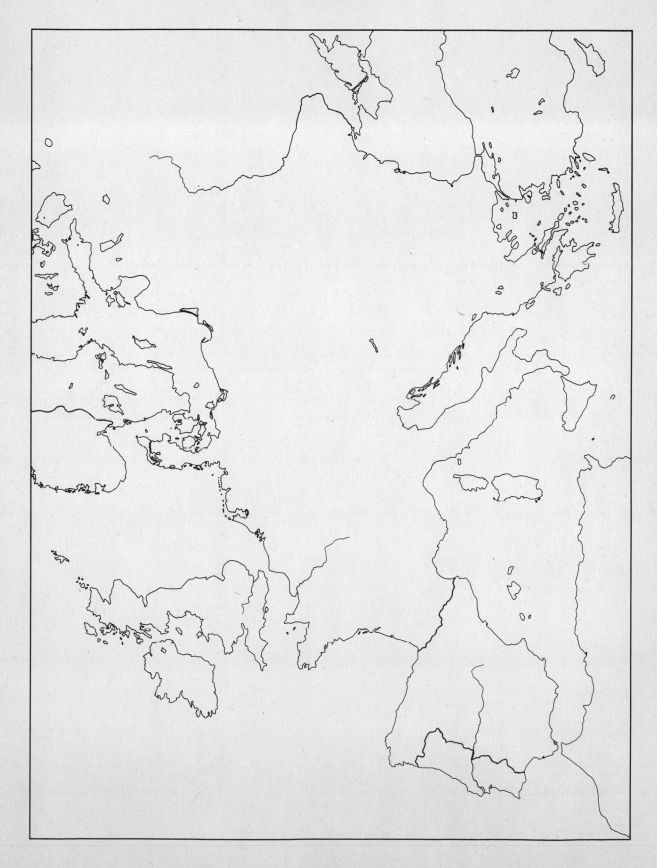